TAILS OF THE ALPUJARRAS
VOLUME 2

First Published in Great Britain 2023 by Valle Verde Animal Rescue

First edition: 2023

Tails of the Alpujarras
Volume 2

Contributions by
Animal Lovers

A Personal Note from the Founders

VALLE VERDE ANIMAL RESCUE IS a privately run and funded association dedicated to helping abandoned and abused animals from the Alpujarra, Lecrin Valley and Costa Tropical.

Valle Verde Animal Rescue has been running since 2015. We have our Facebook page and also our own website www.valleverdeanimalrescue.org

In the last 9 years we have homed over 2000 animals to different countries, such as Germany, Holland, UK, Guernsey and Spain.

Our thanks go out to all of those who have made this book possible, the ideas, efforts and time that have been donated for our cause are as valuable to us as the funding itself.

Thank you all for your ongoing support and the knowledge that together we can build a brighter future for the animals.

Linda, Linda and Krysta
Valle Verde Animal Rescue

Contents

Big dog, little dog
By Jane Bussmann

IT WAS NIGHT BY THE time I dragged the extension lead into the sheep field. The dark bulk of Finbar was hunched over his electric saw, fingering the new blade we'd picked up at the DIY superstore. It was now too dark to see. I could hear my 81-year-old mother's voice in my head, 'Oh for fuck's sake, Jane, why don't you just wait til tomorrow?' Because I'm your daughter. And because I'm part English, part German and part Irish: delusional, pig-headed and, whenever possible, drunk. And because it was January and sleet freezing up the mountain, and there was no way the dogs could last another night.

'Jane! Pass me dat cable, lovey.' Finbar, the only person mad enough to do this with me was completely Irish.

'Finbar, is it switched—'

'So help me, Jane, I might as well tell you straightforward. I've been using dis angle grinder for torty years and if tonight is de night I cuts someone's leg off, well, dey'll just have to arrest me, so.'

Ever since I moved to the hamlet in Spain, I had kept well away from a huge ferocious dog that lived far away up the mountain, barking savagely for us to leave him alone, which I did. Except one day Finbar, being the son of a Tralee warehouseman and unafraid of huge ferocious things, had gone to check on him. He was not a huge ferocious dog far away, he was in fact a tiny dog a hundred yards up, and he wasn't barking for us to leave him alone, he was barking for us to help him. There were two more. Their necks were fixed to short chains that held them running in circles, concentric circles of poo around them where they'd gone as far as they could to keep their beds clean. Dogs will do anything to stay clean. In the January snow, the only place the chain would let the little black dog reach for shelter was a metal barrel with the wind clanking through it. A barrel in a puddle, a puddle that had seeped through the rotten metal, so his only shelter was full of cold water. One dog was just a puppy. I stroked her fur. It felt like she was covered in baked beans. I parted her fur with my fingers. It was ticks sucked full of her blood. The last was an elderly dog, her eyes half closed after years of this struggle.

'They can't stay there,' I said.

'If you take them, they'll poison my dog,' said Finbar. 'They're mountain people.' Expat lore had it that the poor, gnarled goatherds led lives so poor and gnarled that if they abused a defenceless animal it was somehow completely different to men brutalising animals in our own countries, quainter, and definitely not worth jeopardising a life of two-euro white Rioja. Finbar justified this as all expats did, 'Help the dogs after we've moved.' I was getting pretty sick of this mantra, as British and Irish never move as fast as they think they will, and dogs only live short lives.

At the very least the dog needed a kennel. I'm a mongrel but first and foremost British and don't want to cause offence. To this end, rather than simply buy the dog a decent kennel, which would have been patronising, I had racked my brain for an agricultural object I could pretend I was throwing out, that would be waterproof, windproof and big enough to shelter three dogs. Small water tanks were the answer. They don't exist, so two 1000 litre ones were delivered at great expense, 1.2m square cubes that had to be carried up a sheer mountainside to where the goatherd kept his dogs chained up in howling wind. The trouble was we could only get one turned into a kennel and carried up the hill before the goatherd came to work the next morning, and I would have to hide the other before the goatherd saw, as it was clearly a brand new tank that no one would throw out.

It started to rain, the sheep droppings glistening in the moonlight like a thousand diamonds. Finbar turned on the blade and shadowy birds fled above our heads. At last. Then he stopped.

'You owe me bigtime.' A beat. 'You did promise...'

Oh not now. There was no time. In this mission I was on, Finbar had done Spain's dogs many conditional favours. We had driven for hours to find this giant water tank, when normal people in a DIY superstore were stroking Carrerra marble effect splashbacks, we were stumbling under 20kg bags of cement and multipacks of spinning blades. We had sawed off metal bits to fit it in Finbar's truck, given up and paid a lorry to bring it. Finbar didn't mind doing this because he was the older generation, who expected to knacker themselves for a higher cause. But because he was the older generation, there was always payback. He fumbled in his baggy beach shorts.

'...you did promise to fix my phone.'

'Finbar, it's pitch dark...'

'I can't get the Whatsapp, and Roisin at the bingo hall sends me dese jokes... don't look at that one, it's a bit rude...'

'Finbar, I showed you; you just go to the settings...'

'Jane, I'm telling you straightforward, with me and phones you might as well be looking up a bull's hole.'

While I switched his mobile data back on for the third time that week, Finbar ground a dog-sized hole in the front of the plastic water tank.

The tank was the size of a Mini, albeit the 1960s health visitor Mini, not the 2021 junior head of marketing Mini. Despite this size, being Irish, he remained convinced we could effortlessly transport this water tank up the hill on his truck.

'Now if you just help me lift it, I can tie this onto the roof of the truck.' Ten seconds later: 'OK, lovey, forget that, we'll carry it, you and me.' Thirty seconds later: 'OK, lovey, go and ask Paco if he'll give us a lend of his wheelbarrow.'

Paco leant on his walking stick, watching as we wobbled up the mountain in the dark, a grand piano-size water tank lurching on the wheelbarrow, Finbar tall, round and determined, me small, weedy and whimpering, the Laurel and Hardy of animal rescue.

The dogs were still fifty yards away. The wheelbarrow got stuck in the mud. We couldn't lift the water tank. We rolled it up the hill like a snowball. Over and over up the hill in the rain. We reached the stark clearing where the dogs were chained. They went spare. We tied the tank to a tree in the hope the mountain wind wouldn't lift it and throw it back down at us for insulting the mountain people. The dogs had never had a kennel in their lives, and didn't know what it meant to have shelter just for them. They wouldn't go in out of the rain. I took fistfuls of dry dog food out of my rucksack and put it inside the tank along with two sunbed mattresses to try and tempt them inside. The dogs let us give them a cuddle.

Next morning I limped back to my car, trying to keep the discs of my spine in a straight column. There was Paco talking to the goatherd. They were looking at the other water tank. Shit. They've seen the water tank up the hill, and we're going to be poisoned, and worst, Finbar will be proven right.

'This water tank,' said the goatherd. 'Do you want it?'

'No, I've got two, I only need one, take one, it's a spare. I put one on the hill, we were just passing...'

'Yeah, I saw. Do you want a dog?'

'The ones on the hill...?'

'Yeah, I've got three, I only need two, take one, it's a spare...'

Choosing one out of three was a nasty business. I took the chain off the littlest's neck. He hadn't dared go into the tank/kennel. The food was untouched. The little dog I'd thought was a ferocious beast walked quietly away from the circle of poo for the last time and got into the car. He sat on the back seat looking around him, not making a sound as we drove away. I'm coming back for you, I said to the pup and the old dog. I just need to work out how.

Today the little dog lives in a nice warm house in Yorkshire with a lady who says he will always sleep curled up on her bed. The goatherd refused to help the other two, but saw differently when the police paid him a visit. The puppy lives in a warm house in Hastings, tick free, and the old dog lives in the goatherd's farmhouse. It turned out the poor, gnarled goatherd had two thousand goats and a nice warm cortijo all along.

About Jane Bussmann

AT 22 JANE BUSSMANN WAS HIRED by the BBC as comedy writer for radio presenters and at 24 (with David Quantick) sold the BBC two sitcom pilots, What On Earth and Put Out More Fags (1999). Both were produced.

Bussmann and Quantick created, wrote and produced (with Jess Search) the world's first Internet sitcom, The Junkies (2001), later broadcast by Channel 4.

She wrote for over 50 shows, notably South Park (1997).

She was Script Editor on the Emmy-winning series Smack the Pony (1999).

In 1998 Bussmann published the book "Once In A Lifetime", winning Muzik's "Book of the Year", "Book of the Summer" in the Times, "Book of the Year" in the NME and "Book of the Month" in GQ, the Editor-in-Chief James Brown personally reviewing it as "So good it's dangerous".

In 2009 she published The Worst Date Ever, optioned by Film4.

Jane is setting up a small adoption centre for Spanish dogs called Miracle Hill. Still in process but she'd love to help you find a dog to adopt and you can message her on Facebook at jane.bussmann.

Love and loss, joy and pain
60 years with rescue animals
by Richard Skelton

'DOGS – THEY DRIVE YOU MAD then they break your heart.' Or something like that. So said none other than Jeremy Clarkson apparently, and of course it's perfectly true, and equally so of cats.

Another quote for you. I think it was Richard Bach – although it might have been another of those American self-help author-philosophers – who said: 'Make the most of your life because it almost certainly won't end well.' Or something like that. And it's true of animals too. Death is rarely if ever pleasant, to witness or go through. And our animals' lives are most often considerably shorter than ours.

I guess you can tell already this is not going to be another schmaltzy, over romanticised piece about the joys of pet ownership! But stick with me. Living with dogs, cats and other animals may be unbearably painful at times, but it can be wonderful too.

Owning rescue animals is definitely bitter-sweet. Of course, I understand that's a controversial statement from the beginning, arguable as a point of fact as well as decidedly non-PC in this day and age. Do we actually own our pets, or just get to share time and space with them? Anyway, I think it's fair to say we get to take care of them and take responsibility for them. And that's really hard sometimes because we can't guard and protect them from all the dangers they face: they eat things they shouldn't, dogs get loose, cats go out at night and cross roads, and sometimes we make the wrong calls on their behalf. As parents we worry about our kids – and that never stops no matter how old they are or what they achieve in their lives – and we worry about our pets in much the same way.

All my animals have been rescues, and those of my childhood too with one possible exception. But before that particular feline came into my life, a slim and slinky grey and black tabby became part of the family. We're talking mid 1960s here, when I was still at infants' school. My dad popped into the late-night corner shop at the bottom of our road one evening to buy a pint of milk on his way home from work. They were about to close up and evict a young stray that'd been hanging around all day. Dad, a freelancer in the film and television industry, had just been in the call box outside, keeping an appointment to ring a woman called Thelma to find out whether he'd got a job or not. It was good news! Then he went into the shop and shortly afterwards came home with a little cat in a box and my parents named it Thelma.

Then came Samantha, a solid, largish female cat with mixed markings – tabby and white with a splash of tortoiseshell. I'm not completely sure where Sam came from – it's lost in the mists of time – and I'm afraid it is possible it was from a pet shop. But let's let my parents off – the sixties were different times. Samantha – or 'Sam the Prune' as my mother called her for reasons I don't think I ever really knew, was one of those cats who kept herself to herself and maintained her dignity at all times. Tummy tickles and cuddles were not particularly well received, although she'd tolerate a respectful stroke or two, and she clearly admired my mother, watching her unload the shopping as if it were the impressive spoils of a hunting expedition, and choosing to sit with her in the evenings. And she was an impressive hunter herself.

One night's work ended with a whole family of rats of varying sizes, all very dead, neatly lined up in size order on the garden patio of our new early seventies house. It was a deliberate demonstration of her hunting prowess, immediately visible through the patio windows as soon as the curtains were opened in the morning.

But having left for work bright and early by the front door, my dad missed seeing Sam's macabre exhibition, and a neighbour prevailed upon her husband to fetch his shovel and remove the five corpses. It was reckoned Sam must have carried the rats home in relays from new building works on the edge of our estate, a number of the rodents having been seen there a day or so earlier, fleeing from the rubble as an old piggery got demolished. Everybody on our road was greatly impressed, Sam received much positive attention and her expert exterminatory endeavours passed into family folklore.

Despite multiple house moves and living in a busy town centre for a while, both Sam and Thelma lived very full lives. According to my mother, Sam, aged 18, woke up one teatime, stretched, walked towards her food bowl, keeled over and died. Her last thought, presumably, 'Ah, tea!'. Thelma came to live with me and my dad in rural Buckinghamshire when my parents got divorced. She had a good life there except I was out at school all day, and hanging with friends in the evening, and Dad often worked long hours. So, Thelma quite understandably decided Gordon and Martha, the kindly retired couple next door – in all day with the heating on full blast – were a much better bet. I could see her most days curled up contentedly on the rug in front of the gas fire in the lounge. Good on you girl.

So, although those two sixties' cats lived a full span, dying in the mid-1980s, their lives were still very much shorter than those of most human beings. And there are many domesticated animals whose lives are curtailed by illness or accident, and these deaths are perhaps the hardest to deal with. Deaths through road accidents are particularly upsetting, and so too are unexplained disappearances.

In 1982, as a young adult walking home late one night through the mean backstreets of Leeds, I came across an emaciated little black and white cat delicately picking its way along the cemented top of a factory wall embedded with chunks of broken bottles. It miaowed, I reached up, and the little scrap jumped straight into my arms. So, I carried it home, naming her Jess there and then after Postman Pat's black and white cat, an inspired choice, I thought, because the name suited a feline of either sex! And the next day after a checkover by the nearest vet, and the expert administering by him of a jumbo worming tablet, she – for Jess was a female of the species – passed an extraordinary heap of tapeworms in the garden. I bet she felt better for that!

I lived on my own at the time and had a social life split between Yorkshire and Buckinghamshire, so what to do? No problem at all! Jess simply travelled with me up and down the M1 in my Hillman Avenger! She was more like a dog, than cat – I know people very often say that, but it was true. She'd also play hide-and-seek games around the house. We were close friends, but after a while I moved in with my girlfriend taking Jess with me, and she was not remotely impressed by my girlfriend's adolescent kittens. There was a great deal of hissing and hiding behind the furniture.

Then, when we bought a house together in a fabulous countryside setting – cat heaven, you'd think (although one of those kittens, a few years later and fully grown, would be knocked down on the only road for miles around) – there was a great deal of territorial marking, the house soon stank, and a carpet had to be thrown away. We were both working full-time, often late, and it was hard to police the situation, so Jess went to live with friends of ours. They loved her and all went well for a few months, then one day she disappeared. I feel so terribly guilty about that to this day.

Then came another house move, back to Leeds. The seller, a woman known to me a little through work, was emigrating to France. Would I take on her two cats, Joe, a big, gentle black and white tomcat, and Blue, a smallish jet-black male? Of course, I would!

As a kid my mother always told me dogs and cats wouldn't mix. It wouldn't be fair on Thelma and Sam, she said, and that brought an absolute end to any attempt by me to persuade her to let us have a dog. I accepted what she said, only realising many years later how very wrong she was. The real truth, of course, was that she didn't want a dog. Didn't like them. Didn't understand them. Didn't have time for them.

In my early thirties I was single again, and when a new partner came into my life there were strings attached: Bonnie, a young collie-lab cross was part of the deal. Fine by me! Bonnie had been found on a building site. 'A bonny dog, that,' one of the builders had said when Jenny came across her and took her home. And he was quite right. Bonnie was open, trusting and full of love and enthusiasm. She was a super dog. But when she was only seven or eight she became ill and died of kidney failure, which was utterly heartbreaking. Just awful. I buried her in the garden with full honours and still think of her often, and a friend of mine tells me he tips his cap to her when he passes to this day. Anyway, Joe and Blue got on just fine with Bonnie, and in the thirty plus years from that time to this, I've always had dogs and cats living together in my life.

By the time Bonnie died we had another dog. Paphos, a dog from Cyprus. Yes, really. Barely out of puppyhood, scrawny, all legs and as gangly as a newborn lamb, she staggered into the road in front of our hire car in squally rain on the coast road approaching the town which inspired her name. I skidded onto the verge to avoid her and moments later she only miraculously avoided being hit by a huge truck. I collected her up from under the Armco barrier and, back in our apartment, drowned more than 100 fleas in the bath. So gorged were they, none came off her in the car or jumped free to avoid the water.

A trip to a vet led to a visit to a British Army base, where the guards on the gate sent us to the army dog handlers, who in turn put us in touch with a soldier's wife who volunteered for a pet charity for servicemen and women. One of those super-competent dog ladies – not unlike Linda at Valle Verde! – she arranged to transport Paphos safely back to Blighty and gave us a list of approved quarantine kennels in the UK. And a couple of weeks later she flew into Manchester airport before starting her six-month prison sentence.

We visited Paphos every weekend without fail and eventually took her home, and over several weeks she came to terms with her new life, finally having some sort of puppyhood on the way to understanding how to walk on a lead, travel in a car, enjoy home comforts and interact with people and other dogs.

Paphos was two or three, I guess, when we took her to a charity dog show in a local park. A call went out for entries for a best rescue competition, and we entered, wondering if, due to her unusual backstory, she might even win a prize. No chance! It soon became clear it was not enough to have an animal with a highly unusual history. To win Best Rescue at these events it seemed an owner had to tell a good story and turbocharge the sentimentality and wretched emotions of it all; describe all the tail wagging and then cry the tears all over again. It was a lesson, should it be of interest to anyone, in playing the game.

It was clear from the very start Paphos was a disabled dog. Undersized in general at the back end, she had a small, misshapen pelvis and pronounced Queen Anne back legs. But her chest and front legs were strong, and she'd got the smarts all right. Years later we'd meet up with Linda and other friends and sometimes four or five dogs would play rough and tumble games together on a steeply-sloping field. The other dogs all had the legs on her, but time and again she got the trajectories worked out perfectly and would intercept their runs, drop a shoulder, and send one of them tumbling down the hill.

A couple more Paphos memories: one day as I was lifting her into my old Land Rover she broke away and put her paw firmly on the door of my Vauxhall estate. 'I much prefer the comforts of this one, thank you very much!' And then there was the time a sculptor came to the house to sketch her as she was to be the model for a giant steel sculpture of a dog on a motorcycle (it's a long story!). But when he arrived she had completely disappeared. What the? Paphos never wandered off! Anyway, after he'd left I went to close the car door – it was the height of summer and the car was baking on the drive – and there she was, dozing on the back seat, basking in the heat.

Paphos lived to be 13, not a bad age for an undernourished, disabled scrap of a thing running with fleas found tottering about on a Cypriot cliff top. The statue did get made by the way, and I own it, so she is with me forever, immortalised in sheet steel!

Big Joe, I'm very sad to say, was run over and killed and he's buried near Bonnie. It's just so crazy that there were acres of woods and fields behind that house and yet he met his end crossing the road at the front. His mate Blue, on the other hand, lived to a grand old age, and at the vet's being put down, despite being desperately ill, he was still purring and pushing to be stroked. He was a sweet and lovely boy.

Billy was a rather flat-faced ginger and white tomcat who came to live with us without my knowledge or consent, during a period when I was working away in the week and home only at weekends. I wasn't impressed to start with. We already had several cats and a couple of dogs, and I hadn't forgotten all the spraying and marking when Jess had moved in to live with other established cats. Besides, Billy was scowly and bad tempered, an unsociable boy not at all keen to be picked up or even stroked.

Then one day the poor lad had a fit. It was horrible to watch, and the vet reckoned he either had a form of epilepsy or had eaten something terribly toxic. There were no further instances, and he lived a long life, so I presume it was the latter, but we didn't know that when we brought him home that day, worrying if he'd even make it through the night. But survive he did, and he was immediately very different as a result of his experience, waking me up in the middle of that night, nuzzling me vigorously for attention while purring like a tractor before settling down to sleep next to my head. We were the best of mates from then on.

Indeed, when Jenny and I broke up a few years later we divided the animals between us and Paphos, Hector (of whom much more anon) and Billy stayed with me. By coincidence Jenny and I ended up buying properties just around the corner from each other and, having had second thoughts about Billy, Jenny came to my house twice while I was out and took him home with her. But both times he immediately made his way back, crossing several gardens, seemingly determined to stay with me. Billy and I may have got on well, but he and Hector the Staffie-cross were real bosom buddies, and most days Billy would follow me and the two dogs on our regular walks up the lane and across the fields behind my house until, two years later, all three quadrupeds moved with me to make a new start in another new house with a fantastic woman called

Loretta, who had her own motley collection of felines and knew nothing about dogs but was willing to learn.

After a tricky settling-in period, during which he disappeared for a few days and was thankfully spotted by a neighbour (despatched following her call, I carried him home, across fields, purring loudly in my arms), Billy Boo, as he had become known, then enjoyed a very happy life as a senior cat until, many years and adventures later, his organs started failing. The poor old boy became ever thinner, and inevitably began losing his mind too, then one day a passer-by brought him to the door, having spotted him wandering aimlessly in the road. It was time.

So, Billy and I were very close, and he was much loved by Loretta and our daughter, Esme, and all who knew him really! But as with humans it's true to say there are some cats and dogs we come across in our lives that we never really warm to in quite the same way. We respect them, empathise with them, maybe even admire them, but we don't grow to love them fully and unconditionally. It might be that because of a difficult start in life their personalities are suppressed, and they can't interact with people very much.

And sometimes as owners there's guilt on our part because at some points in our lives we're too wrapped up in work or other time-consuming activities to afford an animal the attention we actually really want to give it. I realised after he'd been killed on the road that the last time I'd seen Ginge, a young farm cat we took on in 2012 with his brother, Felix, I'd just given him an absent-minded stroke or two while checking my emails. He had come to see me, and my reaction had been automatic. That was a lesson. Pay attention! When a cat comes to see me now, I always try to engage. That was another strange thing. After he'd been knocked down but before I knew it, I felt his presence near me. A not uncommon occurrence, I think.

Beebee, a rescue dog from Valle Verde is a lifelong escapologist. Bloody dog! The first few months he was with us he got out again and again, and in the end it cost us more than £500 to make the garden secure.

Worse, he's a dog with no road sense at all. Zero. None. He just sails across them without pause so how he hasn't been killed I really don't know. During one of his escapades, he travelled more than two miles, roaming through a town centre and out the other side, navigating along and crossing goodness knows how many roads including two main thoroughfares. Finally, someone grabbed him, read his tag and phoned me. At least escapers seem to follow a pattern. The next time he got out I followed his previous route and caught him early. Then there was the time he ran off at a crematorium when we were attending a friend's funeral and Loretta's ex-husband helped us retrieve him. Don't ask! Despite being terminally gormless, BeeBee has ended up having a very long life indeed for a big dog. He's currently 16 and still enjoying a daily run out around the playing fields near our house, notwithstanding his poor hearing, near total blindness, wobbly legs and general state of advanced decrepitude. And at home he drives us crazy with his incessant Chewbacca-style vocalising.

Roma, an eight stone Rottweiler, vocalised in another way. It was interesting. If you sat down and put your arm around her she growled. Or rather, she made a deep grumbly noise that sounded a bit like growling. But if you ever took her food away from her while she was eating, perhaps having forgotten to add her medication, then you heard what Rottweiler growling really sounded like! But even then she let you do what you needed to do. She was a lover not a fighter and an absolutely fantastic dog. Having said that, in a book I read about the breed it said: 'Do not encourage rough and tumble play with a Rottweiler', and that is very good advice I'm sure. But Roma made a friend of everyone who came to the house, and we enjoy dinner parties and entertaining so that's a lot of people. Everyone adored her, even my mother liked her, and that's quite something.

And although she had no pedigree as such, no kennel club papers, she was an absolutely beautiful-looking dog too. And too smart by far to ever run across a road without looking. What a dog she was, yet in the end she brought heartbreak a different way.

Roma came into our lives when we went to the RSPCA kennels in Manchester having made an enquiry about adopting another small dog. Sadly, Hector didn't get on with him (I'll get to Hector soon) but then Loretta amazed me by asking about Roma, whom we'd also seen on the RSPCA website. The girls at the kennels were delighted. They clearly loved her and didn't hesitate to bring her out to see us. What a great advert for the dog, I thought. They wouldn't do that if they had any doubts about her temperament, especially as we had our four-year-old daughter with us. And Hector? Hector just sat down.

Roma, the manager told us, had been the subject of an RSPCA cruelty and neglect prosecution which had taken two years to complete because the scumbag wouldn't cooperate with the authorities, and since then she had spent a further two years in kennels because no one wanted a middle-aged Rotty with dodgy hips. Now she was eight as after four years of misery and mistreatment, she'd spent four more behind bars. Yet despite all this she was friendly, bright and vibrant, not at all resentful of the human race. Loretta in particular bonded with her straight away and none of us had any doubts she was coming home with us.

Only not quite yet. We had to wait a week before we could collect her – a cooling off period I guess, and a most sensible idea.

When we returned the following weekend Roma pulled her handler across the yard at speed and, bad hips or not, jumped straight into the back of our car. There could be no doubt she knew exactly what was happening. She sat bolt upright, looking out of the window the whole way home, and when we got there she ran round and round the front garden, bounding for joy.

What a fantastic dog she was. What a girl! Once, on a walk in the dark, I lost sight of her on the lane behind our house. I continued, retraced my steps, then continued again. Finally, becoming ever more concerned, I went home to get a torch. But there was no need for that. There she was, sitting on the doorstep. Another time she pushed past me in the doorway to get to the postman walking away down the drive. Just to say hello, but the postman didn't know that! And I was proud of her when she stopped in her tracks and returned straight to me as soon as I called her.

Like a lot of Rottweilers, Roma's hips were clunky and when we adopted her the RSPCA paid for her to be on Metacam for the rest of her life, although we didn't know about this when we chose her. But we decided early on that, if she could choose, this brilliant, intelligent dog would rather have an active life than do less for the sake of living a few extra months. Not that we pushed her over great distances of course.

In the summer months Roma and Hector would often walk through the woods with Loretta to pick our daughter Esme up from school. On one occasion, Loretta had to pop into the class cloakroom for a moment and left Roma tied to the school fence. She was on her way back across the playground when one of the teaching assistants came rushing across waving her arms in the air, shrieking: 'There's a Rottweiler in the playing field!' Now you might think this isn't a laughing matter. But it is. You see, through her many visits Roma had made an army of young friends at the school. She loved the kids, and they loved her. Besides, Loretta was away a total of 30 seconds. And I ask you, would anyone leave a powerful, dangerous dog unsupervised in a school field? Actually, I suppose some idiots would, and that's the trouble.

Roma may have loved everyone but as many of you will know, a guarding instinct runs strong in Rottweilers. On another of our regular walks we would pass a bungalow being extended by a dog-loving man with a Schnauzer. Let's call him Bill. Almost every time we came along, Bill would spot us, come down from his ladder or from behind the wall he was building and come towards us. Seeing him, Roma would trot across to him and let him make a fuss of her. 'Hello, darling,' Bill would say, as he miraculously and unfailingly produced treats for her from his pocket. But it was curious. When I wasn't there and Loretta was on her own, Roma wouldn't leave her side, blanking Bill completely, making him come right over to them and only responding to him when she felt she had Loretta's permission. And then there was Bill's peculiar neighbour – what a twit. One day Roma went over to him for a fuss. Thereafter, he'd always say, 'Keep that ruddy dog on a lead.' No chance pal. You're the one with a problem!

We had Roma for four fantastic years, and towards the end we sometimes had to help her stand up and get moving, and we had long been using a ramp to enable her to get in and out of the car.

But then there came the day when she couldn't stand up at all. It really was hugely upsetting. I got help to lift her back end in a sling and we drove her to the vet knowing she wouldn't be with us on the return journey. Throughout her time with us she would often take my hand in her mouth, pressing gently with her teeth, squeezing it affectionately in her powerful jaws. It was a trust and affection thing. And that last day at the vet's for sure she somehow knew what was going to happen, and while the vet prepared the injection she gave my hand an exceptionally hard squeeze!

By that time, the aforementioned cats Ginge (full name: Gingerelli) and Felix (black with a white chin, bib and paws, obvs!) had come free from a farm up the road. Janet there explained she thought she'd had all the cats there spayed and neutered but there had been a pregnancy nonetheless and Felix had been part of the result. Ginge not so – he had been left on the doorstep with a note: 'Please look after my kiten (sic)'.

And a year or two before then a neighbour who fostered for Cats Protection had asked us to feed her own and various rescue cats while she was on holiday, as her teenage sons couldn't be fully trusted. All went well on Loretta's first visit, but on the second day not so much. A pair of feral white and black kittens escaped from their quarters into a basement utility room and hid themselves behind the appliances. Pete of Valle Verde was visiting us at the time so we both answered Loretta's call to arms and went across the road having donned thick jackets and gardening gloves. Well, there was a great kerfuffle with much shrieking and wailing. And that was just me and Pete! Actually, it was mostly the cats, but it was the nearest I've ever heard Pete et to swearing. The washing machine and tumble dryer got dragged into the middle of the room and the kittens were literally climbing the walls at times, but we got them back into captivity. Back home afterwards we recovered over a cup of tea, somewhat dishevelled and not without painful injury. More than one glove had come off and jacket sleeves had inevitably ridden up, so we were both bitten and scratched quite badly on the hands and wrists. Then the next day Loretta came back from feeding them once more and said she wanted to adopt them!

But Fizz and Milo – yes, Tweenies-inspired! – were damaged little creatures I'm sad to say, poor little things. Having been feral, found in a garage, and their mother having abandoned them (or been scared away?) when they were so young affected them adversely for life. Affection and a stable home repaired some of the damage but not all. Fizz, the female, would never be properly domesticated and she lived mostly in our conservatory, and her brother Milo spent a lot of time there too. But the house backed onto fields, so the arrangement worked quite well, although it did get rather cold in the winter. Milo hunted, or we assume he did – he'd regularly go for two or three-day walkabouts and was always a good weight despite not eating much bought food – and Fizz lived mostly on the top of a display cabinet containing Loretta's badminton and table tennis trophies!

She would come down to eat, only then letting me stroke her, although Loretta got to make a gentle fuss of her at other times too and she'd come to sit near her very occasionally. But neither of us was ever able to pick Fizz up without donning protective clothing. Milo was not nearly so wild.

He would be held, and he sometimes sought affection, but he became uncomfortable if stroked for too long, giving a quick warning bite and trotting away when he couldn't bear the intimacy and vulnerability any longer.

Fizz would only eat cat biscuits, which wasn't good for her at all, but nothing else even tempted her – roast chicken, the most expensive tinned cat food, nothing at all. Then after we moved house and semi-detached conservatory living was no longer an option for her, she took up residence on the top of our piano by the patio doors, nipping outside only to do her business. Or not. We ended up having to have an indoor litter tray. Great! She lived to be 13.

Soon after we moved to our current house Milo broke out and disappeared, returning after three months. We succeeded in keeping him in much longer the second time but once restrictions were lifted he was soon gone again, never to be seen again, or so we thought. But an incredible three years and two months later we received a phone call from a vet 13 miles away. They'd got Milo and had traced us following some clever detective work after reading his chip. Of course, we went to get him straight away and this time he stayed with us for 28 months before disappearing once again quite recently. The last period he spent with us was a much happier time for him, I think, although he liked to be on high surfaces if possible, and not because of the dogs. Felix was clearly more than a little put out by his return and bullied him if he got the chance, but he was much loved by our new Valle Verde kittens Rosko and Minerva who came in 2021, and he had a touching reunion with his sister before she died.

Milo was a sweet, gentle boy who avoided conflict with other felines at all times despite being a strapping tom, surely able to be the household's top cat if it had suited him. He is very much missed.

I've mentioned Ginge and Felix, who weren't brothers although they thought they were! When they came from the farm we set up a base camp for them in the lounge, supplying a litter tray and a feeding station for them, and temporarily banning the dogs. All went well at first, then I made a mistake on day two, leaving the door ajar behind me when I went to check on them during the morning. Roma barged the door right open and followed me in. Ooh, she thought, kittens. How very interesting! Then, immediately afterwards: Ooh food! Much more interesting! As she made for their breakfast bowls, wee Ginge squeezed himself under the long-case clock in the corner of the room and flighty Felix shot straight up the chimney.

It was a chimney in regular use for coal fires and therefore extremely sooty, but thankfully it was fully cold that morning. I stuck my head in the fireplace and contorted myself in order to peer upwards. Felix was on a ledge a few feet up, then he scrambled up even further, completely out of sight, dislodging more soot as he did so. I went outside to see if he would appear out of the top of the chimney stack. Thankfully, he didn't. But it was raining fairly heavily and on my way back to the lounge I caught sight of myself in the hall mirror. Black streaks were running down my forehead and face, and I could feel the same thing happening down the back of my neck.

Later that day Felix and Ginge were due their second trip to the vets for inoculations and fortunately Felix came down just in time for the appointment, Loretta having tempted him with a juicy treat of some sort while I kept well out of the picture.

So, I took a ginger kitten and a matt black one to the surgery that evening, but on my first visit I'd taken a pale marmalade one and a little black and white one. 'Ah yes,' the girl on reception had said, 'Felix and Gingerelli. Which one's which?'

A brief aside about vets. There seems to be quite a turnover at the practice we use, mainly young women, quite a few of them Eastern European. So wot's occurring? Are they fully qualified veterinary surgeons, or specialist practitioners of some sort? Dunno. Are they on short-term contracts rather than permanent staff? Probably.

But one thing's for sure, if the firm's wages are going down at all as a result of its recruitment policy, it's not being reflected in their charges. There must be a formula. Maybe something like, think of a number that sounds half reasonable, double it, add another fixed figure, let's say £6.00. So, a consultation that lasts one minute – that's just £66 please. If it involves any sort of prescription – that's £96 please. Bloods or any other sort of test – that's £146 please. Overnight stay – that's £196 please. You get the idea.

For several years from around 2006 Loretta and I ran a B&B from our home and occasionally, by arrangement, guests would bring a dog. On one occasion a middle-aged couple brought a ten-year-old Welsh Labrador called Ben. The dog was a smasher. Not so much the owners. After clearing away the breakfast things Loretta came back to the kitchen sobbing. Unbelievably, it transpired the couple were emigrating to Thailand in a few days and the dog was going to be put down. 'Oh, we've tried all our friends,' they'd said, 'and the RSPCA won't have him.' Well try harder! Down to one dog at the time, not that that really mattered, we said straight away that we'd have him and fortunately they agreed. Unbelievably, this couple had had Ben since he was a puppy. Some people!

Understandably Ben was a little confused at first, but he settled down quickly enough and fitted right in. He and Hector got on famously, never a cross bark or dispute of any kind. And he was an intelligent lad. I would throw sticks for Ben in the garden, and he would unsight himself by setting off down the steps to the lawn as soon as my arm was raised. But I found I could easily direct him to the stick, no matter where it fell among many others and countless leaves, with just two simple commands: 'No' and 'Good boy'. Working with me in this manner he quickly found and returned the right stick absolutely every time.

Ben went on two or three holidays with us, staying in a posh pet-friendly hotel and at a holiday cottage at the Sussex seaside, especially enjoying the latter. He loved swimming, especially in the sea, and on that break he was in the water every chance he got. Another fond memory I have of him is how he'd sit with my father, who'd come to live with us when he was terminally ill, letting my dad stroke and pat him and providing him with a great deal of comfort in the process. But our time with Ben was destined to be relatively short, just a couple of years. From the start he had quite bad arthritis. He'd suffer the day after a long walk or too much playing. Then I noticed him slowing down in general. A trip to the vet – Ker-ching! – revealed a huge abdominal tumour had developed, presenting us with a choice. A couple of months of suffering and pain management or saying goodbye there and then. I hope you will understand when I say it was a very sad moment, but ultimately not a difficult decision.

Finally, it's time to talk about Hector. We keep Hector in the attic with my dad. They've both been dead for eight years now. I'm talking about their ashes, of course!

Hector arrived in my life when he was aged around six months in the summer of the year 2000. Actually, let me go back even further in time. It must have been 1999 when a characterful young Jack Russell followed me home one evening and stayed the night, before being claimed the following morning by his worried owner. Having that little chap with us for those few hours made me decide I wanted a similar dog and a few months later I finally got round to calling the local dog pound. 'Oh yes, we've got at least three Jack Russells,' said the manager on the phone, 'Come on down!' All too painfully aware of the council pound's death row policy of exterminating all dogs in residence longer than a fortnight, I walked through three large huts full of dogs of all shapes and sizes, some jumping up, some peering through the bars, others barely daring to peep from their beds. It was awful. And there were no Jack Russells. 'Well,' said my young guide to her boss after my tour, 'he doesn't like any of them!' 'Now that's definitely not true,' I said, 'I'd take them all if I could, but there aren't any Jack Russells!' 'Oh yes there are,' the manager insisted. Well, there weren't. Her definition seemed to be that any small terrier was a Russell. We'd have to agree to differ. 'Okay then,' I said, 'there was a small white one, let's go and have another look at him.'

The small white dog, it turned out, was a stocky, barrel-chested little Jack Russell-Staffordshire Bull Terrier cross who had been found wandering the backstreets of Halifax a few days before. 'Nice dog, mate,' the leader of a gang of ne'er do well yoofs called out as we gave him a tryout on the lead on the playing fields next to the kennels. They'd been ogling Hector for the last few minutes. That made up my mind. Yeah, right, mate, I thought. Nice for fighting you mean, and that's not going to happen to this little fellow. I took him back inside and said we'd have him. Boy that was a tough afternoon. There are at least three dogs I left behind that day that I can still recall quite clearly. I've thought about them often over the years. More guilt!

Hector was indeed just six months old, a pretty accurate estimation by the kennel staff that day according to our vet when I got him checked over. You could tell by his teeth, he said. Let's say integrating Hector into the family was challenging. He was a bombastic little-big-guy with no manners whatsoever, coming into a household with several established dogs. As well as Paphos we had Lucy, a great big, galumphing and very loving Labrador cross, and tall Tim, a lurcher who would make hunting and shooting types' eyes pop out on stalks. Although gentle and shy, Tim was a long dog to run down a hare if ever there was one, but don't be concerned, there was no chance of that ever happening. To be honest I really can't remember much about how Tim came to join the family as I was working away much of the time when he arrived, and Jenny, who was well connected in rescue circles, had brought Lucy home one day, at least in part as a reaction to Bonnie's death a few years earlier. Anyway, back to Hector. He would steal the other dogs' food, bark in their faces, nip them to get them to play and generally make a nuisance of himself. And he assumed the cats wanted to play with him too. But he was naughty, not nasty, with no real badness in him, and while the cats were decidedly irritated and unamused, the canine quadrupeds were more bemused than angry with him.

So, Hector – aka Hector Pig, or just Pig, because of his frequent noisy snuffling, or alternatively the White Twit, was quite a character, and we had a difficult first couple of years with him. I was working from home by then so defended his corner when I could as Jenny would throw her hands up after finding yet another shredded cushion, or despair of ever catching him while he raced round and round a car park, refusing to have his lead put on to go home after a walk in the woods. But I had to work long hours so couldn't always help and our relationship was not in a good place in general. At one point Jenny wanted Hector to be adopted by Malcolm, a friend of ours who took a particular shine to him, and I very reluctantly agreed. Malcolm said he'd take him the next day and I found myself lying awake most of the night feeling absolutely wretched, regretting the whole thing. I vowed to ring Malc first thing but instead at 8am he phoned me. He had had second thoughts. Thank goodness! I had grown to love that crazy little dog. Not much later Jenny and I split up instead.

For the next two years I was single again and Hector and I were pretty much inseparable, and Billy the cat was our mate too. Pig was my constant companion, sitting at my feet when I worked and coming with me in the car wherever I went. I took him all over the country during that time, even down to London where he rode with me to the West End on the tube, and I visited numerous people, interviewing them and taking photographs for a project I was working on. He had a winning way about him, making people smile and making memories everywhere we went. And once a week he went with me to the pub, where I had to be alert and manage new introductions because he could occasionally nip when surprised. But don't get the wrong idea, it was just that he was a little bit insecure and, if properly introduced, Hector was everybody's friend (except pub landlord Roger, who'd upset him by coming round collecting the glasses. Really bad judgment on Pig's part, that!).

Another of Hector's unfortunate traits was a tendency to terrible flatulence. He could produce the most horrendous farts and his particular party piece was to release them from under the pub table while a group of us sat around it, heads down, focusing hard during quiz night. The funny thing was his gag-inducing gaseous emissions were extraordinarily directional. It depended exactly where you were sitting and which way his little bottom was pointing (to put it crudely) as to whether you suffered terribly or escaped completely, and it was usually our skipper, captain Jack, who got most egregiously gassed, while those either side of him smelled nothing at all! 'This week,' I would say during the aftermath while Jack's eyes watered and he held a hanky to his empurpled fizzog, 'he's been mostly eating... Sainsbury's own brand!' Or whatever. You'll have to remember Jesse's Diets from The Fast Show to get that reference!

But despite everything, Hector was a really endearing little character whose naughtiness only added to his charm. Even my mum, who was so *not* a dog person as I have explained, became so fond of him on her occasional visits she painted him twice in watercolours!

In what way was he naughty? Well, here are a few minor examples – frequent selective deafness; humping a £1,000 rug at a rich friend's house after I promised he would behave; tearing open several black sacks full of newly-collected leaves and racing around the garden with them, redistributing thousands of leaves all over the lawn as soon as my back was turned; smashing the case of a rare CD and leaving teeth marks on the disc inside as the postman pushed it through the letterbox; biting a woman on the bottom outside the Co-Op; regularly stealing gloves and scarves and other things and running off with them for fun; deciding to have a pop at a German Shepherd that growled at him; climbing on the dining table after a family dinner and licking the butter; bursting a basketball we found in a shed at a holiday cottage – 'Dad, Dad, Hector's got the ball!' 'Don't worry, he won't get his jaws around...' POP!

Then there was the night the cheese disappeared. I'd recently met Loretta and she came to my house one evening to cook a romantic dinner. How lucky was I? Those who know what a good cook she is, as well as being an extraordinary person in general, will not be hesitating to say at this point that the answer is very lucky indeed! Well, after we finished whatever dessert she had magically conjured up that night, which had followed a main course of chicken in stilton sauce and roast potatoes as I recall, and which itself I have absolutely no doubt followed a delicious starter of some kind, she disappeared into the kitchen once more, returning a few moments later carrying a cheeseboard loaded with cheddar and biscuits, but with a puzzled look on her face. 'You haven't seen a piece of brie, have you, about so big?' A tranche of significant size had evidently gone missing.

Working together systematically, we searched every place it could possibly be. Twice. The fridge. No. Every worktop. Nope. All the bags the food had arrived in. Not there either. And, by torchlight, every possible place in the car. Nuffink. Hector was the obvious prime suspect and Loretta originally thought she might have left the brie on the kitchen table, but Hector couldn't possibly reach up there, so that was out of the question. So, we had some cheddar and another glass of wine before retiring to the lounge for coffee, whereupon we came across an incriminating piece of clingfilm on the carpet and lying flat on his back on the sofa with his legs in the air, breathing somewhat heavily, was Hector. We can only assume that a kitchen chair, temporarily pulled out from under the table and momentarily left unattended, had given the naughtiest dog in town all the opportunity he had required.

I mentioned Hector once had a go at a German Shepherd but he was not at all nasty to people, neither was he to other dogs. His attitude seemed to be, okay you, let's play, and if the other dog was frightened and ran, or alternatively attacked him, things could get tricky. But if the other dog said, 'Okay then, mate, come on then,' off they'd go together best of mates.

Hector lived a full life in every respect, living until he was nearly 16. In his last few months, he was having brain seizures caused by organ failure. His body was poisoning itself, and after a while the problem couldn't be contained any longer. But he was a tough old boy. When I took him to the vet the final time it took three times the normal dose of whatever drug they used to bring matters under control. Then they kept him in overnight for observation and the next morning came the news that there was nothing more they could do, and it was time to say goodbye. I went straight away to be with him, held him and talked to him, saying his name at the end. Now, that was hard! I loved that little guy, and I'd got it back in spades from the first day to the last. I remember him with fondness and a smile, but when he first went there was still guilt in the mix. I kept thinking about the times I had been impatient, the times I'd told him off. I guess it's just the same as mourning a human being.

You know how it is, all you can think of are the things you wish you'd said and done, or not said and done… Then as time passes the balance shifts and it's all the good things, the happy memories that more readily come to the fore. Hector was a fantastic little dog with a wonderful winning way about him, despite being so very naughty!

I mentioned Loretta was not a dog person when I met her. It was love me love my dog once again, and Loretta and Hector were to get to know and like each other very much, and she's grown to understand and appreciate dogs in general. But she's a cat person at heart and a fan of long-haired varieties, particularly Persians. I can't say I'm with her on that one, I'm afraid, although Minou, a little rescue cat who spent most of her time on the top of the kitchen radiator cover when Hector was about, was a sweet little thing. My problem with long-haired cats is that they're not capable of self-maintenance, needing regular grooming or their fur gets tangled. What a pain! It's not their fault obviously, no cat asked to be born with easily-matting hair. And Persians to my mind are peculiar-looking creatures. As Loretta's brother once said about one in his best scouse accent: 'That cat looks like it's been hit in the face by a pan!'

The aforementioned Beebee came to us from Valle Verde along with a small dog called Farola – which is Spanish for lamp as I guess many of you will know. She'd been found tied to a lamppost and ended up in one of Linda's network of foster homes. Faz, as she quickly became known, was a giddy little speedster of a dog who loved to chase and catch balls. A Jack Russell on stilts, she's actually a Bodeguero, a Spanish ratter, and her amazing patience and high-speed chasing and ball-catching capabilities together serve to demonstrate the breed's innate methodology and effectiveness. Our party trick when visitors come round and she pushes a tennis ball into their lap, is to tell them to just sit there holding it. Farola will promptly sit down herself and wait for as long as necessary before it's thrown. Not moving a single muscle. Never taking her eye off the ball.

Farola is a street dog at heart and sometimes less than sociable with other canines. And for sure she was not impressed the day we brought Tilly home. Tilly was a Westie cross and another characterful little terrier, a feisty older dog and, like Faz, more than capable of standing up for herself. How did we come by her? Loretta was playing Scrabble with her friend Margaret one Saturday afternoon – I can be sure of that because they play Scrabble together almost every Saturday afternoon – and Margaret was telling her how her neighbour, Pat (not her real name), whom Loretta vaguely knew, had gone into hospital for migraine tests and had been kept in. 'And that poor dog,' said Margaret, 'Pat doted on it, and it's been in kennels these past three weeks and her family just don't care, they haven't even been to see her, let alone take her home.'

Well, you can guess what happened next. After getting in touch with Pat's family we fetched her home with us until Pat got well. But then we found out poor Pat had a brain tumour, and soon afterwards she died, so Tilly ended up staying with us permanently. And do you know what, as the saying goes? When we took her to her vet the first weekend because she was panting – stress, it turned out, perhaps not surprisingly, and it soon sorted itself – it turned out Tilly had an outstanding bill there which Pat's folks were declining to pay.

Like Farola, little Tilly Top was a typical terrier in being strong-willed, single-minded and fiercely determined. And like Faz she was very much Loretta's dog. Cupboard love was a factor I'm sure, as Loretta usually put their food down twice a day, but there was more to it than that. Both little dogs were devoted to her. Sadly, like our other surprise rescue, Ben, we only had Tilly for a couple of years. She died one evening while we were out, finding her dead on the floor when we got back. That was quite a shock I can tell you. Poor little thing. Why didn't we realise? More guilt!

She'd been ill for a week or so although it hadn't seemed especially serious, there having been a misdiagnosis, we now think, by her vet (we had continued to take Tilly to the one Pat had always taken her to). Just a few days earlier he had said she was exhibiting the early stages of heart failure, prescribing medication and saying he was confident her condition could be managed for some time. I actually now think she had canine Covid and the pills he gave us might even have contributed to her death. That was in 2020, and much more recently we got chatting about local vets to another dog owner on one of our walks. 'Oh, Dr Shipman,' he said. 'What?' 'Didn't you know? People around here call him that because he kills people's pets.'

Feral kittens are born all the time in rural Spain and Linda at Valle Verde does a fantastic job of looking after and domesticating them, and finding them homes, while spaying and neutering the parents. By the time of Covid Felix and Milo were fairly senior cats and Loretta had long wanted another kitten, so after Pete mentioned there were a pair of gingers in the latest batch to be born near their house in Spain, discussions with Linda ensued, and in September 2021 Rosko and Minerva made the long trip from Almunecar to northern England while we watched their progress on an app not unlike a Santa tracker!

They were such beautiful little cats, and they brought us so much joy. Indeed, Minerva still does, but almost exactly two years after they arrived, her brother Rosko was killed by a thoughtless idiot, speeding by on the road outside our house. It's not even a busy road and subject to a 20mph speed limit. What on earth are people doing, racing around like maniacs? The open road is the place to get a move on, not a residential street. No doubt he (or she) had a very important job, or urgent business to attend to. Maybe his house was on fire, or a parent was dying, or his wife was going into labour. Yeah, right.

Like his sister, Rosko had spectacular markings. He was a beautiful, handsome cat, and such a friendly, loving boy. Great to have around, happy to be picked up and cuddled, he was soft and affectionate, yet playful and full of fun. And at two he was just calming down and becoming an adult cat after a wonderfully zany kittenhood. By the way, how on earth do young cats know how to play-fight with humans, claws out just enough not to hurt too badly?

Of course, Minerva has had to deal with his loss as much as we have. And with losing her 'Uncle Milo'. She loved being with him, sleeping alongside him when she could, and he was hugely patient with her and her brother, never once lashing out no matter how much he was put upon. It was only a few weeks before Rosko died that Milo went missing again. Poor Milo. Where are you, old friend?

Losing Milo and Rosko in recent weeks has been deeply upsetting, as all previous losses have been. Time, however, is a healer and with feisty Farola, ancient BeeBee, scaredy cat Felix (aka Mr Neat), and delightful little Min Min, we move forward. And what other animals will light up our lives in the future? Animals we're yet to meet, maybe yet to be born. Dogs running free alongside us on our country walks, joining us on our holidays, barking excitedly to celebrate our return to the house. Snooty cats deigning to share their space with us, loving cats rubbing up against us, coming to sit on our laps when we sit down to read or write or to watch the television in the evening. Both species delighting us with the silly things they do.

Jeremy Clarkson's right. Dogs (and cats) will break your heart. But that's no reason at all not to share your lives with them. Do it now. Adopt a cat or a dog. Or both! Your life, and theirs, will be very much the richer for it.

Also by Richard Skelton
Funky Mopeds – the 1970s Sports Moped Phenomenon
A Life Awheel – the 'auto'-biography of W D Forte
Chris Carter at Large – Stories from a Lifetime in Motorcycle Racing
The Vintage Years of Last of the Summer Wine
Royal Enfield – a Global Motorcycling Success Story
Motorcycling in the 1970s (ebook series)

Instructions on How to Raise a Kitten
(From a first time foster parent)
By the Hall Family

1. When the kitten arrives have everything ready: bed, bowl, bottle, toys, camera. (At this age the camera is the most important as they are so cute.)

2. When you get your kitten, make sure you get two as company for each other. When the kitten is undersized, it needs extra warmth as well. (You also have an extra kitten to take photos of.)

3. Bottle feeding is ideal, and you'll need kitten milk from the vets. Then attempt to get the kittens to drink the milk. Discard the bottle as they just won't drink from it. Use a syringe instead. (Take a photo of them covered in milk.)

4. Syringe feeding takes a long time so set aside hours of your time. It's rewarding when they fall asleep. (Take a picture of them sleeping.) Ten minutes later they are awake again, feed them again. Then watch them sleep, again. (Take several more photos.)

5. So after you've had your kitten(s) for a day, you expect them to start pooing. They won't. They need help. Normally mum cat licks their bums. No you do NOT have to do this. (Phew.) Take a damp flannel or cloth and gently wipe their bums. Repeat this again, and again and again. Still nothing? Getting concerned? OK, so quick trip to the vet's. Now stand at the vet's whilst she also tries to get the kitten to poo using a cotton bud. Still nothing? Go home again and continue massaging

their bum with circular motions of the cotton bud. At about 2am the kitten will produce 5mm of poo. Yay! Get some sleep. No, feed kitten again, then get some sleep. (Too tired for photos.)

6. Be proud when your kittens use the litter tray for the first time. If you're lucky they will teach themselves. (Proudly boast to other fosterers about how clever your kittens are.) Excellent – no more cleaning the floor of their little accidents either. (Don't take a photo this time because it'll really embarrass the kittens when they're older.)

7. Be strict about not letting the kittens into the bedroom. This will avoid them chewing your shoes, scratching up your clothes, having little toilet accidents etc. Keep the door firmly closed. Figure out how the kittens got into the bedroom when the door was closed. Pick up any shoes, clothes etc. (Take a photo of the kittens looking at themselves in the wardrobe mirror. They are very cute.)

8. Now the kittens can get into the bedroom, be really, really strict about not letting them on the bed. (Later come back and take a photo of them asleep on your bed.)

9. Kittens start to play at different ages, depending on their rate of development. The first instinctual play is hunting. They start by catching moving objects close to them, like a piece of string or a feather. Their favourite is a moving torch light – go buy a mini laser pointer. (Take a video rather than just boring old photos.)

10. The second type of play is fighting. This becomes very vicious and usually involves fake ripping out the jugular of their opponent. With young kittens you spend a lot of time rescuing the smaller one from their sibling's jaws. (Take any photos before the playing gets too violent.)

11. TV use. At their age kittens must have a limit on how much TV they watch. (Take a photo of them trying to catch Tom Cruise.)

12. Kittens are not IT trained, even though they think they are. They don't always understand what they are typing so beware of unusual searches in your browser or extra words added to that important email to your boss. And of course back up all your documents because their favourite key is Delete. (Obviously take lots of photos because this is super cute, until your computer crashes and you lose everything you've been working on for hours...)

13. Finally give your kittens loads of cuddles and affection. They will return this a hundred times over, especially in the middle of the night when you turn on the light and they are just staring at you waiting for a cuddle. (Of course another photo!)

14. Make sure you store all your photos and videos digitally because there will be hundreds of them. Enjoy!

A m b e r ' s   s t o r y
B y   S a m   B a k e r

ONE MORNING IN JULY 2017 I received a frantic call from my elderly father. He had been walking my sister's dogs in the countryside near Puntalon in the south of Spain on a typically hot July morning. 'There's a dog, a big one, swimming around one of those huge, concrete water deposit tanks,' he said. 'It can't get out, the sides are too high, it's going to drown, there's nobody around, we've got to help it!'

I quickly drove over to Puntalon, picked up my father and we drove to the site. From the lane above the circular tank we could see the dog swimming frantically around inside. The tank had a diameter of about 12 metres and was approximately as deep as a single storey building, rising up from ground level and adjoined to a single storey storeroom. I found a way to clamber up a rusty old ladder attached to the side of the storeroom and on to the roof. From there, the side of the concrete tank was waist height, and I could clearly see the poor dog paddling round and round, becoming more and more exhausted. The problem was I couldn't lean over far enough to reach the dog as the water level was about 1.5 metres below the rim of the tank and the terrified dog would not come close enough to me for me to grab it. I couldn't see if there was any way to get myself out if I jumped in the water to try and get hold of it.

The scenario enfolding in front of me was heartbreaking. The dog was clearly becoming more and more exhausted — only its head was sticking out of the water, its body becoming more and more vertical. Suddenly, I saw a worker's van driving along the track. I stood on the roof of the storeroom and waved frantically, jumping up and down to get their attention – thankfully, they saw me, and pulled over into the parking area next to the tank. I shouted an explanation to the two men, and they rushed to find a key to the storeroom. They brought a ladder out and I hauled it up on to the roof. The younger of the two men joined me and we put the ladder into the water. He stripped off to his shorts and got into the water, but the dog was losing energy and wouldn't come near enough for him to grab it. Just its nose and the top of its head were now visible. I was losing hope of saving its life. It had been swimming for its life for an hour and a half since we had got there, and for who knows how long before that.

The young man, Alberto, changed tactic. He got back out of the water, we pulled the ladder out and leaned it against the highest part of the tank, about 5 metres high. He walked very carefully along the 30cm rim of the concrete tank, avoiding the sharp, metal spikes that were placed roughly every 20cm along it. I couldn't believe what I was seeing. He risked falling off the edge of the tank, 5 metres on to rough terrain. He sat on the narrow edge with each leg either side of the rim and as the dog struggled past, he leant over, scooped it up, grabbing on to its coat and pulled it out on to the rim of the tank on to his lap. I was astounded at his bravery and determination to get the dog out. The dog was large and heavy with a thick, medium length coat. He manoeuvred sideways and attempted to bring it down the ladder without dropping it or falling off. Just then the terrified dog bit him and he dropped her halfway down. The dog attempted to run away but, of course, being totally exhausted it collapsed in a heap at the bottom of a steep hill. Alberto was a hero that day.

We waited with the dog until the rescue service came to collect it. The dog was a girl, the most beautiful, gentle Collie/German Shepherd-type crossbreed. The next day, I collected her from the kennel and gave her a good bath and a brush and lots and lots of love and hugs and took her to Linda and the team at Valle Verde Animal Rescue.

We called her Amber. She had no microchip, and nobody appeared to be missing her, but she was in good health. We will never know how she got in the water tank, whether she jumped in from the side of the hill looking to cool off from the July heat or whether someone had thrown her in, and we will never know for exactly how long she was swimming to keep herself alive.

She was adopted by a wonderful man in Holland who she went to live with in October 2017. She lived a beautiful life with him. We are still in touch, even though dear, sweet, gentle Amber passed over the rainbow bridge in January 2022. She had over 4 wonderful years full of love, comfort and happiness. She is missed greatly.

Benji
By Thomas Bryan

WE HAD LOST OUR BELOVED Spaniel cross Buster to illness and after a suitable break we were ready to give a home to another dog, preferably in need. Our dear friend Sarah got on the case with the zeal of a Breton who had smelt game; before long we got to hear of a young Ratonero who had been found abandoned by the side of the road near Jete. He was being fostered in the Lecrin, so we arranged to go and meet him. Do not let anyone tell you that love at first sight doesn't exist!

He was only about a year old and had a cruelly shortened tail, but he was friendly, looked in need of lots of good food and love ~ he came home with us. That night he slept in his new bed and blanket by the side of our bed where he has slept ever since. It took a good while for him to settle, he was polite but somewhat aloof, couldn't make eye contact, and was very afraid if you touched his rear. He also had real problems with his digestion.

He was seen by the vet who did all the jabs and fitted a chip; we also felt he was young enough to be castrated. Just as he was beginning to settle we moved house and now he had a garden to call his own and long countryside walks ~ he started to grow in confidence.

After about 9 months he would hold eye contact and allow us to stroke him all over; he also started to find his place with us and really became 'our boy'. We called him Benjamin (Benji for short) and he is now completely part of our family and is a loving confident chap who likes everyone. We have loved him from first sight, he keeps us fit and provides lots of affection and laughter. We'd be lost without him!

Canija's story
By Ela Graves and Beth Wallace

Ela Graves:

Canija's story started with her being picked up near Órgiva, in the Alpujarra mountains, on New Year's Eve 2019 by volunteers from an animal protection organisation called No al Maltrato de Animales y Plantas Alpujarra (NoMaypa).

I saw a photo on Facebook of a dog that looked like a concentration camp survivor. She had almost no hair, bits of ears missing, open sores and no flesh at all. So I shared the photo and a wonderful Irish woman living in Órgiva called Beth Wallace agreed to foster her. She did not have a car or speak Spanish, so I volunteered to pick Canija up from the vet and have the medication explained to me. I went there with a friend of mine and her little girl. Canija came out of the inner room, and we all went into shock as she looked so awful, but then she wagged her tail, and I was deeply moved by her. The vet explained she had leishmaniasis but might make it. What we did not know was that she was almost blind.

Beth lived in a first floor flat, and we had to carry Canija up the stairs — it took weeks for her to manage steps. As Beth could not take Canija out into the street, she had to mop up her pee and poo for weeks. Enormous amounts of kitchen roll was the most expensive thing that NoMaypa had to pay for, apart from her medication and food.

Well, Canija could just about walk when the owner of the flat where Beth lived found out she was there and said she did not accept animals. So she then was fostered by Aca, a mother and child living in a caravan who gave her a lot of love but could not stay in the area.

I did not know what to do as we had run out of volunteers. I have a cat that is not happy with dogs, so it occurred to me to invite a Russian woman, Ania, to come and live in our yurt and look after Canija in return for the accommodation. Then the lockdown started and luckily Olenka who lived next door, and who in the end became Canija's main carer, came back from working in England and so all three of us in a mountain farm cared for her.

Little by little she gained weight and strength and could go for short walks, always very cheerful and wagging her tail, though terrified of loud noises. We finally realized that she was almost blind, though as she maps a territory through her incredible memory she fooled us at first. She can see large shapes and some movement but can fall off the edge of a terrace if going too fast. She also started hunting anything that moved, including cats, using her hearing and sense of smell. She can actually go really fast in open countryside.

During the lockdown we went for longer and longer walks and Canija kept improving so NoMaypa advertised for an adoption many times, but no one came forward. Canija did not look very beautiful then! We approached Valle Verde in the hope of an adoption abroad but gradually realized that we were becoming committed to her company and could not bear to have her stay away from us. It was Linda Rane who told us Canija was a Podenco cross which explained the hunting tendency—blind or not.

As we have posted so often asking for help to look after her, she has become well known in Órgiva and people stop us to greet her. The local supermarket Coviran run by the Galvez family have supported us with bones and off-cuts over these years. Thank you so much Marian, Maribel and Bernardo.

One day waiting outside Galvez supermarket with Canija, a French couple stopped and looked at Canija and called her Belle! So we found there was another previous chapter to her rescue, a failed one that led to her blindness. They told us her story: Canija was originally rescued by them three months before she was picked up by NoMaypa. She was permanently tied up at a farm and cried all the time, so they 'took' her and named her Belle as she was so beautiful. The owner found out and got her back but would not give her the leishmaniasis medication they were giving her. In those three months she lost her health, sight and beauty. She also had a puppy that we know nothing more of.

Well, it is now three years later, and many people have been Canija´s third carer. She is now Leish negative after many different treatments, including several natural ones such as CBD oil. In the end she so captured our hearts that Olenka and I have jointly adopted her though it is still very difficult with my cat as I have to keep them apart. Luckily Olenka now lives in Spain permanently, so she has Canija most of the time. My attitude to dogs has changed gradually as I have got to know Canija. I am now fascinated by all of them and stop to greet every dog I meet. I am so grateful to Canija for being so patient with me and giving me time to get to know her and appreciate doggy love.

Funnily enough we rescued another Podenco just the other day, not in such a bad state as Canija but like so many dumped hunting dogs, very neglected and skin and bones. We have named her Dulce. She hopefully has a proper adoption coming up as we really cannot have two!

Beth Wallace
Something broken in me recognised something broken in her.

These are the words that keep reverberating around me in relation to this beautiful creature. I saw her pictures and knew she had to come to me. She came nearly 3 weeks ago on New Year's Eve, literally a bag of bones and skin, unable to walk properly and barely even able to stand, struggling to breathe, needing help to eat by being hand fed. I had never seen something alive look so dead.

And yet over the last 3 weeks she has healed so much, her skin is no longer red raw and bleeding, her hair is re-growing and she has gained 7lbs in weight. What is especially joyful is that her tail now freely wags—she is happy!

I have been reminded each and every day that it is only with the deepest of tenderness and the gentlest of compassion that we can reach the places within us that are excruciating to touch.

I have been reminded that love, time, attention, presence and an open heart is often, though not always of course, what's required for healing to take place.

I have been reminded that healing is usually an inside job and that what's required is an environment in which it is safe for that process to unfold, an environment in which time and patience and space can be given for that.

I have been reminded that love is infinite, there is no end to it if it is truly love — if it's looking for something in return, if it's looking for a transaction of any sort, then it is not love.

I feel very privileged to have been able to share this deep and tender space with her, to have been reminded of my own belonging to myself, to have been given the opportunity to pour infinite love all over and into her, and to receive it from her. Oh, those eyes. I will miss her, so much, as she leaves me today for a new foster mum and a big part of me wishes that my life circumstances were different, and we could stay together but as is often the case with relationships sometimes it is the brightly burning short-lived ones that teach us the most and penetrate us most deeply.

Caramèlo
By Reijer Staats

WE'RE LEAVING OUR LECRÍN VALLEY summer house on a sunny Sunday morning during spring break. Today's goal: the steep climb to the Ermita del Zapato, the chapel high above our Spanish village. As we´re passing the fig tree, opposite the shed in the alley just around the corner, we run into a scene of 8 light to dark brown Podenco puppies with wagging little rat tails. They must be about 4 weeks old. We observe them playing and as soon as they notice us, they curiously run towards us. We're touched!

We complete the steep path of 45 curves up to the Ermita, and the following descent, at record speed, without even taking one moment to enjoy the vistas over the Alpujarras. Within the hour, we´re back at the site where we spotted the litter of pups, where now we find them lying on top of each other, basking in the Andalusian sun.

The actual plan for our short break was to drive our car from Holland to Andalusia, to put it on Spanish plates, and to leave it there for good. I look at my partner, noticing a twinkle in his eyes, and it becomes clear that the same idea occurs to both of us: 'We´re definitely going to rescue one of these puppies, and we´ll just drive back the 2,200 kilometres to Holland by car again!' For help, we immediately turn to our dear neighbour Josefina, who introduces us to a muchacho (young guy), the mother dog's owner.

The next day, the day of our flight back to Holland, we make our way to the shed again. It's been raining all morning, and the alley has changed into a muddy gutter. The muchacho opens up the gate to the dark and damp inside space, where, besides a huge rabbit in a rather smallish wire steel cage, we find the Andalusian Podencos, who are cutely staring at us from two soggy cardboard citrus boxes.

We choose one: a shivering, slightly darker little girl with a white paw and blue eyes. I'm taking pictures as my partner lifts up the little creature, and moments later, I show them to Josefina with a muttering 'Esto es Caramèlo.' I ask her to keep an eye on the caramel coloured pup, while we're in Holland, until we return to Andalusia when the dog is old enough to leave the litter, and we can take her back home with us.

Three weeks have passed, when we arrive at Aeroporto de Málaga. After a vet check, where Caramèlo, or 'Mèlo' for short, is being microchipped and receives a first rabies vaccination, we drive back to Holland by car.

During this long two day journey, she lies at my feet under the glove compartment like a rolled-up fleece blanket, timidly staring at me from below. Crossing the Spanish-French border turns out to be nerve-wracking as it is strictly forbidden with Mèlo having been vaccinated only once, and French customs' controls are strict! But so far so good!

As we're about to arrive at our stopover hotel, Mèlo, while wagging her little tail, decides to make a move from my lap to the luggage compartment, where she marks a brand new white hoodie with a tightly twisted turd, huge for such a small dog. Back home, Mèlo's introduction to our Dalmatian Joey goes very well. She turns out to be completely unimpressed by this giant during their first romp over who gets to be in the best-loved dog bed. Mèlo attends puppy school, and we feel blessed to have her in our family.

Another two months have passed and Mèlo's second rabies vaccination has been given. She's legally allowed now to cross national borders, so we plan a two-week holiday under the Andalusian sun with the dogs. We decide to drive there and fly back, since again, we're absolutely determined to leave our car behind in Spain!

But oops! One of Mèlo's siblings still seems to be roaming around the pueblo, and she approaches us submissively when we bump into her on the stairs under the large avocado tree of our neighbour Horacio. We're touched again! This little girl must be rescued as well! A search for the muchacho is set up immediately, a photo post on Valle Verde Animal's Facebook page is published, and even some celebrity influencers are contacted.

However, it's family back home who lets us know they'd like to adopt Mèlo's skinny little sister: 'Provided it's no problem for you guys to smuggle her in to Holland by car!' A name has already been given: 'Baila!' Of course, we can't refuse…

'Trèèès!' It's our neighbour Josefina. She observes us with horror, with her hands in front of her face and her head shaking, as we're loading the three dogs, Joey, Mèlo and Baila into our car, a compact convertible which is obviously way too small to carry us all. As soon as Johan starts the engine, Baila immediately throws up over my shoes, and immediately afterwards, the two alpha females get into a trip-long catfight that gets on Dalmatian Joey's nerves quite a bit.

That autumn, we would drive back our car from Holland to Andalusia for the very last time. We would succeed in putting it on Spanish plates, and, with an extra mileage of 10,000 kilometres, we would finally manage to leave the car in southern Spain for good. (Two years later, we would even decide to relocate to our Spanish pueblo ourselves, where we would settle just around the corner from the muchacho's shed, with Mèlo back in her natural environment.)

Meanwhile, we've arrived in the now, and we're walking up the steep road towards the upper village of our pueblo with a friendly chatty neighbour. We go slowly, since the plus-size señora turns out to be in bad shape, according to herself for the reason of 'muchos kilos'. The topic of conversation turns to the puppies' muchacho, and we find out that he committed some 35 burglaries in our valley. The señora points out a half-demolished house where the muchacho used to grow marihuana, and adds that he even started some fires out of revenge. According to her, he's absolutely 'loco', and will definitely not be released from prison for the time being.

Although Mèlo puts a smile on our faces every day, she can also be a very oversensitive little lady. We now know why! The señora's revelations explain why Mèlo has never been a big fan of muchachos, and what makes her go berserk every time a Spanish macho comes into our house.

Cat tails
By Gina Watson

VISITING ORGIVA FROM OUR HOME in Almegijar about 18 years ago, we came across a small, black cat, probably about a year old. She was scruffy, thin, and very sad looking, with a terrible infection in both eyes that were stuck with discharge. We wrapped her up, took her home and bathed her eyes as best we could. We took her to the vet, who gave antibiotics.

She was wary of our dog, but soon settled in nicely; some time later, she proudly presented us with four kittens! We kept one and safely rehomed the other three. After the kittens were weaned and gone, another trip to the vet to have her spayed – responsible owners! She was an inquisitive girl, searching round the land for tasty titbits, playing with her daughter and teasing the dog!

Sadly, the eye infections continued to return, although we gave her antibiotics every time. Eight years ago, after my husband died, I moved from Almegijar to Orgiva, and later adopted two more homeless kittens. It was amusing to see her reaction, as she established herself as 'top cat' very quickly, putting the babies firmly in their place!

Three years on and she has had surgery to remove the eye since the last infection did not respond to medication. It did not appear to have had much effect on her and as she was now getting older, she spent most of her time sleeping in the sun in the summer, and on my bed in the winter.

Nowadays, as my 'old lady cat' she has had a few problems with an upset stomach, and recently, what appears to have been an attack from another cat or dog, leaving a nasty wound over the empty eye socket. She has been with the vet for two days for treatment, and today I was told she is recovering well, so tomorrow I get to bring her home again.

I am constantly amazed at how she recovers well from so many things and just keeps going! She has given me a lot of affection, and I am proud of her for her stamina! At a guess, she is now 19 or 20 years old, and continues her chosen lifestyle of mainly sleeping and eating!

Colin
By Keir Duncan

SO HERE'S THE THING, COLIN is a very happy dog. I'd go so far as to say that he brings me joy just looking at him. Since he came to live with us he's even inspired me to write songs about him.

> *He's my baby doggie*
> *Little Colly Bolly*
> *He's very very cuddry*
> *He's very very jolly.*

Okay so it won't win any awards, but he seems to like it when you sing it to him while having his tum rubbed, so that's fine with me.

So, I've established that Colin is happy, joyful and jolly… except last week when he suddenly wasn't.

To give you a bit of background into Colin's daily routine, it kinda goes like this. He wakes up and proceeds to lick himself in places that only dogs can, and some blokes wish they could. A visit to both dads follows, he jumps up in turn and attempts to kiss them awake… bringing a whole new dimension to morning breath. (Dads try to avoid kisses as they know what he was just licking previously.) Once he's established both dads are awake, he heads back to bed till it's time to go for his walk. Once back from his walk, it's time for dindins. This is devoured at a furious pace, then it's time to stare at the door till allowed out to play. He spends his time, barking at stuff, chewing things, searching for cats to 'play' with, eating goodness knows what, collecting huge lumps of wood and dozing on the outside sofa. Every so often he pops into the house to check on his dads, which is always appreciated. Afternoons are spent having a siesta with Daddy John, then it's time for walkies, dindins, post dindins napping and bed.

As you can see his days are pretty full on, and Thursday began pretty much the same, except he wouldn't eat his dindins. (He can be fussy sometimes. Funnily enough telling him about all the starving dogs that would love his food makes no difference whatsoever)... then the vomiting started. Now Col, like most dogs, has the odd chuck up and bounces back straight away. He eats things that are best not described here, and naturally his body just gets rid of them. This was different though. Firstly, he didn't bounce back and secondly his vomit was bright red.

Five minutes later we're in the car en route to the vets. The gods are smiling on us as we get a free parking space outside. The vet sees him quickly, blood is taken, and an ultrasound followed. His tum is empty, no sign of any foreign bodies. (We were concerned he'd ingested something sharp.) The blood tests came back clear. However, his gums were very very pale, apparently an indicator of poisoning. Vitamin K and a stomach calmer prescribed and it's time for home. For the rest of the day Col is a bit quiet, he just dials down his jolly a bit. We give him some white rice for dinner, it's such a relief when he eats it.

Friday morning arrives and Colin has completely lost his joy. He doesn't want to get out of bed, and there's certainly no bedside licky visits. There's no enthusiasm for a walk, just to the end of the lane and back, but he does eat his dindins which we take as a positive sign. The rest of the day he just sleeps — sleep is restorative, so we leave him to it.

Early evening we suggest walkies and he appears keen, it's a relief to see him active so off we go. On the way back he does a pee in the spot where he always pees, I happen to glance down and notice he's peeing what appears to be raspberry syrup. So off to the vets we go, the parking space we got the day before is free again, so we once again take that as a good sign. After more blood tests and a second ultrasound it's established that there's blood in his bladder and some sort of sediment. An antibiotic jab later and we're on our way home. Dindins is devoured and the bowl chased all over the kitchen, someone is feeling a wee bit better.

Saturday morning arrives with bedside licks, enthusiasm for a walk. Dindins are eaten with gusto and the joy levels are on the up. The only downer is his bright red whizz. Later that day, at the spot where he always pees (we call it the pee spot, he also has a favourite place to poo… there's a song about that too… oh my I'm a poet and...) we watch with bated breath and then dance for joy. He's no longer peeing raspberry syrup, it's, well it's just doggy pee pee. Colin looks at us as though we've completely lost the plot.

Today is Sunday, joy levels are back to normal, and once again Colin is a happy dog. This morning on his walk he chased cats, said good morning to the horses and met his Aunt Nete his most favourite human in the entire world… apart from his dads… we hope.

The wonder of this is he doesn't know he wasn't a happy dog. Unlike his dads he's not running it over in his mind, worrying if the tasty smelling crap he finds will make him poorly, he'll just chomp away without a second thought.

He's just being Colly Bolly, very cuddry, very jolly.

Sometimes I wish I could be a little more Colin.

Cooper
By Paula Jones

WE ARE HEARTBROKEN TO SAY that our boy Cooper, Coop Doggy Dog, the Coop meister, Coop de Doop has passed over the Rainbow Bridge.

For those that don't know, we first met Cooper when he was brought to Valle Verde Rescue after being found at the side of the road, hanging on to life, barely any hair, and skin and bone. He had been reported as missing by the owners 6 years before, but they very cruelly didn't want him back. Their huge loss and our complete gain!

Dave and I volunteered at the rescue, and he immediately stole our hearts. He won the entire Dog Show at Valle Verde, we were so proud of him. He used to have a kennel next door to where our girls would stay, he was practically family before we even took him home. We already had 4 dogs and thought an extra one would be too much, but we got upset leaving him there and so we agreed to foster him. Of course, we failed spectacularly at fostering, and he was ours in no time!

His health improved, his coat grew in, and he was such a huge character. Our little Teddy bear. An avid swimmer, he used to dive to the bottom of the river and pick up pebbles.

I will never forget the day that Dave and Alex decided to shave him to look like a lion! with a big ruffle around his neck. He was the soppiest lion you ever could meet.

Thank you for loving us so much, Coops, you were a very good boy, and we will miss you forever. Now go run free with Hunny, until we see you again xx

Fede's story
By Ana Lenceria (English version)

HELLO.

MY NAME IS ANA AND I am going to tell you the story of a kitten named Fede, one of the many that I feed and care for.

He was very special. I think he was the one who loved me the most.

Fede appeared at the door of my store one day. I saw that he did not belong to anyone in the area.

He always followed me everywhere and tried to enter the store — he wanted to be protected and asked for a welcome while he recovered from sterilization. My friend Maria took him to her house, but Fede wanted to come back with me and one day he ran away, and he was lost for 5 days, but he came back to look for me on the sixth day and he found me.

But he needed a home and I already had five cats.

My friend Lisa adopted him. The next day she called me and said that he had escaped. I left my job, and I went to look for him. I could not find him but when I returned sadly home, 'surprise', Fede was waiting for me at my door. I promised him that I would never be separated from him.

He lived with me always. But the years passed and Fede got sick.

He had calicivirus and I didn't separate him from any of his brothers.

The day of Fede's farewell arrived. He waited for me to get up at 7 in the morning. I saw he was very bad. I hugged him while waiting for the vets to arrive. He looked at me very fixedly, he closed his eyes and left calmly, as he lived and as he wanted.

~ * ~ * ~ * ~

Fede's story
By Ana Lenceria (Spanish version)

HOLA

ME LLAMO ANA Y OS voy a contar la historia de un gatito llamado Fede de los tantos que alimento y cuido. El fue muy especial pienso que ha sido quien mas me ha querido.

El Fede apareció en la puerta de mi tienda un dia. De momento vi que no era de los habituales de la zona.

El siempre meseguia con la hidada e intentas entrar en la tienda, queria estar protegido pedí una alogida mientras se recuperada de la esterilizacion. Mi amiga Maria se lo llevó su casa, pero Fede queria volver conmigo y un dia se escapó y estuvo perdido 5 dias volvió al sexto dia a buscarme y me encontró.

Pero el necesitaba un hoga y yo tenia ya cinco gatos.

Mo amiga Lisa lo adoptó. Al dia siguiente me llamó que se habia escapadó. Dejé me trabajo y me fui a buscarlo, no lo encontré. Pero al volver a casa tristemente 'sorpresa', Fede me estaba esperando en mi puerta. Le prometí que jamás me iba a separar de el. Vivió conmigo siempre. Pero pasaron los anos y Fede era enfermo.

Tenia calicivirus y no lo separé de ninguno de sus hermanos. Entre ellos Linda mi perrita Linda que es mi compañera inseparable, tambien rescatada.

Llegó el dia de la despedida de Fede. El esperó que yo me levanté a las 7 de la mañana. Lo vi muy mal. Lo cogi en brazos esperando que llegaran los veterinarios. El me vió muy fijamente, cerro sus ojitos y se fue tranquilamente, como vivió y como el queria.

Mi niño Fede siempre en mi corazon.

From beast to prince
By Saskia Wilstra

IT WAS A WARM SUMMER day. The sun was beaming brightly over the mountain as the crickets filled the air with a peaceful sound. It was the middle of the day when my sister and mom decided to go for a walk.

As they were walking along the trail they noticed something in the distance: a dog. The dog was scared, weak and hungry. He was cowering behind a water pipe sticking up above the dry ground. He tried his best to lick up every drop leaking from it, waiting long intervals to quench his never-ending thirst.

The dog's usually strong body had lost almost every muscle, showing off his bone structure in an unpleasant way. His usually black, shiny coat now looked rotten, leaving skin flakes behind where he walked. The claws on his paws were so long that they seemed beastly, digging in to the ground underneath him.

As they approached the skeleton-looking creature, he started shaking. He was scared, seemingly trying to get away. But he couldn't. Maybe he had already given up, or maybe, he felt the enormous amount of care and worry coming from my sister and mom. He gave in and let them come closer.

The dog seemed powerless as my sister picked him up. His disgusting, skinny body was close to hers. Every step she took was carefully taken, so as not to disturb or hurt the creature. Although the weight of carrying the dog became more unbearable for every minute, they kept on going. Not wanting to give up on the frail beast.

When they heard the dogs barking, they knew that they had arrived. That the dog had a chance. A chance to survive, a chance to live. They were quickly greeted by Linda and her dogs as they hurried inside. My sister kneeled down and carefully placed the frail creature inside the soft, purple bed. As he laid there, he seemed content. Almost as if he knew that he was in good hands, that he didn't have to fight alone anymore. For the first time in his life, the dog felt like a prince.

How to catch a cat... or not
By Janet Hassell

MANY OF YOU WILL HAVE read and chuckled over the legend which does the rounds, on how to catch a cat (for example to go to the vet) and the lengths they will go to, to evade capture. Let alone what damage you and your home may sustain. And all that presupposes it is a) your cat and therefore nominally used to being handled and b) in an enclosed area — your house.

Catching cats in Spain is a different matter entirely since it mostly involves trapping an unwilling and definitely not tame feline and outdoors to boot. It makes the former sound like a picnic. A cat trap is a long wire cage with a trapdoor at one end and a plate at the far end attached to a wire which in turn supports the door when raised. When the cat treads on the trip plate it pulls the wire off the door lever and the door drops down into place. Bingo, one trapped cat.

Who promptly goes into orbit and bounces off all available walls hissing spitting and exuding murderous intentions to anyone foolish enough to get within paw and claw range of the mesh. So watch out when you go for the handle to pick it up. But I digress, as first you have to tempt the bugger in there, and I might add, the ONE YOU WANT in there.

So imagine, identify a suitable area where the cat will go. The trap has to be baited (general practice is a tiny amount of something very tasty and preferably smelly like sardines) at the far end which for people like me means lying on the floor and putting my entire arm in. It also means doing so sufficiently gently not to set off the mechanism because it's mostly easier to raise the trip plate first and put in the food than to put in the food and then raise the trip plate, sending the food scudding off in who knows which direction, usually ending upside down under the trip plate.

Then, you wait, but not where you can be seen or you will frighten them off, but not too far away that you forget all about it and find one of your cats in there for an hour and very very cross about it. Or within earshot to hear a) the clanging of the door and/or b) the anguished wailing which normally follows along with c) the sound of a metal cage being more or less knocked over by someone trying to get out.

See previous paragraph for description of typical trapped cat behaviour and also warning re fingers, legs and anything else within paw/claw reach. Cover up entire cage to quieten the captive and search for the handle without getting under the cover and losing a finger or two. Endeavour to lug heavy metal cage containing cat to wherever your car is and attempt to fit it in and drive rapidly to the vet. Lug the trap and contents in, hand it over and breathe a massive sigh of relief that paying for this is going to be preferable to having to try to get the bugger out and onto an operating table. Go home and lie down. You see there are some similarities to that How to Catch a Cat thing after all...

Sounds okay so far? But consider this: chasing a cat round your house shutting doors as you go not only restricts the available area but generally involves one identified animal. Now try putting a trap on your terrace when you have (quick count) 9 cats of your own, none of whom need to be neutered, and another 9 or 10 who are not really yours but think they own you too.

All of whom DO need the snip (apart from the one daft enough to go after a cat toy in the trap before he was old enough to know better) although the youngest 3 are probably safe for another few months or so yet. So whilst the priority will always be girls first before they turn into Patch (well Patch is actually no. 1 on the hit list for the trap but far too canny to fall for it), what are the odds when the present targets include only one known female other than Patch? And if you trap later in the day then the cat would have to stay in the trap all night and the next morning, which hardly seems fair let alone likely to end well if they remember afterwards.

Cats are curious animals and are likely to investigate something new, especially interesting food smells, but when they see what happens to one of their number in a trap, they run a mile and it's hard work persuading them to come near it again.

If that was not enough of a problem, try adding this in: the vets normally operate afternoons when the surgery is closed, so you need to get the cat there before 1.30 which means a morning capture. So weekends are out (Sat no evening surgery and Sunday closed), on Tuesdays I am not there either to trap or deliver, which leaves Monday, Wednesday, Thursday and Friday and then only if nothing else needs doing, then there may well be too many already booked in or emergencies.

The day I caught Cheeky and took him in, feeling very pleased with myself, I was greeted by the receptionist who said they might not be able to fit him in, my face must have been a picture. You can't guarantee when you will actually succeed so you can't book them in or plan when...

Anyway, that's the reason for dilly-dallying over the trapping business really, it's not that easy and you can easily find reasons why today is not the day. I'd digress by mentioning the nightmare which was trapping the original Sooty and her four kids who were all feral, but you can read about that elsewhere, suffice to say it was a nightmare but nothing like the present problem in terms of numbers or variety. And the point of telling you all this, is that yesterday, much to my amazement, I trapped Sparky who is the one known girly apart from her mum (Patch) and I wasn't even trying.

This is how that happened: she's of an age where if we didn't get things done there would surely be kittens, and given how much time Horace has spent following her around, I thought sooner rather than later. Then that big black tom cat who hangs around and fights with all my cats has been yowling as well as pursuing her and she has been unusually skittish.

He (the would-be rapist) has a hurt leg and is limping badly which made me think yesterday that perhaps getting him would be a good idea as the leg needs attention plus having his nuts off might give Sparky a break, plus catching her was bound to be harder than catching him... so I baited the trap and put it away from the terrace and outside the window of the disused olive press which is where he'd been hanging out.

Imagine my surprise when Sparky went to have a look at it and went in... I held my breath, and clang, there she was... and she pinged off all the walls and I covered her up and sprayed the happy cat spray and tried to get hold of the handle without losing any blood and then struggled to get the trap in the van and to the vet, and then we had to decant her into a smaller crate for overnight as I was keen to take the trap back and try for the tom cat today.... and she's now in the spare room while the drugs wear off, but she must be really woozy still as I can't hear any sounds of distress or destruction.

She does come indoors, as they all do, but isn't used to it, so this is make or break time for whether she is going to do like Nelson and turn tame or whether she will race away as soon as possible and hate me for a lot longer like Smokie and Stumpy did, and those three had to be caught again for moving house not once but twice and only since we came to this house did Smokie decide to turn tame. (Poor Stumpy died still hating me.)

I forgot to mention that once the trap was covered and liberally sprayed with Feliway, I found Smokie rolling on the end of the blanket looking deliriously happy, and had to fend off various other people who came to investigate before I got the trap in the car, not least of which was the black tom cat yowling his head off no doubt looking for her again.

The postscript to all this is, of course, that the black tom cat hasn't gone anywhere near the perishing trap all day and I can't leave it open all night in case the wrong person goes in... and the reason he hasn't gone back to his stamping ground is revealed in the next blog post, in which yet again I have to acknowledge this lot have me for a mug. I don't know about catching cats, but those cats know how to catch a human.

James and Sherlock
By Paula Van Oudheusden

ON A SUNNY AFTERNOON IN the Lecrin Valley we received a call from the local vet. She asked us if we were willing to take in two little kittens that had been found that morning in a trashcan in a nearby village. The kittens were just a day old and one of them was very sick with high fever. They knew we already had other dogs and kittens in our care and did not really have the space, but we were the only ones she could think of who were willing and able to take such a big risk with kittens so young and sick.

At that time we had 5 dogs and 3 cats to take care of, but we decided to at least try to save them. It was mid-pandemic and only necessary travel was permitted, so the vet made a note for Daniel to show to the police if he got stopped on the way and we at home started setting up the 'kitten nursery' again. Luckily our two kids, 16 and 18 at that time, were being 'homeschooled' and had time to help us to take care of all the babies. Our son Tim helped out with the dogs and our daughter Joy did the night shift with the kittens.

When the kittens came home everyone was super excited to meet them. They were so small they could both fit in our hand. They were still deaf and blind and very very sleepy. The bigger of the two is a classic tuxedo cat, black and white, and the smaller one is a very handsome tabby. We called them James, after James Bond the tuxedo-wearing chatty spy, and Sherlock after

Sherlock Holmes the tweed-wearing smart detective. We did not know at that time that their names were going to fit them so perfectly!

The first couple of days we kept them separate from our other animals. After a couple of days they really wanted to meet their new family and we integrated them with the rest. Bimba (grey and white ragdoll-looking) and Simba (orange tabby) were just a couple of months old and babies themselves but already had experience with other kittens we fostered. They integrated perfectly! Simba took over the role of big brother. He bathed them and taught them how to play. Bimba kept them warm at night. Our dogs Zorro (Collie mix) and Suzy (Pitbull mix) were not too interested in the new visitors, but very unexpectedly Diego (Waterdog mix) really took an interest in them and almost treated them as his children. He was super patient and gentle with them. He would lay down and they would climb all over him and even tried to nurse on his nipples.

Our intention was, as it had been before, to put them up for adoption. But after a couple of months there had been no interest, and they became a part of our family. When one day the vet called and asked if they were still up for adoption I kind of insinuated they weren't and she took the hint!

In memory of cats

Anon

ONE OF THE MOST UPSETTING things about living in our village was the fate of the many cats, some feral and some abandoned, that lived in the streets. I mention here a few of the special ones for whom, sadly, I was unable to offer refuge.

My first encounter was with a black cat who had obviously been domesticated because she was so friendly and unafraid. My dog and her got on well and usually they sniffed noses, which was unusual, because my dog normally had no interest in cats other than to chase them. I fed this lovely cat daily and one day when we had a load of tiles delivered in the square and it was my task to stay with the load while others hiked it down the path, I sat on the roadside and the cat sat on my lap. Our decision was that we couldn't take on a cat one reason was that we had heard of other cats previously living at our property who had met quite nasty ends... and also because we couldn't take on any more commitments. So, I continued to offer food and a fuss.

The local women consistently told me to take the cat home and had I realised then what I know now, I would have done something. At that time I had no knowledge of animal rescue groups and if they had been in existence then, I would certainly have approached them for help.

One day the cat completely disappeared. I asked a local man where it was.

"It´s gone to the lower barrio," he replied. Of course, now I know better that in the towns and villages there are people who carry out regular culling of the feral animals and now I know where the lower barrio is.

Heart breaking.

There were various other cats after this, including a group which I fed regularly. My husband called our car the chuck wagon because every time we parked up, a group of cats would appear begging for food. Of course, they always got some. This led to an awful accident one day when my husband drew up in the car and the leader of the pack rushed across the road to the chuck wagon. A car hit him, and he just managed to climb back over the cat wall. We never saw him again.

Further culls thinned out the remaining pack, but one always seemed to survive. There was an old gentleman who my friend named Brown Cardy... for obvious reasons... who lived in a run-down house. He fed cats and this one benefitted from his care. Then Brown Cardy passed away and it seemed the one remaining cat still survived. I called her Mummy Cat because she was always having kittens who never survived. More about her later.

The house next to our friends was empty and had a vine which wound its way up the wall to an open window. A pair of cats had climbed up and made themselves a home in the bedroom and before long they had a family. We could watch the kittens climbing along the perilous roof. I usually fed this group, and they often followed me to my home meowing fiercely, with their tails standing erect like meerkats.

Then the house was sold. Understandably the new owner didn't want cats in the house, so that was the end of them. That house still remains empty and still has an open window at the top of the vine.

One day the most beautiful fluffy, ginger cat appeared. I imagine she was dumped because she was definitely tame, and I took on responsibility for feeding her. We had been house-sitting for a friend further up the valley and I had walked down to check on our property when the cat appeared frantically meowing and very pregnant. She followed me to my house, and I gave her a tin of tuna. I never saw her again. However, a few weeks later a local lady found a group of kittens near to where I had last seen her. One looked just like her. The kittens all found homes, so for that I am grateful.

One day as we entered the village we saw a Siamese cat struggling across the road. 'Stop the car!. Stop the car!' I yelled at my husband. I caught the cat although he was trying hard to run away. He was pretty badly injured. I took him home and gave him some food and then cuddled him on my lap. He had the most incredible blue eyes, so I called him Blue. I decided to see if the vets had an appointment, to see if there was any way we could save his life. It turned out that he had a broken hip in three places, and I was advised that he would be unlikely to survive surgery. As we left the vets with his body, somebody who saw how upset I was, asked me how long he had been our cat. About three hours I replied! We buried him in our garden and placed a lovely stone from the campo on the top. I can't imagine how much pain he must have been in.

Back to Mummy Cat.

She moved from Brown Cardy to another elderly couple in the adjoining house who fed feral cats. Eventually they too passed away and just Mummy Cat was left. She eventually had a surviving kitten and I asked Linda if Valle Verde could take it in. They could. I was so happy that I could at least help this one kitten and went back to their 'living area' to find it. I did find it – it was dead. So I took it home and buried it next to Blue.

Every time I went to feed Mummy Cat she would rush to me meowing frantically, but never ever would she let me come near her. When I went on holiday my friends fed her and so she became our surrogate cat for some time. Not long before I moved from the village I went to feed her, and she appeared with her nose literally hanging off! She was quite a fighter which is perhaps how she survived for so long, but this was the worst battle scar she had ever had... it looked terrible. However, she seemed to cope with it somehow, until one day she appeared with an obviously broken paw as well as the nose injury. She couldn't really walk and certainly couldn't run or fight. I visited the vets to see if I could get a sleeping tablet which would enable me to catch her and bring her for a vet's appointment. I had previously tried to catch her but even in her injured state she was too clever for me. I was advised that if I gave her a sedative it would take a while to have an effect and by then she would have crawled back into the undergrowth where I would never find her.

So it was Plan B. I mixed paracetamol with tuna! I saw her the following day and it was obvious the paracetamol was working, and I gave her some more laced tuna. I never saw her again. Nowadays that house is restored with a smart driveway where once she lived in the undergrowth. I feel I did the right thing.

If this tribute to the many cats I have met sounds in any way that I have been heartless, I can assure the reader that it has all quite devastated me. I am grateful to Valle Verde for helping me rescue one kitten who I met on the bus stop roof. I did manage to catch her and although she responded to me with purrs and snuggles, she didn't respond so well at the refuge.

Happily though she has a forever loving home now.

In many countries there is a problem with feral cats and dogs. In Spain the attitude is very slowly changing to recognise that animals are sentient beings, but for a difference to be made I think we can only hope and pray. Meanwhile, I have found it very hard to come to terms with all of these and many other animal experiences. As an animal lover, it has spoilt my experience of living in Spain and caused me great sorrow. I will always be thankful and grateful for Valle Verde.

Please support their endeavours.

La gata que habla
By Katrina Edbrooke

WE CALLED HER THE CAT that talks. La gata que habla in Spanish. She would stroll across the terrace, looking around and chattering away. If I was talking on the phone to a friend I would ask her to say hello and she would meow into the phone as she walked past. Tail high in the air. She made us laugh. We also called her Pretty Cat. She looked like an Egyptian sphinx when she sat like a statue, back arched, green eyes, beautiful markings, a tabby Siamese mix maybe. She never begged for food, and we never fed her.

We did not encourage her or any cat that strayed onto our small farm. We were not cat people. There were a lot of cats. People came to their holiday homes in the Valley of the Swallows where we live, they would come with kittens and after a long summer leave behind cats.

One day while eating sweet smelling sticky ribs, made with a marinade of marmalade, garlic and chilli from the farm, we found ourselves surrounded by them. They seemed to multiply, sneaking in from the Nispero field on one side and the avocado plantation on the other, they crept forward as if they were playing grandmother's footsteps, freezing in their tracks when we looked at them like the weeping angels in Doctor Who. They were all shapes and colours, some with sparkling emerald eyes, others with eyes as blue as the Spanish sky. Only Pretty Cat broke away from the pack and walked boldly past, stopping to do a quick roll on the floor in front of us, flashing her belly and as always talking away. Still we didn't feed them. We did not want cats.

A few times that winter a sick or injured cat would pass by and I succumbed, making a nest for them on the terrace sofa, leaving plates of food. Friends joked that now I was going to have a cat, but they always moved on, off into the fields and were never seen again.

We didn't see Pretty Cat that winter, but she appeared again in spring, rubbing herself against the glass doors, no longer chatting but crying. She was in a sorry state, weak and thin. We broke our rule and opened a tin of tuna which she devoured. The following day she reappeared but she wasn't alone. Four beautiful tabby kittens stared at us through the glass, eyes wide and frightened, mouths open crying. Our hearts simply melted. We fed them, all the time reminding ourselves we did not want cats.

The next day they returned and there were seven of them. The tabbies had been joined by three more kittens a black one, a black and white one and a Siamese. They were not Pretty Cat's kittens but still she nursed them along with her own, stretched out on the floor, exhausted looking at us with pleading eyes. If she can care for them we reasoned then so can we. We went out and bought cat food.

We knew nothing about cats. They were insatiable, eating everything we put down, sleeping together on the terrace sofa, lounging on the cushions and absolutely terrified of us.

One of the kittens was different, she didn't join in their games and when the others ran off into the pear garden to play she would take a few steps and give up exhausted and crying. She let us stroke her, too weak to run away. We were getting worried she would not survive.

We had heard of Valle Verde, seen their stall in the Sunday market and spoken to them already hoping they could rescue our kittens, but they were full to overflowing and could only advise us to do our best to domesticate them, take photos and look for people who wanted to adopt. Meanwhile, the sick kitten was getting weaker. Take her to your vet said our friends with cats. We didn't have a vet; we didn't know a vet and we were dealing with frightened wild cats. I called Valle Verde again desperate for help with the sick kitten and they agreed. I cried when I took her to them, shaking with relief that they knew what to do and how to care for her. At least we had been able to handle her, she was too weak to protest, and we were able to pick her up and get her in the cat box donated by our friend Mark, whose elderly cat had just died. We had turned a corner; we knew we needed to domesticate them if they were all to survive. We named them after their colours and markings, so they became Patches, Stripes, Grey, Blackie, Black and White and Siam. Meanwhile it was becoming obvious that Pretty Cat was pregnant again. Our friend Sarah came to help me catch her and in a flurry of claws, vicious hissing and flying fur we got her in the cat box and to the vet to be neutered. Followed by a trip to the A&E where Sarah, blood spattered and very brave was being treated for multiple scratch wounds.

It took Pretty Cat a long time to forgive us for that and no longer came near us or even talked to us, however, the kittens were becoming braver. Patches was the first to jump on my lap, giving me the shock of my life when it happened, followed by Grey who put his paws on my chest and would stare up at me purring in adoration. There was no going back.

The black and white kitten, since renamed Belen, was the only female and she was neutered without any fuss, as was another adult female who we believe is Pretty Cat's mother. We call her Blanca.

That summer we were joined by five adorable Siamese kittens who would skip down our driveway every time food was put out. They soon became friendly enough to catch and three of them were successfully adopted with help from Valle Verde.

At one point we were feeding so many cats we lost count. There were casualties. The original Siam disappeared after a failed attempt to catch her. We never saw her again. My darling Grey was run over and was buried in the pear garden where he played. They all caught cat flu, and we lost a few more despite antibiotics and frantic visits to the vet.

Pretty cat is now talking to us again and rubbing herself against our legs and even wanders into the house occasionally looking for her grown up kittens who are now part of the family. Blackie and Belen rule the terrace while Patches and Stripes are practically house cats coming in to sleep on the piano or cuddling up with us on the sofa as we watch TV, and they all talk to us.

It's not the end of the story, stray cats still turn up, spring will bring more kittens and we will continue to befriend and neuter them and hopefully find them their own families. We are now officially cat people.

Lana (aka La Negra)
By Dominique Henderson

ONE SEPTEMBER IN MONDUJAR (IN the Lecrin Valley), we're walking in the street with Bikkie (a stray dog found 15 years before). I notice a black dog, Labrador cross, very thin and looking frightened. We are about to go back to Paris, can't do anything for her but as I'm near a shop I rush in and buy a big tin of dog food. She wolfs it down on the pavement.

We return to Mondujar the following May. Unfortunately, our lovely Bikkie had died peacefully in February, aged 17 and we have decided we will never get another dog. I notice the same black dog we had met in September. She comes up to me, wagging her tail, seeming to recognize me. She looks well fed, a small flea collar round her neck. We are delighted that she has found a home. Later, we discover that she is still out on the street, but the owner of Celia 2, the small shop, feeds her regularly and has equipped her with the flea collar.

Unfortunately, he already has 4 dogs of his own. She starts following us everywhere, and sleeps outside our door. It's cold, we hear her coughing at night... and guess what? First we decide to get the vet to examine her and give her whatever treatment she needs to help her stay in good health, then 'maybe we'll take her on board when we come back in September'. He laughs, says she will probably be taken away to a perrera and put to sleep, so we decide to put her in a kennel in Durcal for a couple of months until we find a solution for her.

We then set off for an expedition in the mountains. On the way back, and just before leaving for Paris, we stop by at the kennel to check everything is okay. She is obviously well treated there, but she expresses so much canine joy and adoration when she sees us that we can't resist and end up leaving with her and driving back to Hendaye.

Nightmarish journey at the start. It's so difficult to get her into the car that after a couple of kilometres we realise that we have left the front door of the house wide open and have to turn back. Lana is terrified of cars, jumps around (we are so ill-prepared we don't even have a dog net in our rented car), and we feel we have really made a big mistake! Then, miraculously, she settles down after an hour. On our way north, we stop in a pet-friendly B&B.

She still hasn't 'done her business' and we're getting a bit worried. Finally, after much walking about with no success, we decide to let her off the lead, she darts off and we are desperate that she'll never come back. In the distance we see her crouching behind a bush, she sniffs around a bit, hesitates, then trots back happily.

At the French border in Hendaye we leave the rented car and board a TGV train, she gets in with no difficulty and hides under our seat for the whole journey. Arrival at the Gare Montparnasse, football fans all over the station, loud voices and trumpets, the dog panics. She refuses to walk down the stairs, and my husband has to carry her down (25 kg) while I look after the suitcases. No taxi accepts us with the dog, and we end up in the metro. Colin and luggage already in the carriage, Lana refuses to get in and I have to drag her into it just as the doors start to close on us, everybody glaring at us (no dogs allowed on the Paris metro, normally!).

Linda
By Ana Lenceria

FOR THIRTY YEARS I HAVE rescued, fed and cared for stray animals.

It doesn't matter if it's cold, rainy or I am sick, they have never run out of care. My daughter is my great support. Without her I could not have rescued one of the best dogs in my life.

I rescued her 15 years ago from the surroundings of Orgiva. I had seen her a few days before in Orgiva. I saw her very defenceless and scared every night, so I went out to look for her, to take her somewhere safe.

They told me that she was from the neighbouring town of Tablones, but I didn't take her to the pound.

That day I caught her with the lasso, I left my job and rescued her, but I didn't know where to keep her while I was looking for a place for her.

We realized that she had some problem. 'Surprise' she was pregnant, so we decided to sterilize her and put in a chip.

One day I heard stories that I did not want to hear. Linda was very seriously ill. She had very little time left. She had a lung tumour and heart problems.

We started treatment and after three years she is still by my side.

She is very happy and is more like my spoiled girl. She does not lack the affection of the whole family.

She gets along great with all the animals; she is a great mother with the baby kittens that we rescue. She washes them and takes care of them!

Hopefully her illness will go away so that she continues living because she doesn't want to be separated from me. Nor I from her.

~ * ~ * ~ * ~

Linda
by Ana Lenceria

DESDE HACE TRENTA ANOS RESCATO, alimento y cuido a los animals callejeros.

Da igual que haga frio, llueva o esté enferma ellos nunca se han quedado sin cuidadoMi hija es mi gran apoyo. Sin ella no habria podido rescatar una de los mejores perros de mi vida.

La rescaté hace 15 años de los laceros de la perrera que venia a Ogiva. Yo la habia visto unos dias antes por Orgiva. La vi muy indefensa y asustada todas las noches. SFui a buscarla para llevarle a un espacio seguro.

Me comentaron que era de Tablones pero yo no la llevé a la perrera.

Ese dia que la cogieron con el lasso, salí de mi trabajo y la rescaté, pero no sabia donde llevarla mientras buscaba un sitio para ella.

Nos dimos cuenta que tenia algun problema y la llevamos al vete. 'Sorprisa' estaba embarazada. Decidimos esterelizarla y poner chip.

Mi nombre la adoptamos y sigue con nosotros desde ese dia.

Un dia empezaron cuentas. El vete confirmó lo que yo no queria escuchar. Linda está muy grave. Le queda muy poco. Tiene tumor en el pulmor y problemas cardiacos.

Empezamos tratamiento y ella despés de tres años sigue a mi lado.

Ella es muy feliz y yo mas — es mi nina mimada. No le falta el carino de toda la familia.

Se lleva genial con todos los animals es muy madre con los gatitos bebes que rescato. Las lava, suega y cuida Linda. Mi querida Linda siempre a mi lado.

Dice la vete que sigue viviendo porque no se quiere separar de mi. Ni yo de ella.

Muffin (cat) and Zanti (dog)
By Vivien Sutcliffe

MY NAME IS MUFFIN. I didn't know my mother; she died before I was born. My twin sister and I were saved, though, thanks to being delivered by Caesarean. We were both adopted, but sadly my twin didn't survive.

Now I am eight years old, healthy, happy and dearly loved by my mum and Zanti dog. I like the rain! And the freedom to come and go as I choose, announcing my return at the top of my voice. I love my mum and her daughter, am wary of anyone else, except Zanti dog, my brother and best friend. His story is below mine!

My name is Zanti. I was thrown out of a car eight years ago and landed in a ditch, umbilical cord still attached. I was brought to my best friend on a banana leaf. She tucked me inside her shirt to keep me warm and took me home.

That night she made me a hot water bottle. Friends brought me puppy milk and and advised her how to care for me.

Forever grateful!

Boycie's tale
By Sandra Cronin

MY NAME IS BOYCIE, AND my sister is called Marlene. We were born in the campo, and we were lost, lonely and hungry. When we were about 6 weeks old we ventured into the village and came across a big group of similar beings to us, who we discovered were being fed by a human lady.

One day, I saw the human lady in the street, and I ran up to her, jumped up and threw my paws around her neck. She took pity on me and my sister, and she took us both into her home.

One by one she brought in a few more of us – some were very unwell. Marlene and I weren't very keen at first (their fur coats were ginger and grey, so common! Marlene and I have pure white ones!), but we could see they needed help, and the kind human lady fed them and took them to the cat doctor and made them well again.

We got used to these furry beings eventually, and they are now very good friends. We are all nearly two and three years old now. When we have a tummy ache she takes us to the nice cat doctor who gives us medicine to make us feel better, but sometimes he puts this big needle into our fur coat. Ouch!

When we were younger, he took some bits from our bodies. I'm not sure what that was about! I have to have special food as I have only one working kidney. I'm okay though, I get the best food in the world!

We are so happy and lucky. She even gives us these things to play with.

Our wish is that — one day — all our furry friends in the whole wide world will be able to have lives like we do.

Yours, Boycie.

Nube/Zaza
By Paula Van Oudheusden

WE HAD JUST MOVED FROM the Netherlands to Spain when we had our first experience with abandoned animals. It must have been around September when Joy and I were walking through the village and spotted a sturdy white dog in the streets. It looked like it was following some girls home, but they didn't pay it any attention and the dog seemed to be in a rough state.

We followed the dog for a while, but we didn't want to seem like creeps following some girls around town, so we lost track of the dog. After a while we went home to have some dinner and told Daniel and Tim we had found a dog that needed our help. They decided to join the search and rescue party and eventually we found the dog.

It followed us home, but didn't want to enter. It took some time, so we took the opportunity to see what we were dealing with. It was a female Pitbull mix and she seemed to either be pregnant or just had babies. She looked defeated. She was full of ticks and had scar tissue all over. Her fur was dull and dirty, she looked like she had given up. It was a look that we did not know we would see so many more times in the eyes of abandoned and abused dogs.

The first couple of days she was in survival mode. She ate and drank what we gave her, slept on the floor curled up in the corner and wouldn't really move. Our dogs, Zorro and Suzy were curious but mostly left her to herself.

After a few days her personality started to show... she would make weird growling noises and wag her tail when we came home or went for a walk. She started to play fight with Suzy (also a Pitbull mix), but very clearly did not have any understanding of her strength and Suzy's boundaries. Suzy really had to teach her how to be a dog and how to live inside a home with a human family that took care of her. They became best friends.

Zorro didn't dislike her, but also wasn't her biggest fan, so they just tolerated each other.

Lola, our cat, on the other hand was a bigger problem. The first couple of days, when she was still adjusting, it had not been a problem for Lola to enter the house and be with us. But after a while Nube showed signs of aggression towards her. She was excellent with people and even other dogs on the street, but cats and other small animals were not safe around her. We talked to our vet and started a more rigorous training. The training did help a bit, but we and Lola had to be constantly vigilant. Nube would 'live' downstairs and Lola would enter the window on the first floor from the neighbours' roof.

It worked for a while, but we had to come to terms with the fact that we could not keep Nube in our family, especially after an incident where Lola nearly lost her life.

It is very difficult to get a dog or cat adopted in Spain. Especially an older dog, a breed that has been marked as potentially dangerous and has problems with cats. Another thing to be concerned about is the bad people who only want that kind of dog for dog fights or other types of abuse. It is a real thing in Spain, we have seen the scars and trauma. So we tried everything possible to find a loving home for Nube, but there was no interest.

In January, we had a trip planned to the Netherlands. We didn´t really have a network of people that could take care of our dogs and cat, so we had to take all of them with us in the car during our three day trip! We made it to our place in the Netherlands. We were going to stay for just 10 days meeting with friends and family.

Two days before we were going to drive back a friend visited us and got to know Nube. She immediately called a friend of hers who had lost a similar dog some time ago and was looking for a new family member. That night my friend took Nube to her friend to see if they were a match and they were!

We decided right there and then, after visiting the friend, that she would adopt Nube. She had already been spayed, vaccinated and chipped and had a European passport. We did the paperwork and said goodbye to our beloved Nube, now called Zaza. Even though we miss her sometimes, we know she is in a much better place where she gets all the attention she needs and has a loving family who really know how to take care of such a powerful and wonderful dog.

Paco/Dollar/Pepe
By Paula Van Oudheusden

WHEN WE FIRST MOVED TO Spain we lived in Nigüelas, a small mountain town at the foot of the Sierra Nevada.

We loved to walk around town, getting to know all the streets and little bars and terraces, and often took the kids and dogs with us. On one of those walks we suddenly saw the biggest dog we had ever seen! He was playing with some little kids from town and they didn't really know what to do with him. He did not belong to anyone, but he had been in town for some days, and they decided to call him Paco.

Paco was skinny and still a puppy, though very big. He liked us and our dogs so we took him home to see if we could try and find his owner. He settled in right away. He got on the couch (and left no space for anyone or anything else) and ate all the food (he needed a lot of food!). He tried to climb onto the bed and sleep with Joy in her bed, but he was just too big.

It is funny to have such a big dog acting like a little puppy. He wanted to chew on things and had sudden bursts of energy. These are hard to handle in little puppies, so imagine coping with one that can easily rest his head on the dining table.

Paco was the kindest and sweetest dog we had ever known. Careful with the kittens and very obedient. His biggest flaw was his size and not wanting to ever be alone. He would be fine with any other animal but would escape and try to find another living soul if he was left alone. At our place this was rarely the case, but if for some reason he was alone in the garden he would break out and go into town.

After a couple of weeks we got a call from the local shelter saying that his owner had come forward. He had been looking for him ever since he escaped his cortijo in the mountains near Nigüelas. Since Paco was not chipped he had to prove his ownership with photos and other info and eventually we agreed to hand him over, but not before he got chipped and vaccinated. His owner, Francisco, informed us his name was Dollar and he had found him when he was very little and decided to keep him at his cortijo. He showed us pictures of him with Paco/Dollar, his kennel and all the space he had and even though we knew Paco/Dollar was going to be sad to be alone at the cortijo again he seemed to have a good home with a caring owner.

Some weeks later, just when the pandemic hit and the whole country was in lock down, I got a call from Francisco. Dollar had escaped again, and he was wondering if he had found his way to our home. We hadn´t seen him around, but since that day we spent hours on our terrace seeing if we could spot a big dog somewhere in the mountains and in every trip Daniel made to the supermarket he took a little detour to look for him.

We were really worried because it gets really cold in the Sierra Nevada and Dollar was very sweet but also incredibly stupid. If he took a wrong turn somewhere or went the wrong way he could be lost in the mountains forever without skills to survive or find his way back to a populated area.

After 6 weeks of nightmares we got a call from the vet. They had found Dollar. They knew him because he was chipped. They sent us a picture and I started crying. He was skin over bones! He had been lost for 6 weeks in the mountains until some couple hiking found him and took him to the nearest vet. We took him home immediately and called his owner.

The owner was very happy he was found, but also realized he couldn´t take good care of Dollar. He could not be alone, and Francisco did not have any other place for him other than at his cortijo where he went every other day to tend to his crops. We decided Dollar would stay with us and we would try to find a new home for him.

Luckily we found a new loving home for him in a nearby town. The family had just lost their own dog at 16 years old and saw a picture of Dollar online. He reminded them so much of their old dog that they wanted to try to adopt Dollar. We agreed he would spend a week with the new family and that they could bring him back to us if it didn´t work out, but within a day the family asked us to arrange the paperwork to sign him over to them. We contacted the old owner to legally sign him over. They renamed him Pepe and send us a picture every couple of weeks. Pepe had finally found his home. A big garden and a lot of grandchildren to play with!

Spanish life and animals
By Paula Jones

THE DAY WE VIEWED OUR house in Spain was the first day we saw how differently animals can be treated here. There were little puppies chained up in absolute squalor in an abandoned sawmill, right by our house. We already had two dogs, so seeing this really upset us. Little did we know that very soon we would be rescuing them from a life of suffering.

So here began the upsetting, but extremely rewarding path of rescue. The chained ones were now being used by the local goatherd. He already had two other dogs and he wasn't very nice to them and hit them and only fed them stale bread. So we used to take food each day and treat them for ticks and fleas, walk them with our dogs and show them love.

One day we saw a little pup wandering down the valley looking lost, so we picked him up and brought him home. Then there was a cry in our garden, then some more little barks, and before we knew it we had 10 puppies! It was chaos but fun. The goatherd didn't care about them, so we began training them, gave them vaccinations, lots of cuddles and walks and began searching for suitable homes.

We were delighted when the last puppies left for their new homes, so much so we went out to dinner to celebrate. On arriving home 2 new pointed puppies were on our doorstep! We should have known then how this story would progress.

Years have now passed, and we've rehomed so many puppies, and kept a few that pulled on our heartstrings. We've climbed into collapsed buildings, scaled the side of mountains, run down the centre of the road, volunteered at a refuge, driven them to their new homes in another country, run fundraisers, even kidnapped some in the night! All to give them a better life.

Our advice, if you love dogs, hate cruelty and you are coming to live in Spain, get ready to open your wallet and home, as there is nothing your soppy hearts can do about it!

Guapita's story
By Line Eskildsen

I DIDN'T EVEN HAVE A name. I was living outside for most of my life. They took me away from my mum when I was no more than a month or so. I was a birthday present to a sweet girl. But when her holiday ended and she went back to school, her dad didn't care much for me. He left me outside the house all day and all night.

Suddenly, a family started noticing me. I was waiting at the gate every morning and every afternoon for them to come by and give me water and food. I think they got worried about me, because one day a team from the police came and cleaned the courtyard. At last, it was a bit clean again. But they left me there, and the family kept looking out for me. Feeding me and giving me water.

Little did I know that the family were just on their holidays and tried to somehow find a more suitable place for me to be. Apparently that didn't work out the way they had hoped because one day the lady crawled over the fence and left a note for the man I lived with. I didn't know that the note said she was willing to help in whatever way possible.

The next day the man took me to the lady and her family. I stayed with them for five days. I slept in a bed; I got dog snacks and toys and had the best time of my life. However, one day the lady took me to go away with another woman from a place called Valle Verde.

There was something about me not being old enough to get the injections I'd need to go home with them. I stayed at that place for about a month and, when I was least expecting it, the lady and her family came back for me. Today, I have a name. And I love it. I'm called Guapita. I think that they think I am really pretty. And I have a wonderful life: I sleep on the couch and the bed (although my humans say I shouldn't really). Two long walks every day and plenty of food and cuddles and my own little dog brother called Eddie. (He's cute but sometimes so embarrassing.) Life is so good.

Thank you so much Valle Verde.

Tess

By Sue Mcgeoch

WE FOUND TESS AT A dog rescue in the UK. She had been rescued from gypsies in Ireland and was missing an ear. She was a blonde rough coated Lurcher (probably Whippet cross). She was incredibly nervous and especially distrustful of men. For the first week she would not eat unless I sat on the floor with her food on my lap. I took her to dog training and agility, and it was at agility that she realised that not all men would beat her. All the dogs loved her, and she had a special love affair with a Collie who nearly pulled his owner over every time he saw Tess.

Tess loved life in Spain and the freedom which was nearly her undoing. She joined the boar-hounds one day in full cry up the mountain. Fortunately, she came back without any incident. She then had an altercation with a wild boar early one morning at dawn. She was barking and I called her, then there was a crashing like a herd of elephants and a yelp from Tess. She got back to me, and it was only later I realised she had two deep puncture wounds on one of her thighs (from tusks). I was advised never to let the dogs out until proper daylight.

A few years later though at 2.00 in the afternoon all three dogs went racing off down the terraces. The other two came back pretty quickly, but when Tess arrived she was covered in blood and had an awful wound to her shoulder. It was a Saturday afternoon, and the vet was not amused. It took about 6 weeks

(3 visits a week to the vet) to recover. She went through quite a few T-shirt protectors!

Another time she caught a fox on our land, and she had it by the throat on its back. My grandchildren were yelling to their father to save the fox. He called her off. When he went to examine the 'dead fox' it got up and ran away!

Although such a hunter, she was very devoted. I became ill with polymyalgia and could not get out of bed. Tess and our terrier slept on my bed. My husband went downstairs to feed them. Tess would not leave me. My husband left her breakfast in an ice-cream box with the lid on it on the work surface. Later, Tess went downstairs removed the box from the work surface brought it upstairs, took the lid off and ate her breakfast in my bedroom.

Tess was one in a million. She was a real lady, as my husband pointed out when walking the dogs in town, she walked like a lady while the other two were (are) always sniffing to see what disgusting thing they can pick up!

We miss Tess very much. In conclusion I would say the kindest thing you can do is to give a rescue dog a happy home. The second kindest thing you can do is to know when to take the heartbreaking decision not to prolong life and suffering.

Teun
By Annalies Van Boven

IN 2020 MY RESCUE DOG LOLA from Spain passed away at the age of 9. Looking for another dog we met Teun. She was also from Spain, was found as a puppy in a garbage bag and came to the Netherlands at 4 months. There she lived in a family for 2 years, but it didn't work out there.

When she came to us I saw a terrified dog. Afraid of people, afraid of loud noises. She spent the first 2 weeks under the table. For the first six months she walked outside with her tail between her legs. We chose to let her come to us. And that paid off. Little by little we gained her trust.

In 2021 we started travelling with the camper and Teun came along. Being close to us 24 hours a day made her into another dog. She became playful, she ran on the beach, she even started to trust other people more and more. We finally moved to Spain in 2022. Teun was back in her native country and doing so well. She was a happy dog and gave us so much love.

Unfortunately, Teun passed away very suddenly just before Christmas last year. But how she had come out of her shell. We are so grateful that we had gained her trust and received so much love from her. It turns out that even those dogs with a past can become the best companions with a lot of patience and love.

The Chase
By Karen Evans

IT IS A BEAUTIFUL MIDSUMMER morning in England, and we are up and out early to beat the heat of the day.

Muttley loves his walks and is keen to get going, bouncing and frolicking down to the gate and back, trying to hurry me up. We go down the shady gravel track and across the muddy lane which is now hard packed and dry, a complete contrast to its wet and sticky winter conditions. At the end of this lane, Muttley usually edges a little further ahead of me. There are usually baby rabbits and squirrels down there and he likes to get his paws on one. He stalks them, his tail dropped down, his body slightly closer to the ground and a look of total, uninterruptible concentration on his face. He used to make me laugh when he did this, he is so patient, slowly inching forward to begin his chase from a closer distance.

We turn the corner at the end of the lane and have the whole of the Lambourn Downs spread out in front of us, softly rolling grass and arable fields, chalky tracks and distinctive pine trees. There is a string of racehorses up to our right being put through their paces, silhouetted against the horizon as they sprint up their sandy gallop. For us, an easy trot downhill now and around the back of the old pig farm. The grass is quite long on our track and still has a little dew on it, making Muttley's white, fluffy muzzle and paws damp where he is tracking animal smells in the grass. He almost doesn't need me, he knows where he is and what he is looking for but at the cross tracks he hesitates and looks back at me, just checking where we are going today.

We're now making the climb back up hill, this track is not so well used so there is a profusion of wild flowers, knapweed, hogweed, buttercups, rattle and more, an overall spread of tall white, yellow and purple heads dotted amongst the long grass with wispy heads full of seed. The butterflies are beginning to make an appearance, Meadow Browns, Chalk Whites and blues.

As we walk and look and sniff I'm aware that Muttley is not quite with me now, he's picked up a scent and is in the longer grass at the edge of the track. I can't see him, but I know he is there from the way the grass is moving and then the occasional view of his tail or head just popping up. That's it, he's exactly where he wants to be, this is a great walk.

Now I'm approaching the top of the hill, I'm not one hundred per cent sure where Muttley is but I'm pretty sure he's not too far away. A wide sweep of gallop grass crosses the track ahead of me, fine, springy and neatly mowed. As I approach I see a hare sprinting at full speed from right to left, low to the ground at full stretch, his back legs overtaking his front legs as he speeds along. He is followed some seconds later by Muttley doing the same thing! A happy dog doing absolutely what he loves best. I have the best eye level view. Dog and hare are above me and I watch in awe.

No time for a camera but the image is permanently imprinted in my memory, the beauty of the chase. Not just the chase but the beauty of the fresh day, the location and nature.

Muttley is always happy to flush out a hare or a rabbit who always dodge out of his reach. He walks many miles across the downs and when he started to chase he used to bark in a happy 'I'm chasing a rabbit style'.

On many occasions I have watched our little dog and best friend disappear into the distance, a little white dog in a sea of green or harvest gold. Thankfully, he has always returned, totally puffed out. We would have a lie down to cool off before we set off on our way again. As Muttley got older he would still enjoy following the scent and making the flush, but he became wiser to the chase, he knew when he was beat. Of course, each chase seemed to be repeated later in the day in a doggy dream with yapping, growling, twitching and tail wagging.

Muttley was our greatest friend, we found him by the side of a road in the Lecrin Valley in Spain when he was a puppy and contrary to all our future plans, we rescued him on condition that he did what we did.

He had a long and happy life with us touring all over Europe in our campervan. Sadly, he is no longer with us, but we have so many great fun memories of him. What a great little dog.

A Love story
By John Butts

ONCE UPON A TIME, IN the beautiful Alpujarras of Spain, there lived a cat named Mica. Mica was a cat with a remarkable personality. She had a mischievous streak but was also incredibly affectionate and loyal. The strange marking on her back looked like a question mark. Her owner was an old lady called Juana. Every evening, Mica would sit on her lap, they would sit on her terrace and watch the sun go down. Juana would think about the old times when she was young, and she lived in Granada. She had been a flamenco dancer in the Sacromonte and had had many adventures. During the sunset, Mica would think about catching mice and eating sardines, which were her favourite food.

Mica's home was a small village in the Alpujarras mountains. Life in the village was simple and slow, and Mica spent her days exploring the cobblestone streets, chasing the village chickens and trying to catch lizards. The villagers loved Mica and she was always around to greet them with her enthusiastic purr and a rub of her head against their legs.

One day, as Mica was out exploring, she noticed that there was a wonderful smell of fish coming from the van that was parked in the main square. If she had been able to read, she would have noticed that the van had the words 'Pescado de Ramón'written on the side. She jumped into the back of the van, and she started eating some delicious sardines. After about five minutes, she heard Ramón say, 'Adiós. Hasta la semana que viene.' Suddenly, the van door shut, the engine started, and they were soon speeding along the curvy mountain roads of the Alpujarras.

Oh no! She was trapped. How stressful! Mica was very worried, but she did what all cats do when life is too difficult... she went to sleep.

About an hour later, Ramón arrived in Almuñécar, a small seaside town. Ramón opened the door and Mica jumped out. Mica had never been to this place before, there were no friendly village people. She was next to the beach where Ramón kept his small fishing boat and his net. There were some men playing petanca and a group of young people were doing exercises in a fitness class.

The sun was going down.

Mica felt very alone, and she wondered where Juana was. She was sad and hungry and went to sit down under one of the fishing boats on the beach. Cats don't cry, but Mica was very lonely and upset.

The next day, she wandered around for what seemed like forever, but couldn't find her way back home. Everywhere she went, there were strange sights and unfamiliar scents that scared her. She felt like a tiny speck in a big, scary world. Mica had never been totally alone before, and it was a terrifying experience. How would she ever find her way back to the village? It was impossible.

Life was much more difficult at the beach. She was hungry most of the time. Fortunately, there was a kind old woman called Victoria who would bring leftovers and scraps from the local restaurants for all the stray cats every morning. Victoria was a retired nurse who lived in a small apartment looking over the sea. She was a very caring person and couldn't bear to see the stray cats suffering or going hungry. Mica would go to be fed by Victoria at her house and they got to know each other. Victoria named Mica 'Question Mark' because of the markings on her fur.

One day, Mica was exploring the line of rocks where the fishermen sit and cast their lines into the sea. The fishermen use small sardines as bait to put on the end of their hooks. Mica smelt the sardines. She could not resist and snatched one of them from the fisherman's basket. The fisherman flew into a rage, picked up a stone and threw it at Mica. The stone hit Mica on the paw, she let out a big scream and ran as fast as she could. She ran and ran. Cats don't have good road sense and she ran straight across the road. A car had to swerve to avoid her and made a loud screech as the tyres slid on the asphalt. The driver shouted out '¡Caramba! ¡Maldito gato!' Mica carried on running. She ran to the house of her only friend...Victoria.

It just so happened that at this moment an Englishman called John Pidley was walking along the seafront. He was doing a walk called 'the Almuñécar fat burner' to test his fitness. He had recently retired after running an antiquarian bookshop in Granada for many years.

He was a very pleasant, amiable man who had a slightly posh English accent. His presence on the scene at this particular moment has a big bearing on this story.

In the latter years as a Flamenco dancer, Juana had started to suffer from pains in her feet due to the years of 'taconeo'. This word describes the energetic stamping of the heel into the ground which produces a staccato sound, accentuating the flamenco rhythm.

Juana had previously worked in John's bookshop for years to reduce her hours of flamenco dancing and thus relieve her aching feet. In fact, John Pidley had been secretly in love with Juana for a long time but as John was a gentleman, he had never declared his love for her because she had a boyfriend. He had looked after Mica a couple of times when Juana had gone to dance in Paris, so he remembered the distinctive question mark pattern on Mica's back.

John suddenly realised that the cat running down the road was Juana's cat Mica. He abandoned his hike and followed Mica. When John arrived at Victoria's house, Mica was already eating the stolen sardine. Fortunately, she had not been badly hurt by the stone. John told Victoria that he recognised Mica and that she belonged to Juana. John still had Juana's phone number even though he had not seen her for over a year. He phoned Juana and told her that he had found Mica.

When Juana heard the news, her eyes widened in amazement, and tears of joy started streaming down her face. John decided immediately to take Mica back to the village. With Victoria's help, he put Mica into a cat box and within minutes, he was driving along the bendy roads of the Alpujarras. Eventually, John arrived at Juana's house, and when they opened the cat box, Mica suddenly realised that she was back in the village and her life of suffering was over. She was so happy that she went to her favourite chair, started purring and then went to sleep.

Juana asked John if he was hungry and if he would like to stay for a meal. John gratefully accepted. Juana went to the kitchen and started to make gazpacho. John went into the kitchen and took out three knives and forks from the kitchen drawer and started to lay the table for the meal for three people: himself, Juana and Pierre, Juana's French boyfriend.

Juana and John had not seen each other for some time and John did not know about recent changes in Juana's life. Juana told John that he only had to lay the table for two people because Pierre had died peacefully in his sleep six months previously.

Juana and John had a lot of news to catch up on. They talked and laughed, and they both realized that they had a lot in common and that they had missed each other. The conversation flowed effortlessly, and they began to realize that there was something special about their connection.

Something snapped in John's brain, and he decided to tell Juana the truth. John took a deep breath and looked into Juana's eyes. 'Juana,' he said softly, 'I can't keep this in any longer. I need to tell you that I love you. I have loved you for years.' Juana's eyes widened in surprise and delight. Then, she smiled and took John's hand in hers. 'I love you too, John,' she said. 'I've been in love with you since the day we first met.'

As you can imagine, the story has a happy ending. Juana and John became great friends and lovers. Mica enjoyed her old life in the village. Victoria, Juana and John would sometimes meet up and watch the sun going down over the bay in Almuñécar.

John sometimes thought to himself how lucky he was that he was passing the road just at the moment that Mica ran in front of the car. Then he realized that unlikely things can sometimes happen.

The Road to Salobreña
By Linda Rane

PONGO

WE HAD LIVED IN SPAIN for 8 years and travelled 'the road to Salobreña' many many times from our house above the little village of Itrabo. It is a very windy road and the short cut we use goes through lots of orchards with an irrigation canal running alongside them. There is also a rubbish tip on the opposite site of the orchards where stray dogs and cats can sometimes be found scavenging. I have seen stray dogs and cats wandering along this road many times, but normally I don't stop unless I feel that it is an extreme case or that the dog or cat is not coping with life on the campo!

One such time I saw an extremely emaciated male Dalmatian on the side of the road. Since it is rare to see stray Dalmatians, I stopped and opened the passenger side door. The dog immediately jumped in, which made me think he had an owner. He was covered in sores and so so skinny. I took him to my vet, who found he was chipped. He had been reported missing about 5 months before. The vet phoned the owner, and we made arrangements for me to take the dog, who was called Pongo, to meet up with his owner, Claudio (the local policeman) who lived in the village of Itrabo.

When I got there, Pongo didn't show the slightest bit of interest in Claudio and did not seem to recognise him at all. I told Claudio that Pongo would need to go to the vets to examine all his cuts and to buy him some special food to build him up. As soon as I mentioned this, Claudio asked me if I wanted to keep the dog as he didn't want him anymore! And since Pongo didn't seem to like Claudio, I agreed and took Pongo home with me. He stayed with me for 3 to 4 months during which time he put weight on, and we managed to find him a new home in Germany. He was a lovely and easy dog to look after and was my first foster Dalmatian. (I have had about another 6 or 7 rescue Dalmatians since then!)

About one or two weeks after Pongo had left for his new home in Germany, my husband got a visit from Seprona (the police who keep an eye on animals and land issues). I was out at the time. They wanted to check all our dogs' chips (and we had 23 dogs there that day) as someone had told them that I had been stealing dogs!

Anyway, all the dogs were very well behaved (even Lucky Lady!) and allowed the police to read their chips. Unfortunately there were 4 dogs who didn't have chips (they were foster pups who had no homes to go to yet so we had not chipped them) and also one of my own dogs Blondie, whose chip they couldn't find (we have since discovered it had moved down her leg). It is illegal in Spain to have dogs without chips so the following week we received a denuncia in the post.

We had to make a trip to Granada with all the dogs' passports and explain why some of the dogs didn't have chips. Luckily we were not fined and my friend Kathy, who came with us explained why there were so many dogs there and that I rescued them and found homes for them. But to this day I still don't know who reported me to Seprona as having 'stolen dogs' but it was a strange coincidence that it happened just after I had rescued Pongo, who had belonged to the local policeman. Just coincidence? I wonder.

BROKEN JAW

ON ANOTHER TRIP DOWN 'THE road to Salobrena', I came across another extremely skinny brown and white Pointer type of dog. I couldn't drive past. I stopped and tried to give him some cat biscuits (it was all I had in the car that time) but even though he wanted to eat them, he didn't seem able to manage them. I decided to take him to the vets. He was another one who didn't protest at all about getting into my car. I think that some of these animals are so desperate that they will accept any help.

The vet found he was unchipped, and we also discovered why he couldn't eat the cat biscuits. His jaw had been broken (possibly from a car hitting him) and obviously some time ago for him to get so thin. So sad. The vet told us that she would have to re-break and re-position his jaw and then he would have to be fed liquids for 5 to 6 months as his jaw would be wired. The operation would cost 400 to 500 euros and there was no guarantee that he would be able to eat normally afterwards.

Pointer cross dogs are not particularly easy to rehome in Spain especially if they have a disability. They are mainly used by hunters and discarded at the end of the hunting season to be replaced by new ones. We came to the sad decision that the best thing for this poor dog was to end his suffering. 'Broken jaw' now lies in my pet cemetery on my terraced land. I will never forget him, and this is his story.

LITTLE EVIE

ANOTHER DRIVE, THIS TIME ON our way home after shopping in Salobreña one New Year's Eve, I spotted a small whitish dog. She didn't seem to be able to see anything and was frantically running backwards and forwards across the road. Although the road isn't a particularly busy one, I could see that there was something wrong with her other than the usual starved and skinny look of most stray dogs. I shouted for Pete to stop the car, and being the obedient husband that he is, he did!

We both got out to try and catch her, but she was so scared that she kept running away from us. I could tell that there was something wrong with her eyes and her feet. For the next hour we chased her backwards and forwards across the road, through olive tree groves, vineyards and nispero groves. Eventually we managed to corner her as she was getting tired. I held her down but when I tried to pick her up she bit me, so keeping my hands well away from her mouth I just kept her quiet and calm while Pete went back to the car to get a blanket. Once she was wrapped in the blanket and in the car on my knee she was calm.

We turned and went back down to the vet in Salobreña which luckily was still open. The vet took one look at her eyes (she was blind) and her claws which were so overgrown that they had grown back into the pads of her feet (which was why she couldn't walk very well) and said that she had leishmaniosis.

He said that it was such an advanced state of the disease that she would not have lasted for more than 10 days. So we agreed that she should be put to sleep. Evie, as we called her because of finding her on New Year's Eve, is also now sleeping in our pet cemetery along with Broken Jaw and numerous other poor dogs and cats who just didn't make it.

PIPPA

I WAS RETURNING HOME FROM Salobreña. I had just dropped off one of my foster dogs with a pet transport company called For the Love of Dogs and Cats who were taking him to his new home in the UK. So my dog numbers were going down at Casa Montana at last, or so I thought.

I was just driving around one of the bends after the olive groves and saw a small beige browny dog right in the middle of the road. Obviously I stopped, opened my car door and called. The puppy came running up to me. There was one house nearby, but the puppy was so full of fleas and ticks and extremely dirty, that I thought even if she did belong to that house, they were not fit owners to allow a young pup like her to wander in the middle of the road and not keep her clean and free of parasites.

So I 'puppy napped' her. She was one of the most endearing and loving pups that I have ever fostered. We called her Pippa. I cleaned her, deticked, defleaed and dewormed her, and she stayed with me in foster care. Once she was old enough we posted her photos onto Facebook and soon someone was interested in adopting her.

She now lives a very happy life in the far north of Scotland and is called Luna. She is doing really well and even has a new brother called Cosmo to play with who was also rescued from Spain a year after Luna. A happy ending for one of 'The road to Salobrena' dogs! But I will always remember the other two, Broken Jaw and Evie, who weren't as lucky as Pippa and Pongo.

The Stolen dogs
By Linda Rane

I GOT A CALL ONE day from a friend who lived above Salobreña about three dogs who were in a bad way. Two little Yorkshire Terriers locked in a small area, eyes gunged up and fur totally matted. Plus another bigger dog chained up next door to them, a female German Shepherd cross.

I agreed to go and have a look to assess the situation. My friend didn't want to get involved as the dogs lived very close to her house and she was worried that if she got annoyed with the neighbour, he might harm her own dogs. This was in 2014. In those days Seprona (the animal welfare people) were not really concerned about helping and the police were not interested at all. (Nowadays they are much better and such cases like these can now be reported to them.)

I went up the next day and the two little dogs were in a small, locked and fenced area which looked as though it hadn't been cleaned for weeks. There were a couple of bowls with very smelly water and some dry dog biscuits. The dogs were indeed in a terrible state. They couldn't really see because the fur had grown over their eyes, plus their eyes were almost totally closed, probably due to infection.

The bigger dog seemed in slightly better condition and was behind a gate next door to the Yorkshire Terriers on a chain. She could get her nose under the gate, and we could stroke her. She was very friendly. There was no way we could get into the Yorkshire Terriers' enclosed area. And there was no house nearby to knock on a door to see if the owners lived close by. The first option would be to speak to the owners and ask them if they could take better care of the dogs. Since we couldn't do this I had to go home and think of an alternative.

I spoke to my Spanish friend who also lived up in that area and she agreed to come with me again. This time we went prepared! I put two cages into my car, a smallish one for the Yorkshire Terriers and a big one for the German Shepherd. My friend came along with wire cutters. We parked just alongside the fenced area and my friend went around the back of the area and used the wire cutters to cut a hole in the fence. Both the two little dogs came running up to the hole and she handed them to me one by one. I got them into the cage and then we unhooked the German Shepherd off her chain and got her into the car too, leaving as quickly as we could. Stealing dogs is an offence and we didn't want to end up in jail.

Once away from the area, we pulled over to check if they had any microchips. If they didn't have any we would be fine because it is illegal to have unchipped dogs in Spain and the owners could be fined. But if they were chipped, then we would definitely be in the wrong. The German Shepherd had no chip (phew!), but the two Yorkshire Terriers both did. We were horrified and didn't know what to do so I took all three dogs to my house until we could decide on the next step.

After a sleepless night thinking that the police were going to turn up and arrest me, I spoke to my friend again and we decided to take the two Yorkshire Terriers to the local vet and tell them that we found them on the road (which was sort of true). So we did that, the chips were read, and the details found. Amazingly both dogs had different owners.

The vets called up the owners and it was discovered that both dogs had gone missing about 2 to 3 years ago, obviously stolen. One was a female and one a male, were unneutered so it looked as though they were being used for breeding. The old owners were absolutely delighted to get their dogs back after so long. So in the end the dogs had been stolen twice, once in a bad way and the second time in a good way.

These days (as I mentioned above) I would not take such drastic action but would immediately call up Seprona and let them deal with the situation. But if we had gone down that route, the people who were using the dogs might have taken them away somewhere else to hide them before Seprona had managed a visit. I took the female German Shepherd a long way out of the area to a foster home where the people eventually ended up keeping her. So a happy ending for all three dogs.

Waiting for a cat with Sir Philip Sidney
By Rebecca Reynolds

I'M STAYING IN A SMALL town in the Alpujarras, south of Granada. If I open the windows of my first floor balcony I can hear the sounds of people chatting in the small square below (if they are not drowned out by music from the man who lives opposite). A few cars are usually parked there, and neighbours or some of the town's youngsters sit on benches to chat and smoke.

One morning the cries of a cat filled the square. It sounded distressed so I went down and walked around, but could not tell where the sound was coming from... inside a room? From a balcony? They continued through the morning and an hour or so later I went down again. This time a friend happened to come along, and we looked together. 'Here,' she said eventually, 'it's in this car engine!'

Cats often find refuge in car engines because they are places of safety from predators and can be warm. I got some tuna, and we sprinkled it under the car to tempt the cat out. Meanwhile, I went back again to post a picture on Facebook and ask if anyone knew the car owner, and to ask for help. When I came back my friend said the cat had come down to eat a morsel of tuna... 'It's so skinny!' ...and had jumped back up.

Next thing I knew a neighbour appeared (he had read the post), promptly lay down and pulled himself under the car to investigate. 'It's definitely in there,' he said, 'I can hear it.' But he couldn't tempt it out. He even tried to remove the grille at the front to get into the engine, while I tried to think what to tell the car owner if they returned.

The car couldn't be left. What if the owner came back and drove off with the cat still inside? I knocked on the doors of houses around the square, but no one knew who the car owner was. There was nothing for it but to wait. I fetched an essay I was working on for my Literature Masters and sat down on one of the benches... possibly the only time someone has sat in a public square in Spain writing an essay on sixteenth century sonneteer Sir Philip Sidney while waiting for a cat.

After about an hour and a half a tiny tabby kitten with painfully bony haunches emerged and scooted into one of the houses, head down. I had knocked there earlier to ask about the car owner. Now it was answered again by the same elderly man in a white vest.

I explained the situation to him, to the accompaniment of miaows from inside the house. We went inside and kneeling down I saw a dark shape and two yellow eyes blinking at me from under a kitchen cupboard. 'Cepillo,' said the homeowner, swishing a broom around energetically under the cupboard. But as any cat owner knows, you can't catch a cat with a brush. Kitty streaked out and squeezed itself under a sofa near the front door.

I explained I could go and get a 'jaula trampa'... trap cage. I came back with it, to find he had built a plastic bag barricade to stop the cat getting out of the room. He took my phone number to call when puss was caught.

That night my phone rang at 11 p.m. My Spanish wasn't good enough to get the whole story, but from the man's urgent tones I gathered that there had been an escape. I went down and sure enough the cunning kitten had run to a room upstairs. I set the trap cage again and told the man I would be back the next morning.

Next day the owner opened the door beaming and gestured at a certain tiny furry creature meowing loudly inside the cage. We were delighted. Back upstairs in my spare room, the kitten gave me little nips when I tried poking my fingers inside. I opened the cage door and he paused, doubtful, before taking refuge under the bed.

Later he disappeared as part of the well-known game 'stray cat hide-and-seek', finally turning out to be in the tiny space behind an electric heater. He took some fragments of tuna, and amazingly, started purring when I stroked it. The moment a cat 'turns' and becomes friendly is always memorable.

He accepted a second course of raw anchovy, then squeezed into a tiny space on top of a pile of sheets. Next day he was more confident and bounded out to investigate my permanent feline housemate, Indi, who hissed, chased and took a swipe. I swapped them over so that Indi was in the spare room and the kitten in the lounge. The kitten sat under the laptop, playing, sleeping and watching me.

In a rare stroke of stray cat good fortune, friends of friends were looking for a cat. They came round to pick him up and Luque, as he is now called (after Barrio Luque, where he was found) is today a contented, confident and much bigger animal, regularly terrorising and playing with his housemate Caramelo among the olive and orange trees at a finca a couple of miles away.

But I will leave the last word with Philip Sidney. His *Astrophil and Stella* is a sequence of 108 plaintive, pleading, sometimes angry sonnets written by Sidney as Astrophil to his unresponsive beloved, Stella. It turns out that Stella was an animal lover. Sidney starts Sonnet 59 by complaining: 'Dear, why make you more of a dog than me?' and compares himself with that dog:

Bidden perhaps he fetcheth thee a glove,

But I unbid, fetch ev'n my soul to thee.

In other words, the dog will fetch a glove if you tell him, but Astrophil brings his soul to Stella without being asked. He then laments that the dog is allowed to touch Stella's bosom and lie in her lap, whereas he is not; and this canine 'sour-breath'd mate' can 'taste of those sugar'd lips' whereas Astrophil can come nowhere near. I'm not sure whose side Luque would be on... human or dog. But he would certainly approve of extended complaining... since his cries got him his new life in cat heaven... and he might say to Sir Philip: keep going, you never know what might happen!

Slawit

By Craig Briggs

MY WIFE MELANIE AND I moved to Spain in May 2002. We travelled here with our dog Jazz, a Collie cross we'd rescued from the Halifax branch of the RSPCA.

Eight years later, when Jazz passed away, we were determined to never again put ourselves through such emotional trauma. Our resolve lasted four days.

Melanie and I divide our time between Galicia in the northwest corner of Spain and the Andalucian coast where we spend 3 months over winter.

Since publishing my first book, *Journey To A Dream*, in 2013, The Journey series has grown to 10 books. I am currently working on book 11. The series follows the ups and downs of our life-changing move to Spain. The following extracts are taken from book 8, *An Excellent Vintage* and book 9, *Life In A Foreign Land*. They begin with our first encounter of Cuca and recall some of our setbacks and triumphs.

------o---0---o------

The rescue centre was situated off the main N-VII highway, close to the city's municipal cemetery. We pulled up outside a gated compound and looked around for signs of life. High fencing and a tall hedge made it difficult to see anything, but barking dogs signalled we'd arrived. The day was hot and humid, and the morning sun had started burning holes in the wispy cloud cover. It was only a matter of time before standing around outside would be intolerable. Someone had seen us arrive and walked up to the gate.

'Hola, soy Craig (Hello, I'm Craig),' I said.

'Hola, soy Emilio (Hello, I'm Emilio).'

Emilio was a little older than I'd expected. He unlocked the gate and opened it just enough for us to squeeze through. Within the compound were half a dozen large pens. Each had an enclosed run with a kennel at the rear. Cuca was in one of them along with a very frisky terrier.

'This is Cuca,' said Emilio, leading us to the pen.

If anything, she looked more peculiar in the flesh than she had in the photos. Neither dog paid us any attention. The little terrier had other things on his mind and Cuca seemed more than happy to submit to his amorous advances.

'Hola, Cuca, ven aqui (Hello, Cuca, come here),' I called.

I pushed my fingers through the railings and waggled them.

'What do you think?' I asked.

'She doesn't seem very interested.'

Cuca had other things on her mind.

'Can we look at the other dogs?' asked Melanie.

'These are the puppies,' said Emilio, as we strolled along to the next pen.

The two puppies Maria had offered us were absolutely gorgeous. Tiny fluffy bundles of jet-black fur.

'Aw, aren't they lovely?' said Melanie.

'Look at the size of their feet,' I whispered.

They were ten weeks old, and their paws were already the size of my fist. Maria had described them as Labrador, German Shepherd cross but they looked more like Galician Mastines to me. If you're unfamiliar with the breed, the adult dogs are as tall as a Great Dane and built like Staffordshire bull terriers. Can you imagine how much food they'd eat?

'It would be better to take them both,' said Emilio, fumbling with the keys to the pen.

Crikey, that hadn't taken much encouragement. I wasn't surprised. As tiny balls of fur they were an easy sell but in another ten weeks he'd have two giants on his hands. Emilio's enthusiasm was all the encouragement Melanie needed to put the brakes on proceedings.

'No, no, they're far too big for us, Emilio, but they are adorable.'

Emilio looked disappointed and moved on.

'This is Blanca,' he said.

Sadly for Blanca, she was also too big. They had other dogs, but we had our hearts set on a bitch.

We wandered back to take another look at Cuca who was still being mounted by her randy admirer.

'Can she come outside so we can take a better look at her?' asked Melanie.

Emilio opened the gate. We waited with open arms. Cuca ran straight past. Melanie and I looked at each other dumbfounded. She wasn't exactly endearing herself to us.

She'd gone to run with the pack and looked really happy playing with the other dogs, which was hardly surprising. A bitch on heat is a popular attraction and before long they were chasing her around the compound. She didn't seem in the slightest bit bothered despite most of them being twice her size. Emilio was a little more concerned and went to rescue her. For a short time, the others kept their distance, all except one: a little short-haired terrier. He was by far the friendliest of the bunch and wandered over to say hello.

'What do you think to this one?' I asked.

'He's very friendly but we did want a girl.'

We did, but this little chap was the only dog to show the slightest interest in us. Emilio returned dragging Cuca by the scruff of the neck.

'You can't have him. He's mine,' he said.

Bang went that idea.

'Can we take her for a walk?' asked Melanie.

From the moment we'd collected Jazz from the RSPCA she'd been the perfect companion except for one short-lived flaw. She'd spent the whole of her life locked away in someone's cellar and the excitement of being allowed outside was too much. On a lead she would pull like a husky, so much so that she'd walk down the street on her hind legs. We soon remedied that with an easy walk harness.

'We don't have any leads,' replied Emilio.

'We've got one.' Melanie had come prepared.

Somewhat hesitantly he agreed. Did we really look like dognappers?

Melanie hooked her on and we strolled back to the main gate and headed up the road towards the city cemetery.

'What do you think?' I asked.

'She walks really nicely.'

Cuca had Melanie's seal of approval.

The dog seemed really happy to be outside and apart from a slight arch in her back, she looked fit and healthy. I did wonder if that had developed from cowering. She seemed very timid and wary of sudden movements, but Cuca was growing on us.

'She is a cute little thing. Do you like her?' I asked.

'She's very different to Jazz.'

'Perhaps that's a good thing.'

'Perhaps it is.'

By the time we'd walked back to the compound we'd made up our minds. We'd even chosen a new name for her.

THE FIRST YEAR WE MOVED to Galicia, we nearly adopted a stray dog. She wasn't too dissimilar to Cuca. Jazz took to her straight away despite her being a bitch. We started calling her Slawit which to most people means absolutely nothing. However, anyone living in and around Huddersfield will know exactly what it means, or indeed where it is. Five miles outside Huddersfield, nestling in the Colne River Valley, is the village of Slaithwaite, known locally as Slawit. The name also has the added benefit of being pronounced exactly the same in Spanish as it is in English. She didn't know it then, but Cuca was about to become Slawit.

Emilio was waiting for us on our return.

'We'll take her,' I said, and that was that.

Emilio phoned a local vet who issued her with a new passport under the name Slawit, inoculated her against rabies, and inserted a microchip using a device which looked like a leather eyeleting tool. I couldn't help but wince as he punctured the back of her neck.

Slawit didn't seem in the least bit concerned. The fee for this service was a paltry fifty-five euros. They congratulated us with a warm handshake and off we went.

I opened the tailgate and tapped on the rear bumper.

'Come on, lass,' I said.

Slawit stood there looking extremely nervous.

'Come on, Slawit, up you get,' said Melanie.

As if to show willing, she placed her front paws on the bumper and peered into the back.

'Go on then,' I said, encouraging her to jump.

It hadn't occurred to us that she might be wary of travelling.

'Come on, lass,' I repeated.

At which point she jumped back down. More encouragement was needed. For the next few minutes, she jumped up and down, up and down, but whatever we tried she couldn't bring herself to take that leap of faith into the back. In the end I picked her up and plonked her inside.

'There you go. Nothing to be scared of. Now, sit down. Go on, sit down.'

Once again there was no response. If anything, she seemed more anxious.

'Leave her. She'll sit down when she's ready,' said Melanie.

Gently, I closed the tailgate and we set off home.

Every so often Melanie tried to check on her, but it was very difficult to see anything from the front seat.

'She's very quiet,' said Melanie.

'She's probably asleep.'

A little over half an hour into our journey we'd reached the village of Montefurado, famous for its Roman tunnel.

'Tell me that's not what I think it is,' said Melanie.

I felt certain it was and pulled to the side of the road. We jumped from the car and walked around to the back. Bright sunlight bounced off the rear window, making it impossible to see anything other than the dog's head.

Slowly, I opened the tailgate. Our worst fears were realised. Slawit had thrown up, not once but at least three times and by the look of it, she hadn't long eaten her breakfast. They hadn't mentioned that when we said we'd take her. It had never crossed our minds that Slawit might get travel sick. Jazz had loved riding in the car. Fortunately, we'd had the foresight to place a large bath towel in the back. While Melanie did her best to fold the mess into a small bundle, I took Slawit for a short walk to try and calm her stomach. As I lifted her into the back, her ears drooped.

'Poor thing,' said Melanie.

'Poor thing! What about the car?'

Gently, I closed the tailgate, and we took our seats. I turned off the music and we pinned back our ears. Before long, we heard more guttural rumblings. Stopping was pointless. The sooner we got home the better for all of us. For a small dog she certainly had a big stomach.

Back at El Sueño we gave her the freedom of the garden. We didn't have much choice as she flatly refused to go inside the house. The journey had left her a little shaken and very apprehensive of us. The reason she had been abandoned was a mystery, but Maria had told us she'd been found locked inside the cemetery. We thought it best to leave her be and let her familiarise herself with her new surroundings at her own pace.

------o---0---o------

Nothing quite compares to the homecoming welcome of a dog. Be they parted for five minutes or five hours, their greeting is always overwhelming. We couldn't wait to see the reaction of Slawit on our return.

'Where is she?' asked Melanie.

I hadn't a clue. Surely she hadn't escaped. How could she?

We leapt out of the car and ran to the gate. Melanie was searching through her handbag for the key. I looked around the garden but couldn't see her anywhere. There was no way she could have climbed the five-foot-tall fence, was there? As soon as Melanie found the key, I caught a flash of ginger out of the corner of my eye.

Slawit came bounding towards us. She'd been hiding behind the pampas grass in the corner of the garden. We breathed a sigh of relief but couldn't understand why she hadn't come to greet us when we first arrived.

Slawit's greeting was everything we'd hoped it would be. She whined with excitement, wagged her tail and jumped up at us. We were just relieved to know she was alright and still here. Melanie led everyone through the house and onto the back porch. I held back to have a look around the garden. The first thing I noticed was a hole scratched out of the lawn underneath the conifer. The previous day, she'd hidden in a flowerbed. It would seem she liked to scrabble about in the dirt.

From the conifer in one corner of the garden I walked across to the pampas grass in the other. What I found was even more alarming. Behind the bushy grass was a two-metre-high bamboo fence which, along with the side gate, enclosed the front garden from the back. From what I could see, Slawit had eaten her way through the bamboo in search of an escape route. Thankfully, the back garden is also fully enclosed. It was time to find out what she had to say for herself.

'Come here you,' I said.

Slawit was lying on the lawn. She looked. Her expression said it all: dipped head, floppy ears, and remorseful eyes.

'What have you been up to?' Her head dipped further.

'What has she been up to?' asked Melanie.

I explained what I'd found, much to everyone's amusement, except Melanie. Having once jumped into the pool fully clothed to rescue Jazz, she knew exactly how dangerous it could have been.

'Slawit, come here,' said Melanie.

'Aw, don't be cross with her,' pleaded Janet.

As if we could have been.

Melanie gave Slawit a talking-to but even if she'd understood I doubt it would have made any difference.

Two people missing from our little soirée were Roy and Maria. They'd had another lunch engagement, but news travelled fast, and we hadn't been home long when Roy phoned to ask how we were getting on with our new house guest. I invited them down for refreshments and within half an hour, they too were fussing over Slawit.

'What are you calling her?' asked Roy, in his broad Somerset accent.

'Slawit,' I replied.

'Slaver-it.' Roy was teasing.

As the evening wore on, the wine flowed. When dusk turned to night, Melanie raided the fridge and rustled up a bowl of ensaladia (Russian salad) and plates of patatas bravas (bite-sized chunks of deep-fried potato), and I lit the barbecue. It wasn't until the clock ticked into a new day that our guests departed.

'I'm going to check the wine before I turn in,' I said.

'I'll take Slawit out. Slawit, come on.'

I'd like to say that Slawit spent the evening outside with us, but she was more aloof than that. Every so often she'd wandered over looking for attention. She'd taken quite a shine to Bob, but her impromptu appearances hadn't lasted long.

Calling Slawit was like speaking to a wall, except a wall is more responsive.

'Slawit, come… Slawit. Can you see her?' asked Melanie.

'Slawit, come.' My tone was more commanding but equally ineffective.

We waited and waited.

'She's not inside, is she?' I asked.

'I don't think so.'

Melanie made two steps towards the kitchen door when I caught a glimpse of her through the darkness.

'There you are. Come on, lass. It's time for bed.'

------o---0---o------

By the time we'd got home, the clock had ticked around to midnight. As we pulled into the driveway, Slawit appeared at the glass-panelled French doors wagging her tail. It wasn't until we opened them that we realised something was wrong. As Slawit came running out, I noticed a length of black rubber lying on the dining room floor.

'What's that?' asked Melanie.

'I'm not sure.'

Slawit was beside herself with excitement, jumping up at Melanie and whining with pleasure. Melanie did her best to calm her down. I picked up the rubber strip. It looked like a section of the weather seal from around the doorframe. Had there been an attempted break-in? Surely not; this was sleepy Canabal, for heaven's sake, not the East End of London. I stepped back outside and inspected the doorframe. Not a scratch. How strange.

'Well?' asked Melanie.

'Everything seems fine.'

By then, Slawit had calmed down. Melanie picked up the lead and clipped it to her collar.

'Come on then,' she said, leading her towards the gate.

Pushing the door closed revealed a probable cause. Far from it being an attempted break-in, it was in fact an attempted breakout. Slawit had peeled back the corner of the aluminium doorframe and pulled out the rubber seal. Her teeth marks were clearly visible on the frame and that wasn't the only thing. Having failed to escape through the French doors, she'd jumped into my armchair and tried to eat her way out of the lounge window. The evidence was smudged in blood along the window frame, and she wasn't finished yet. Undeterred by her lack of success, she'd jumped down and started chewing her way through the lounge door. There were teeth marks in the architrave, and deep scratches in the door. She'd really been going at it. I slumped into my armchair, staring at the damage. Moments later the culprit returned.

'I know where that piece of rubber came from,' I said.

'Where?'

'Look.' I stood up and showed Melanie the damage to the French door.

'Aw, Slawit.'

Slawit looked guilty. Her tailed curled under her tummy, her ears flopped down, and her head drooped.

'That's not all, look at that.' I pointed at the window.

'What is it?'

'Blood. She must have cut her mouth trying to get out.'

'Aw poor Slawit, come here and let me take a look at you.' From condemnation to commiseration in under ten seconds.

'Poor Slawit! Just look at that door and the architrave.' I pointed at the bottom of the lounge door.

'Oh, my word, Slawit.' Talk about a rollercoaster ride; Melanie had gone from condemnation to commiseration to consternation – what next?

To be fair to Slawit, she'd been left alone for almost the entire day in an environment she was still getting used to.

------o---0---o------

It took six days for Slawit to settle into her new bed. Actually, that's not strictly true. The exact opposite happened. Parts of it settled into her. We returned home one day to find she'd taken a bite out of it. A rather large bite.

By the end of October her travel training had progressed from sitting in the car with the engine running to driving through the village, a round trip of four kilometres. It was a relief to get home without her throwing up although the back was awash with slaver. Later that day we tried again. On that occasion we drove almost five kilometres to the village of Sober. Once again, she managed to keep her stomach contents intact, but a splattering of saliva illustrated her anxiety. At her current rate of progress, it would take one and a half years to train her to travel the 1100 kilometres we were due to drive in less than five weeks. What were we going to do?

To add to our troubles, she still wasn't sleeping. Melanie had been up at least once every night since we'd brought her home and frequently more often. Slawit would either cry, or tap on the lounge door until we took her out. If we didn't, she would invariably leave us a puddle to clean up. Melanie had the patience of a saint.

'Can you hear that?' whispered Melanie.

I was barely awake, never mind listening for unusual noises.

'What?'

'Listen… There it is again.'

'She's just trying to get comfortable,' I replied.

It sounded like Slawit was ruffling her bed. Melanie wasn't convinced. She pulled on her slippers and went to find out.

'Aw, Slawit. Look at that.' Whatever she'd done, Melanie wasn't impressed. 'That's a bad girl, a very bad girl.'

'What's she done?' I called.

Melanie pushed open the bedroom door. She was holding Slawit's new dog bed, or what was left of it. Not satisfied with taking a chunk out of it, this time she'd ripped it to shreds.

'Oh my word.'

'If you think that's bad you should see the state of the lounge. There are pieces of foam everywhere.'

'It's a good job it wasn't expensive.'

'That's not the point,' she snapped.

Anyone would think it was my fault.

The day went from bad to worse. The progress Slawit had made in the car was undone when she threw up on a round trip to Sober. Undeterred, later that day I climbed into the back with her at mealtime. To say it was cramped is an understatement. Slawit started trembling before Melanie had picked her up.

'Fetch me some kitchen roll, will you?' I asked.

For the next hour I sat in the back shifting my weight from one cheek to the other in an effort to stop my bum from going numb. Slawit's shaking became so bad you would have thought she was sitting in an ice bath, and foam dripped out of her mouth like suds from a washing machine.

'Come on, lass, eat your food,' I said, doing my best to calm her down.

Slawit seemed determined to ignore me. Whatever I did, or said, made no difference. After an hour, Melanie came to see how we were getting along. I felt so stiff I could hardly move. As for Slawit, she was a trembling wreck.

'You'd better let her out,' I said.

The minute her feet touched the driveway, she shook herself from head to tail and wandered off as if nothing had happened. All we could do was press on. We vowed to take it in turns to spend one hour a day in the back of the car with her until she improved.

-----o---0---o-----

The following morning, we woke to bright sunshine and the sound of waves breaking on the shingle beach below the cottage. Playa del Río de la Miel hadn't lost any of its charm. I could have sat on the balcony all morning, staring out to sea and daydreaming but Melanie had other ideas.

'Let's take Slawit for a walk along the beach after breakfast,' she suggested.

'Are you sure?'

Jazz used to love paddling in the water and barking at the breaking waves. This would be Slawit's first encounter with the open sea and if her response to the lake at A Rúa was anything to go by, she'd hate it.

'You never know, she might like it.' Melanie was nothing if not optimistic.

From Casa Maria we walked around the bay, down past the old paper mill, and onto the beach. We had hoped to bump into Paco, but he must have had better things to do on a Friday morning.

Once on the beach, Slawit flatly refused to go anywhere near the water. Worse still, she seemed absolutely terrified. Water was her nemesis, and this endless sea was not only wet, but it moved to and fro, up and down, and made an almighty noise when it broke on the beach and retreated through the shingle.

'I'm not sure this was such a good idea,' I said.

Melanie was having none of it. Undeterred, she walked along the water's edge with Slawit straining at the limit of her five-metre retractable lead. No amount of persuasion or coercion was going to change that. Our morning walk was brief and before long we were trekking back home.

Life continued at a lazy pace and by the end of the first week, we'd slipped into a relaxed routine.

'I'm taking the dog out. Are you coming?' asked Melanie.

Mornings at Casa Maria were a peaceful affair. We'd wake when Slawit wanted to go out and then drift back into dreamland for an hour or so. Melanie would make a coffee and we'd sit up in bed staring through the open door and out across the Med. Having downed our coffees, we'd slope out onto the balcony for breakfast and our first glimpse of the morning sun. Warm rays and the rhythmic note of breaking waves would contrive to sap our motivation to move. Thankfully, we could always count on Slawit to shatter that illusion.

'Where are you going?'

'Down to the beach.'

If only Slawit had known, I doubt she'd have been as keen to disturb us.

'OK.'

It's believed that Podencos are hunting dogs and Portuguese Podencos, like Slawit, were bred specifically to hunt rabbits. Whether it's true or not, I'm not sure, but it would certainly explain her curiosity. Nose to the ground and tail in the air, nothing gets in the way of her searching out her quarry, which more often than not is anything remotely edible. She would happily scale a cliff face with all the confidence of a Himalayan mountain goat. Fear was reserved for an open car door or body of water, the latter being anything from a puddle to the undulating Med.

'Come on,' called Melanie as she tugged on Slawit's lead for the umpteenth time.

'What's she eating?'

'Slawit, drop it!' shouted Melanie.

By the time she'd dragged her close enough to discover what she'd found, Slawit was licking her lips. Down on the beach, I waited at the entrance while Melanie tried in vain to coax her into the gently rippling sea. Slawit was having none of it. Suddenly, Melanie's scream shattered my daydream.

'What's the matter?' I called, instinctively rushing towards her.

'Slawit's slipped her lead.'

Melanie was standing at the water's edge with Slawit's collar swinging from the end of the lead. I'm not one to panic but my heart was racing. The bay was hemmed in by cliffs at the far end, steep enough to deter most humans but not a fearless Portuguese Podenco.

'Where did she go?' I asked.

'I don't know. One minute she was here and the next she'd gone.'

I could hardly blame Melanie. If I'd been paying more attention I might have seen where she went. I scoured the cliffs for any signs of life but nothing. My heart skipped from a canter to a gallop. Lining the back of the beach was a thicket of wild sugar canes, impassable to humans but a veritable adventure playground for an inquisitive Podenco.

'Slawit!' I called. 'Slawit!'

'Slawit, come on, lass!' shouted Melanie.

'You go that way and I'll go this.' Splitting up increased our chances of success.

Melanie marched off towards the cliffs calling her name and I did the same in the opposite direction. I was beginning to think we might never see her again when the anxiety in Melanie's voice changed to joy.

'There you are, come on, lass.'

We weren't out of the woods yet. On more than one occasion Slawit had returned to within touching distance only to sprint off again. For her, this was one big game. Melanie's quick reactions saved the day as she grabbed her by the scruff of the neck. I went to lend a hand and between us we managed to get her collar back on. I suppressed the urge to overtighten it.

'Come on, trouble. I think that's more than enough excitement for one day.' Slawit's response was to wag her tail even more vigorously.

------o---0---o------

We spent the final two days of our stay in and around the house, sitting on the narrow balcony and staring out to sea. On the evening before our departure, we'd set the alarm, just in case, but hadn't needed it. In the morning, Melanie slipped out of bed to put the kettle on and take Slawit outside. When she opened the bedroom door, bright sunlight angled into the room.

'Aw, Slawit.'

Melanie's tone suggested she'd left us a present to clean up. I decided to keep quiet; there was ample time for recriminations. I heard her filling the kettle and then opening the front door. A few minutes later, Slawit dashed into the bedroom and leapt onto the bed.

'What have you been up to?'

I raised my voice in anticipation of a reply from the kitchen. It's always easier asking sensitive questions through a third party. Melanie said nothing nor did she need to; Slawit's drooping ears spoke louder than words.

'She's thrown up,' said Melanie, as she walked into the bedroom with our cuppas.

Slawit waited in vain for her morning treats. What had started as a training tool in recognition of good overnight behaviour had become a daily routine regardless of it. If we hadn't been travelling, I suspect Melanie would have caved in to Slawit's hangdog expression.

I felt a bit sorry for Slawit. The most likely cause of her upset stomach was anxiety brought on by watching us packing. Poor thing, she couldn't win.

'There's no treats today, lass. We're going for a drive along the coast but as soon as we get there, you can eat as much as you like.'

My offer fell on deaf ears.

'Do you think we can get away without sedating her?' I asked.

Such was Slawit's aversion to travelling that before leaving home the vet had given us four sedatives to be used as and when required. Without them, we would all have had a torrid time on the drive south. The dose induced a semi-comatose state and despite Slawit showing no ill effects, we would all be happier to avoid it. To make matters worse, the drug had to be administered by injection and Melanie's dislike of needles meant that responsibility fell to me.

'I don't see why not,' said Melanie.

At 10:15 am we squeezed the last few pieces of luggage into the back of the car, said our goodbyes to Casa Maria, and set off on the 118-kilometre drive along the coast to Santa Maria Village in Elviria.

------o---0---o------

The drive along the coast had taken a little over an hour and a half. Throughout the journey, Slawit had been standing motionless in the passenger footwell with her front paws on Melanie's lap. From the moment we'd set off, she'd been panting heavily, and a constant stream of saliva had dribbled from her open mouth. The smooth road surface, constant speed, and even pitch of the engine had helped to control her motion sickness but as soon as we left the highway, all that changed. Her anxiety increased and she began to fidget. Thankfully, the supermarket was nearby. As I pulled into a space in the carpark, panic filled the cabin.

'Quick, stop! She's going to throw up,' cried Melanie.

I slammed on the brakes. Melanie grabbed her collar and flung open the passenger door. In Slawit's eagerness to escape she took Melanie with her and the pair of them tumbled out onto the pavement. Before Melanie had picked herself up, Slawit barfed. I jumped out and ran around the car to help. Laughing was not an option.

'Just wait. Slawit!'

Melanie was on her hands and knees, hanging on to Slawit's collar for dear life. If she escaped, there'd be no telling where she'd end up or if we'd ever see her again.

'Grab her,' pleaded Melanie.

I forced my fingers through the collar and wrapped my free arm around her neck. Melanie could finally let go and get to her feet.

'Blooming 'eck, Slawit, couldn't you wait?' she said, as she clipped the lead to her collar.

She passed it to me, and I released the lock on the extension. The cord whistled out like a hooked fish on a rod as Slawit ran into the adjacent rough ground. When the cord reached its limit, she almost pulled my arm out of its socket.

'Are you alright?' I asked.

'I think so. You stay here and I'll get what we need for lunch,' said Melanie, dusting herself down.

She headed off towards the supermarket and I turned to Slawit. Having realised escape was not an option, she'd turned her attention to the surroundings. Nose to the ground and tail in the air.

The patch of waste ground was dry and dusty. Well-trodden footpaths wound their way between stunted southern pines. These contorted trees reflected the harsh growing conditions and resembled exhibits in a natural sculpture park. Slawit wasn't interested in following pathways and headed off wherever the scent took her. The morning air felt warm and humid as we strolled through the pines. Patches of shadows turned the reddish-brown earth into darker shades of ochre. After a while we wandered back to the car. As we neared, Slawit sensed danger and began to pull away.

'Come on. You don't have to get in until Mummy gets back.'

Listen to me, or rather, thank heavens no one was.

I strolled past the car and Slawit came scampering after me. Back and forth we walked until Melanie finally showed her face.

'Right then, you get in and I'll pass her to you,' I said.

Melanie put the shopping into the back and jumped in. Slawit knew exactly what was about to happen and tried to pull away.

'Come on, lass, not far now and then you can have something to eat.'

On this occasion I was telling the truth, but she didn't believe a word of it.

'Stop being silly,' said Melanie, as we manhandled her into the footwell.

------o---0---o------

In this final extract, our friend Sue had come to stay with us. On the final day of her week-long holiday, we'd decided to eat out for lunch. Under normal circumstances Slawit would have come with us, but unusually inclement weather meant dining outside would not have been an option, so we left her in the apartment. This is what we found when we returned.

------o---0---o------

'Get ready,' said Melanie, as she pushed the key into the lock.

The deadlock clunked and then clunked again. It seemed inevitable that Slawit would try to escape so we readied ourselves for the charge. Slowly, Melanie pushed open the door, enough to put her arm through but too narrow for Slawit to escape. Sue and I crouched down with our arms apart. If Slawit slipped past Melanie, we were the last line of defence. We waited for her nose to appear, but it didn't. Melanie turned to me and I shrugged my shoulders. Something was wrong. She couldn't have escaped, could she?

Perhaps she was waiting until Melanie flung open the door before making a dash for freedom. As the seconds ticked by, a feeling of foreboding landed in the pit of my stomach. Had her home-alone antics been so destructive she was terrified to show her face? Melanie opened the door and peered inside.

'Where is she?' I asked.

Melanie turned and pressed a finger to her lips.

'Shh. I bet she's asleep on the sofa,' she whispered.

One by one we tiptoed inside. By the time Sue had closed the door, Melanie was ready to pounce. Poor dog, she wouldn't know what had hit her.

'What are you doing on...'

Melanie's raised voice stopped mid-sentence.

'What is it?' I asked.

'She's not here.'

'Shh. What's that?'

The room fell silent. The sound of paws, clawing gently at a door, floated into the room. The three of us turned to face Sue's bedroom. It couldn't be, could it? I walked across the hallway and opened the door. Slawit shot out, darted past me, and ran straight to Melanie. The poor thing looked terrified. Melanie bent down to give her the attention she craved.

'Aw you poor thing. How long have you been locked in there?' asked Melanie.

I could only think that Slawit had pushed open the door, wandered inside, and somehow closed it behind her.

'What's the matter?' asked Melanie.

She'd caught me staring into the room.

'Craig, what's the matter?' she repeated.

Shock had momentarily rendered me speechless.

'You'd better take a look at this,' I said.

Melanie could sense that something was wrong. She stopped fussing the dog, walked past Sue, and stood next to me.

'What?' she said, looking aimlessly around the room.

'There.'

I pointed at the foot of the door frame.

'What is it?'

'Slawit, come here.'

Slawit knew she was in bother. She'd sloped off to her bed and was curled up in a ball. Her whole frame was shivering as if her bed was made of ice.

'Come here!' I bellowed.

Melanie had entered the bedroom to take a closer look at the door frame and Sue also wandered over to find out what had happened.

'I definitely closed the door before we went out,' she said.

In her desperation to free herself, Slawit had tried to eat her way out of the bedroom. The bottom six inches of the architrave were chewed beyond recognition and deep teeth marks were embossed into the frame to the height of the door handle.

'Slawit!'

Gingerly, she got to her feet, trembling like a shaven polar bear in the Arctic. Slowly, she walked towards me with her ears drooped and tail tucked tightly under her body.

'Aw, don't be cross with her,' pleaded Melanie.

'Look at the state of it,' I replied, pointing at the damage.

'She didn't mean it.'

If she hadn't meant it, I couldn't imagine what it would have looked like if she had.

'What's that?' said Sue, pointing at a pile of rags on the floor.

The crumpled pieces of fabric were actually the voile curtains that should have been hanging at the pair of door-length windows. Melanie picked them up and my heart sank. Slawit had dragged them to the floor with her teeth. They weren't ripped but the fabric had pulled, and they were covered in teeth marks. Sue's distraction had given Slawit the opportunity to retreat. Melanie stepped out of the bedroom holding the curtains.

'Slawit, come here!' Now there'd be bother. 'Come here!' she screamed.

I scanned the door frame looking for any mitigating circumstances and noticed that one of the retaining screws which held the strike plate to the door frame was missing. At least now we knew how she'd gained entry. By now Slawit had risen to her feet and was creeping slowly towards her fate.

'That's how she got in,' I said, pointing at the latch.

'That's not the point,' replied Melanie.

'Don't be too hard on her. She must have been terrified.'

The persianas, or plastic window blinds, were shut tight. With the door closed the room would have been pitch black.

Slawit had crept the length of the apartment and was cowering in front of Melanie.

'Look at this.'

Melanie grabbed Slawit's collar and pushed the curtains under her nose.

'That's a bad girl, now get on your bed.'

Disciplining the dog brought tears to Melanie's eyes. Rescue dogs have probably suffered enough without their new owners giving them a hard time but behaviour like that couldn't go unpunished. I'm not a fan of corporal punishment. It's often administered out of frustration rather than a desire to correct unacceptable behaviour. Slawit scampered back to her bed and lay down. If I had to guess, the only thing she'd learnt was that being confined in a darkened room was not fun. As for eating her way out, given time I suspect she would have made it.

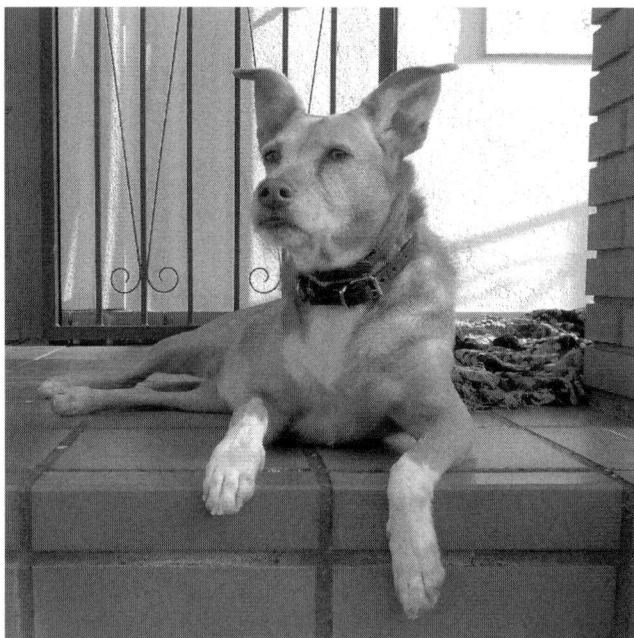

Hunny
By Paula Jones

TODAY MY HEART HAS COMPLETELY broken into a thousand pieces. I don't think it will ever mend. I currently look like I've been in a boxing ring and pummelled to death. Oh gosh, here goes.... How do I find the words? ..... You've been my constant companion for the last 16 ½ years and I don't know how I'm going to cope without you, Hunny.

The house already feels empty. From the age of about 8, I remember it like yesterday, school assembly for guide dogs for the blind, encouraging a sponsored walk. A golden retriever called Honey. I was in awe, and said to myself I'm going to do my best and try to raise lots of money and one day I'm going to have a golden retriever just like her, but I will spell her name the Winnie the Pooh way! Hunny.

Years later with two young children, I searched for you. I found you by Stonehenge with Kim Ellis, who had a waiting list as long as her arm, I felt I had no chance, but she had a little pup who had failed the test to become an assistance dog. You wouldn't let go of the chew toy! That didn't change and I'm grateful about that. Their loss was absolutely our gain. I fell in love instantly with you, my Tenfield Sea Queen. I was only allowed to have you if I traded off for caravan holidays (I bloody hated camping!) but I agreed, anything for my girl!

You came on family holidays (not caravan holiday!), Cornwall being your favourite, the ultimate surf dog. You adored Reece and Charis and there is nothing you wouldn't do to protect them and me. We visited Kim and your brothers and sisters, grannies, mum, aunties... A beautiful sea of goldies running across the Salisbury Plains, the most spectacular sight that has always stuck with me I should have known then that I was destined for a houseful of rescue dogs.

You got a new daddy when you were only 3 years old, the two of you hit it off from day one and he was just as crazy about you as I was. He loved you so much, I could not have asked for a better guy, in fact all my friends and family loved you, you were so caring and gentle, that was your way. You moved houses and even countries with us, saw me through some of the best and darkest times of my life and were my absolute rock, always by my side looking after me, you understood it all and never judged me, just there to give a soothing paw. You knew every word I said and just when I needed a cuddle.

At age 6 we nearly lost you to pyometra, but we caught it in time and after an operation you came back to health, although we felt you were slowing down a bit (little did we know!), so we found a little companion for you, Lillie, a little pocket rocket! That woke you up, she was a real live wire and you put so much energy into training her well. In fact when we started our path of dog rescue you trained them all, the wise one of the pack showing how things are done around here. We could not have done it without you, Hunny.

You are such a kind and happy soul, embracing life and sharing your huge heart with everybody you met. A prolific swimmer, one sniff of water and you were diving in it (muddy or not!).

We even had a shelf built in our pool just for you, as you used to launch yourself in it, and in later years struggled to get out. Your favourite spot has always been by the pool watching the family have fun and enjoy the water too.

Sadly for the last couple of years you struggled with dementia. It's been a bit like a nursing home around here, with an old lady barking the orders, having a bit of a wobble now and again and wanting things done her way. Of course we've always been happy to be there for you, no matter how tired we have felt, it's been our pleasure to return the love you have shared with us. I've always promised you that your last day would not be your worst, we owe you that much, after being our faithful friend for so long.

Yesterday you had the best day, a rice pudding breakfast, a picnic down by the river with the other pups and a steak dinner, it was your perfect day. You loved it and smiled from ear to ear. Sadly you were coming close to the bad days overlapping the good and this morning for the first time you looked at me and told me you were tired... it was time.

Today you passed peacefully in your favourite spot overlooking the pool, after having a doggy massage you happily snored away, listening to your favourite music. You were surrounded by your family and doggy and kitty friends, a room full of love just for you. I could not have hoped for anything more tranquil. It's always been you and me together Hunny, against the world, my bestest bud.

Parting is utter agony and you have taken a huge chunk of my heart with you. Goodnight, God bless my sweet girl, thank you for looking after me and loving us all so much. I will love you forever and if there is a bridge, like I told you earlier, I promise I will find it and one day we will be together again, run free with Sherrie and the Tenfields my love until we meet again xx.

Dotty's story
By June Davies

WE MOVED TO SPAIN IN 2011 after retiring with no thoughts of having a dog or any other animal. Little did we know that within a year we would be dog owners.

There was a dog wandering around our village that had obviously been abandoned. Every day when we went out we would see this poor dog looking for food or shelter from the hot sun. A few people were feeding her, but she looked so sad. Lots of friends commented on seeing this dog and suggested that we should adopt her. (It seems that all Brits living in Spain have to own a dog or two or more.) After a lot of discussion we decided that 'yes' we would take on this dog.

The following day we went out to get the dog and bring her home but, alas, she was nowhere to be found. Where could she be? Every day she'd been along the road. We asked a few local people who all gave us different answers—'She's been taken to Granada,' - 'Her owner has come for her,' - 'She's been poisoned.' We were very upset as we had no idea what had happened and had geared ourselves up to owning a dog. We guessed it was just not to be.

A few days later a friend was walking her dog up in the mountain when she heard a dog whimpering and spotted a dog tied to a tree. She came to us saying that she is sure it was our dog. We quickly drove up to the spot and there was our dog looking frightened and so sad. She had dug a hole to lie in to try and stay cool as it was so hot. She had no food or water. We untied her and she came readily with us to the car and jumped in. A man turned up to see what we were doing and said that we couldn't take the dog as she belonged to his friend from a nearby village. We gave the man our phone number and said to pass this on to the owner and to let him know that we had his dog if he wanted to come and collect her. No one came.

That day we had to go shopping and was worried about leaving our new dog in the house alone as she had probably never been inside before. So we took her to our campo and tied her to a tree with a long length of rope with some shade, food and water and went shopping. We came back with dog food, bowls, a collar and lead and a soft comfy dog bed. We returned to the campo to retrieve our dog to find the rope had come undone, but the dog hadn't run off. She was still there and greeted us with her short stumpy waggy tail.

We took her home. She was a bit nervous in the house and slept by the front door but gradually got used to her bed and two meals a day. When she seemed more settled we had her spayed and chipped.

We have since learned that our new dog was from a litter of superior hunting dogs but on their first hunting expedition this dog was so terrified of the whole experience and loud bangs of the guns that she ran off. No one bothered to look for her as hunters are not going to waste money feeding a dog that is of no use to them. She does still have her hunting instincts and will run off 'hunting', given the chance, with any other dog willing to join her. She will not go alone. One time, during a visit to the vet, she needed an x-ray. The vet called us in to look at the x-ray as it was full of small shot pellets. She had been shot at some point in time, probably when she'd run off. She now has a tracker so that we know where she is if she runs off again though we try not to let this happen.

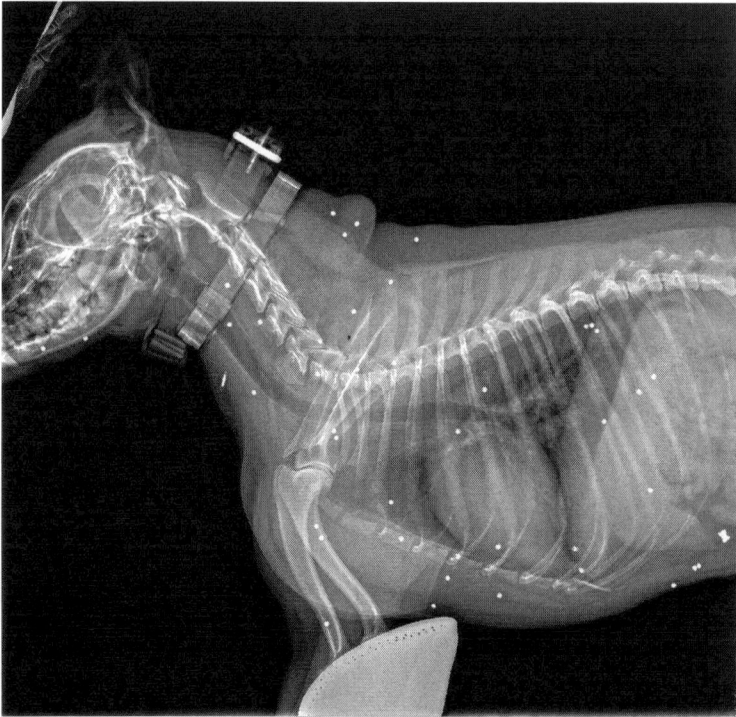

That was 11 years ago. She is the most loving and lovely dog you could ever wish for. Her name is Dotty, and she is a Portuguese Podenco, and we wouldn't change her for the world.

Dotty now has a 'brother', also found wandering the same streets but he is another story.

Cyril's story
By June Davies

CYRIL IS A SMALL, SCRUFFY, mucky dog with a huge personality. He was a campo dog in a neighbouring village with his doggy friend Benny. When the campo owner got too old for the work, he abandoned his campo along with the dogs.

Cyril could be found hanging around the bar at night looking for scraps of food. During the day he and Benny would roam the streets. Every morning when I took our dog Dotty out for her walk I would see them and give them a few dog biscuits. Some of the local people were also feeding them. They would often join me and Dotty on the walk along with our campo neighbour's dog Ricky. I usually ended up with quite an entourage by the time I got home.

Someone from the local dog charity thought that if we could catch these dogs then they could be homed. 'No problem,' I thought. Cyril was used to me so the next day I went out armed with food and a spare lead and brought him home. He very quickly made himself comfortable. A nearby family thought they would adopt Benny if I could get him to them. They lived off grid with plenty of space for a big dog. 'No problem,' I thought. Benny was used to me. So the following day we walked Benny down to his new home. Sorted!

We took Cyril to the vet with the dog charity lady to get him checked over and to have various inoculations and then took him back home until an adoptive family could be found for him. Benny's new family thought they might take on Cyril too as the two dogs were such good friends and it would be a shame to separate them. But Cyril had other ideas. When Benny and his new mum came for Cyril all hell broke loose. Cyril started growling, barking and showing his teeth at poor Benny. We thought it was because we were inside, so we went out onto neutral ground. Still the same. Cyril was not going to go with Benny.

Cyril got on very well with Dotty. They were very fond of each other. Maybe we should just keep Cyril? They would be company for each other and as everyone kept telling us, 'If you have one dog then you might as well have two.' So, guess what? Yes, we adopted Cyril. He could be quite aggressive towards other dogs and men, especially men carrying sticks, so he had to be kept on a lead when out. When meeting these men, I would give them a couple of dog treats to give to Cyril. This helped enormously. Cyril soon got to realise that not all men were bad... some had treats for him. We also had him castrated which calmed him down a bit.

After having Cyril for a while we noticed that he kept flicking his head as though trying to catch flies. At first we thought this was what he was doing but when the weather got cooler and the flies disappeared, he kept on doing it. We discovered on the web that this was a recognised condition. We videoed him doing this and showed it to the vet.

Cyril had a form of epilepsy which could be controlled with medication. He had to have regular blood tests as the medication could affect his organs. Also, getting the correct dosage was a bit problematical. Too little did nothing, too much and he'd be falling over and crashing into the furniture. We now have the dosage sorted and he is fine.

Dotty is a hunting dog and would pester Cyril to go off with her. She can be very persuasive. Cyril is not a hunter. He is more of a couch potato breed. When they do go off they always stay together and come back home together. One day Dotty returned home alone and injured. We rushed her to the vet who said it looked like she'd been in a fight but nothing serious. Some antiseptic spray and an injection and all was well. But where was Cyril? If there was a dog fight then you can bet your boots that Cyril would be involved. By midnight we were really concerned. I slept on the sofa in the living room with the front door opened so that if he returned he could get in. I really thought that this was the end of our Cyril. At 5.30 a.m., in staggered a very injured Cyril covered in blood.

It was very hard to see what was injured as he has so much hair. As soon as they were open we were at the vet's. Some stitches, injections and antibiotics and we were back home. No more hunting for these dogs.

Sometime later we discovered that Dotty was full of shot pellets, as mentioned in the previous story. We asked the vet to X-ray Cyril too as we now thought that the dog fight may not have been a dog fight. Yes, Cyril was also full of shot pellets. They hadn't been in a fight, but both had been shot.

Cyril is not a dog that takes personal hygiene seriously. He is a mess that likes nothing better than to go in the acequias and then roll in the dirt. He has the type of fur that everything sticks to. The name 'Velcro' would have suited him better. We thought an appointment with a dog groomer would be good so off he went for his first visit to the beauty parlour. We thought he might have to be sedated as he wasn't keen on having his hair brushed or matted bits cut out. As it happened he was as good as gold. So we were told!

When he came out we didn't recognise him. He was now half the size and had a pretty blue ribbon in his head to complete his new look. He now has regular haircuts.

We have had Cyril now for 7 years. He is very laid-back and everyone's friend. He is affectionate and very loving and follows me everywhere. We still meet Benny occasionally, but Cyril kicks off whenever he sees him, even if Benny is in his car. I guess they will never be friends again, which is a shame.

Pietje
By Ivon Stelloo

IT WAS A GREY DECEMBER afternoon when I decided to go for a walk along the beach in Almuñécar, not knowing that that walk would change my life forever. After a while I made a 'pit stop' at a chiringuito and when I walked onto the terrace there was also an elderly man with a very small puppy. Not wanting or liking any barking around me, I sat far away from the couple.

The old man left, alone, and the puppy was tied to a pole on the terrace by a waitress. Assuming it was hers, I said to the waitress that I would keep an eye on it. Next thing I knew is she'd put the puppy on my lap and said, 'Do you want to have a dog?' It seemed that the puppy had walked into the chiringuito the day before and until now she had fed it with tapas and had hidden it in the kitchen. I had never had or wanted a dog, so I offered to take the little one to a vet, to see if it had a chip or had been reported lost. Unfortunately she hadn't been, and the vet said they would keep her to see if something or someone would turn up. That night I couldn't sleep and kept thinking about her, and even named her Pietje. Next morning I went by the vet's to see if she was okay and found her caged in the shop window next door. The explanation was that maybe the owner would walk by and spot her. Feeling very sorry for the little one, I offered to take her out for a walk during their closing hours, and they agreed. After 2 afternoons walking with her, one of the employees of the vet didn't agree any longer and we got into an argument, which ended up with me, and Pietje under my arm, on the street.

I thought I was an utter fool taking her, but my heart said otherwise. The next few days I sought hard to find her owners and later on looked into ways to have her adopted. This resulted in me finding an organisation that organises adoptions between Spain and Holland. Within hours a new home was found for Pietje, and she was reserved and planned to fly to Haarlem 3 weeks later. That's when I met Linda and Valle Verde. Because she needed the necessary shots and so on, and Cantalobos dog shelter was overcrowded, Linda asked me to foster her until she left... I reluctantly agreed. There was me, with no experience of dogs and a 3-month old puppy that needed all the training necessary, but my heart screamed yes! Her departure date was getting closer and closer and every day my love for her grew more and more, how could I ever hand her over? During this period Linda helped me out enormously and guided me all the way and I started to feel more confident as a 'dog owner'.

Desperately wanting to know about her new owners, I was allowed to get in touch with them via email. I hoped I would feel connected with these people and at ease with her new destination, but it was the opposite. Their only question about Pietje was about her size and if she would fit into their bike bags. That was the moment, now 8 years ago, I decided we would stay together, and I would never ever let Pietje go.

Sophie the bin puppy
By Marina Bourgaize

OUR STORY BEGAN ON A sad 5 November when we had to say goodbye to Dexter our rescue dog, who had been found abandoned by the side of a motorway in the UK 15 years earlier. We had the delight who was Dexter for 15 wonderful years.

That evening, feeling devastated, I went to my yoga class and happened to mention what a tough day I had had to Rachel, the lady behind me in the class. She could see how sad I was and mentioned that she knew of some puppies that had been rescued that day in Spain. They had luckily been discovered by a passerby who, when using a bin, discovered a bag containing 4 newly born beautiful puppies! It had taken some effort to climb into the bin to get them and we thank them to this day. I really do believe in fate.

The puppies were rushed to the vet in Motril and Laura contacted Valle Verde animal rescue to see if they could help.

They were fostered and bottle-fed in loving homes in Spain. Unfortunately the male puppy didn't survive the trip to the fosterer's home, but the three remaining female puppies did.

Rachel, who does all the home checks for Valle Verde, mentioned to her friend Linda, who was looking after two of them, that we were interested.

There and then we knew one of these girls was destined to become the latest member of our Bourgaize family.

I got in touch with Linda the moment I got home, and she sent me the most adorable photograph of these two little puppies which she thought were almost certainly Podencos. We did not mind the breed of our next puppy; we just knew this was meant to be.

We chose our girl who we found out had been named Sophie. The cute white stripe on her nose was what won us over. We loved her name and kept it. We had regular updates from Linda about Sophie's progress. She had the most beautiful green eyes and her ears started to pop up, typical of Podencos!

We followed her on videos and had regular photographs of her and her sister Maddie. There were three other dogs in Linda's home, much larger than Sophie, and one of them, Freddie, a male, mothered them, even cleaning them when they were tiny, just as their own mother would have done. It makes such a difference to have a rescue from Valle Verde as volunteers choose to bring the puppies up in their own homes, so different to other situations.

A house without a dog is just not right. Four months seemed like a long time to wait but it was well worth it. We filled out all the relevant paperwork to secure her and had a home check which turned out just fine.

It was a tough time to get a rescue from Spain since Covid had put the world on hold. But with help from Valle Verde and Maddie's soon-to-be mum Liz who was so organised, we managed to secure a date to get our girls over, which turned out to be Valentine's Day and the best present I have received in my life.

I started to shop for our girl and researching Podencos it seemed they could grow very tall, so I bought the biggest bed and dog bowl we could find. Little did we know she was a small breed of Podenco but so perfect. We even walled in the garden so she would be secure as we heard they can jump pretty high.

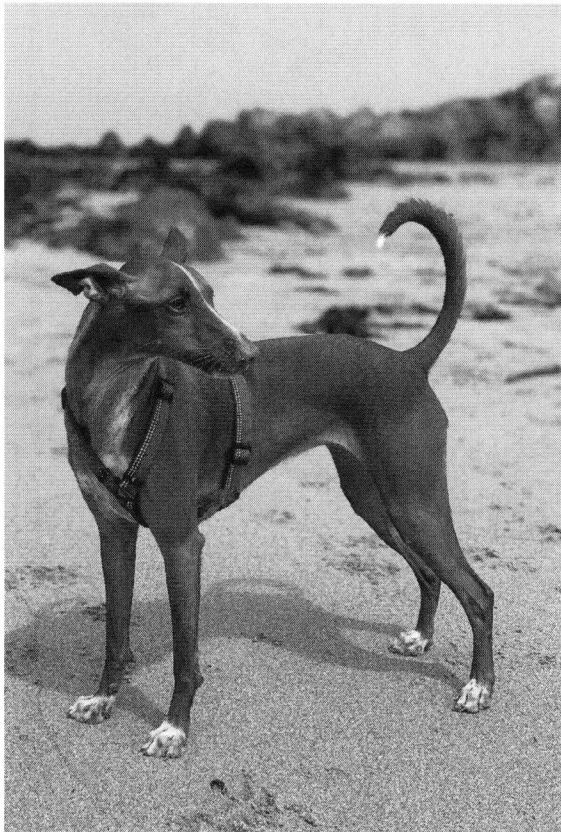

Their journey was a long one, but we could track it, which made it special. Once they arrived in Bournemouth they spent the evening with the wonderful Simon Horwood who had the girls to stay for a night after they were dropped off in the early hours. I hear they did not get much sleep as the girls kept them busy!

They flew over with Channel Jets on their final leg of their journey. When they arrived in Guernsey and were carried off the plane we saw the ears first(she has grown into them now). They were standing up on their hind legs looking so adorable, like two meercats the staff at the airport said.

We brought Sophie home. She was so affectionate and obviously wondered what her life was going to be like. We had a rescue cat we had got from Manchester in the house already, and slowly introduced Sophie to Shadow as Podencos are not typically great with cats, but they became firm friends. Unfortunately we lost our boy only one year later in a road traffic accident.

Sophie became lonely in the house on her own so again I messaged Valle

Verde and they had just taken in a mother and her kitten who were found on the streets in Granada. We received the photograph and knew Daisy, as we called her, was going to be the next member of our family.

She arrived with her mum Misha, who was homed with Sally who also fosters for Valle Verde in Guernsey. Misha looked so happy when she was dropped off first, no more kitten to take care of! They came over with Simon Horwood this time on the boat three days before Christmas... again the best present ever.

We kept them separate for nearly a week as we did not know how Sophie would be with another cat, but now she and Daisy have become best friends although Daisy is definitely the boss!

We are so pleased we have rehomed two beautiful girls from Spain, I had never really heard of Podencos but what a wonderful breed of dog they are. I've been told they can run at speeds of up to 35mph, and Sophie can really run!

Due to Covid we could not take part in puppy training classes, but she learnt recall so quickly, as well as sitting for her treats. We wanted her to have friends to run with, so Sam Barry who runs a local dog walking service, Walkies, took Sophie on her first walk after a few months of her settling in with us. This definitely helped with her training.

Sam researched the breed, so she knew what she was taking on. The first day she went out with Walkies they were worried about her running off, but she jumped out of the van and followed the other dogs and had the most fabulous time. She now goes out with her pack three times a week and has so much fun.

We managed to get her interested in a ball as last spring on a lovely walk on L'Ancresse common in Guernsey she caught three rabbits in a week! If she sees any birds on the beach she will take chase but as soon as she goes over paws deep in the water she gives up.

Definitely not a swimmer.

She still gets the scent on walks as I am sure all Podencos do, but her recall is fantastic, and she loves fetching her ball. So many people stop us and say what a beautiful dog she is.

Treat is definitely her favourite word. We have always taken her out to shops and restaurants. I have two sons so having a girl to go shopping with is wonderful!

She has had one holiday to Herm, a small island off Guernsey. She was not keen on the boat trip but loved the walk on the island, where dogs are free to run since it is car-free.

We are so happy with our girls from Valle Verde and cannot thank them enough for all they do and are just so happy we have changed two lives.

I wish more people would consider taking on a rescue.

Sweet Pea
By Miguel Lore

THIS IS THE STORY OF a little dog whom we called Sweet Pea who had been so neglected and abused that he was on his last legs when he came to us. We were told by the animal rescue people that he had been confined in a crate so small that he couldn't stand up or move around. I think he was a year old, maybe a year and a half. When he arrived at our door he was listless and still, very little movement. We were told that the vet said his organs were beginning to shut down. This tiny little dog had given up and was ready to go. So sad and terrified. I remember him shivering in my arms and on my lap for hours We had wrapped him in a blanket with his beautiful head sticking out and we took turns sitting in a chair with him on our laps. We stroked him and told him we loved him. We sang to him and just held him until the shivering finally abated, then stopped. This was eleven years ago now, but I remember him just looking at our faces. Gradually he started to accept water and finally, after a few days he started licking food off our fingers. The miracle was that after all his abuse and neglect, he decided to trust us and never looked back! Trust, after all he had been through. He became the happiest, most joyful and loving dog! He started playing catch in our hallway, at top speed! He was our constant companion and travelled with us outside in a shoulder bag with his head out watching the world go by!

Sweet Pea

Never underestimate the power of patience, love and trust! Sweet Pea made friends with everyone and every other dog he met! He eventually found his new home in Holland with a little boy, an older dog and a horse on a small farm where he is known as Snuffy! Our miracle Sweet Pea!

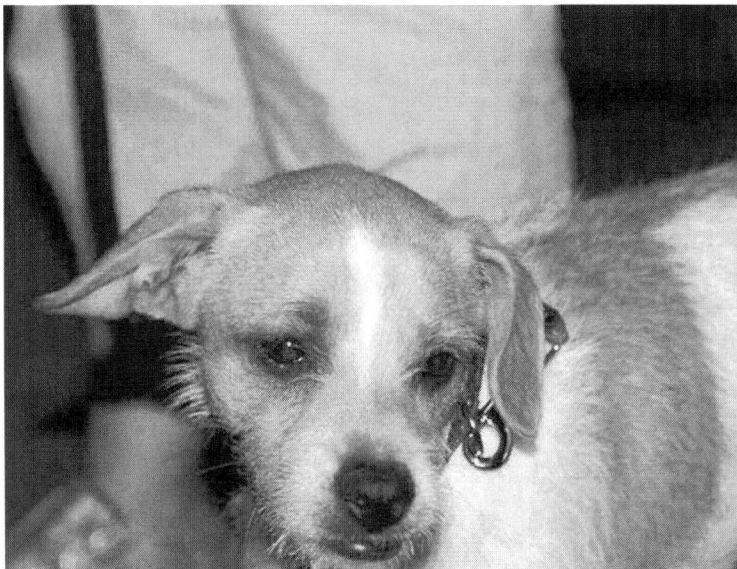

Squeaky
By Debs Shanley

AS WITH MANY RESCUE ANIMALS in Spain, she had a miserable start to life.

In September 2022 I was walking our rescue dog Brutus who was animatedly sniffing a mound on the side of the road. On inspection it turned out to be a flattened black kitten. 'Poor little soul,' I thought, and made a mental note to pick it up on the way home and dispose of it.

An hour later, with pet undertaker duties completed, I was walking past our vecino's property. Their little girl was sat on the pavement, looking at her parents' car. There was an animated squeak coming from the wheel arch. '¿Un gatito?' I enquired. 'Siiiiiiiiii,' she said, rolling her eyes at the crazy British lady.

Her mum and I spent a fruitless half hour trying to extract said kitten from the wheel arch. Hands were scratched and food ignored. In the end my neighbour decided to reverse the car, very slowly, and out she shot – straight into dense thicket, behind metal railings.

I spent the next 36 hours enticing her with frankfurters – which she would grab and retreat back into the vegetation to eat – and leaving water.

She was obviously a very small kitten and mindful that time was of the essence I grabbed her the next time I saw her outside the thicket. She was most indignant and tried to get away. 'Be still, you ungrateful beast,' I chided. 'Your life has just gotten immeasurably better.'

And so, a little jet black bundle with a white tummy flash, came into our lives. I believe she was about 4 weeks old at that point as she was unable to retract her claws.

A feisty kitten from the start, she terrorised her dog-brother Brutus, and annoyed her other rescue cat-brother, Sooty. Sooty was slow to accept her and there was much hissing and posturing.

Brutus was anxious about the little furry loon careering about the house too, but he was also very protective of her, and would put himself between the kitten and Sooty when Sooty got too bossy with her.

She was given several names – Sweep (well, we had a Sooty), then Queenie (after her Maj died), but we eventually settled on Squeaky, because that's what she did. Almost constantly.

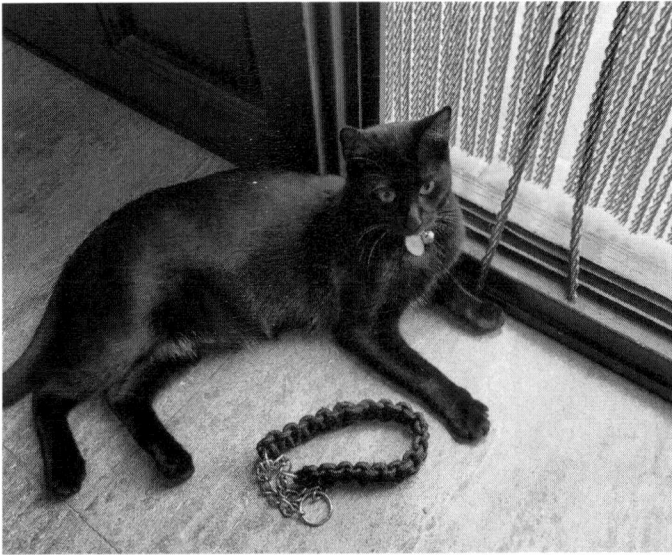

We also discovered she has an alter-ego: KleptoKat. She has morphed into an avid collector of the things our neighbours 'carelessly' leave on their balconies.

To date her hoard comprises: a one spot domino, a small dog metal choke chain, two dog tug toys, a small green diplodocus, several Kinder egg toys, a brand new shoelace, a tennis ball, two odd trainer socks, two odd gloves, a necklace (not precious metal), a child's terry towelling beach poncho (at least 3 times as big as Squeaky), a metal, clothes' hanger, a pair of ladies knickers, 4 random football cards, a cloth from a spectacle case, 2 darts complete with their flights, and a dart flight, minus its dart.

Initially we asked around our neighbours and managed to return some items, but since Knickergate, my husband, being of a sensitive disposition, is too embarrassed to ask.

Consequently we now have her treasures in a 'found' box and have informed the President of the urbanisation in which we live of Squeaky's predilection in the hope that should a neighbour mention random things are disappearing from their balcony, he can send them to see us.

And no, she hasn't yet brought home a 50€ note!

My rescues
By Linda Rowe

I CAME TO SPAIN IN 2002 with my two cats, tortoise and lizards. I set the lizards free on my top balcony against a mountainside as they basically had returned to their natural habitat. Purdy the tortoise died after a few years; I thought through not having the right food. I was extremely upset but found out years later that not all types of tortoise live to great ages and his lifespan was normal for his type. He was a feisty little boy and loved chasing my friend's dog, who was terrified of him.

For many years, I just had cats. Gizzy was found in a margarine tub in the rubbish and had kittens before I managed to get her neutered. Get them done earlier in Spain as so many strays around makes it risky otherwise!

Then I decided to get my first ever dog. I can remember as a child begging my parents to let me have a dog or a horse but as my father had a bad experience with a dog he was very afraid of them.

Zowie was adopted from Seacrest in Nerja.

'I think I'm going to get a dog,' I said to my mother when she was on one of her visits to me.

'Come on then,' she said, 'let's go and find one.'

I was imagining a medium-sized black dog, but my mum saw this sweet-looking dog with different coloured eyes cowering in the background and that was it. 'You have to have that poor little thing that looks so scared,' she said and so I adopted Bertha. We changed her name to Zowie Bowie Rowe because of her eyes.

For the first three days she hid under the bushes in the corner of my garden and didn't make any sound. Then suddenly something passed by and out came the deepest bark! She gradually came out of her shell and became the most affectionate loving girl possible and my constant companion. She even got on with my four cats.

Next came Ossi whose owner was in trouble with the law. I said I would take him for the week if he got on with my cats. He already knew Zowie and he did. The week turned into 18 months so when his owner was free to take him again I said no, he's mine now and I think Jochen was quite relieved really.

Unfortunately Zowie became ill with cancer and died. Ossi was obviously grieving and missing his best friend, so I started to look for another rescue dog to keep him company.

Once again Seacrest came to my aid with another of their rescues.

Prince, as I named him in honour of the artist Prince who had died that week, had been tossed over a wall and landed in the yard of some people having a barbecue and so was taken to Seacrest for them to find him a good home.

So Prince became part of my family of cats and dogs and soon became firm friends with Ossi who loved his new friend. He was quite wary of the cats.

Ossi and Prince used to set off each evening to herd my chickens back to their coop for the night. It was very amusing to watch.

Then came an appeal on Facebook from Julia in Lanjaron who had found six newborn puppies next to a rubbish bin. She appealed for anyone who was willing to take some of them to bottle-feed.

Along I went up to Lanjaron and chose the runt of the litter, and a little fatty white one. This was when I was contacted by Linda Rane from Valle Verde who kindly offered to help. I would have found it much harder without her.

So these two little monkeys, after several name changes as their characters developed, became Freddie Mercury, small but feisty, and Georgie Michael a little white ball, quick to finish his bottle of milk and still always first at the food.

Prince absolutely loved them; you would have thought he was their dad the way he protected them both so of course I kept them both — how could I not?

This was the start of my involvement with Valle Verde animal rescue, and I have fostered many more puppies since Freddie and Georgie.

I did adopt another abandoned at birth baby, Roxy. Beautiful Roxy was with me until she was about 14 months. She wanted to be top dog and started attacking the little ones and even had a go at Ossi, so I had to make the heartbreaking decision to rehome her as an only dog. She's happy now in Germany with a lovely owner and a wonderful life.

Sadly my beautiful Ossi succumbed to old age and incontinence, losing mobility in his back legs, so I had to make another distressing decision to let him go. I had some wonderful years with him and fifteen isn't a bad age for a largish dog.

The vet came and he went peacefully on his favourite sofa on the terrace and I'm sure he's joined Zowie and the cats, Tonto, Louie, Nico, Gizzy and her twins Bella and Beau in animal heaven.

Prince is still just a big soft puppy at heart, and I was told he will never change. He's so good natured and inquisitive and playful. He gets super excited and exuberant at certain words but at 45 kilos he is quite a handful when bouncing around like a puppy.

Freddie is a true character, feisty, fast and can be ferocious. He absolutely loves newborn puppies and other than feeding does everything for them.

Georgie takes over when puppies start running around and teaches them to play, including with his many toys. Georgie loves cuddly toys and doesn't usually want to share them except for with pups.

Fostering, whether of a dog, puppy, cat or kitten is an essential part in animal rescue.

Freddie and Prince

Ossi and Georgie

Kai's epiphany
By Kathy Sparrow

WE KNOW VERY LITTLE ABOUT Kai's previous life apart from the fact that he was born in Germany and ended up living with a young homeless couple on the streets of Spain. When the couple eventually found work and were unable to take him with them, they handed him over to the Asociación de Animales in Berja, to rehome.

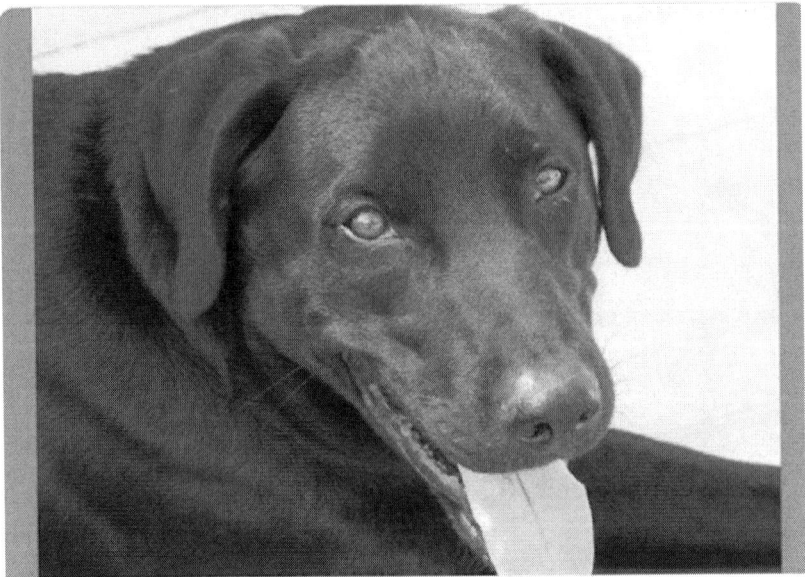

Asociacion de Animales de Berja. Reg No. 5272
12 June 2015 · ⊙

KAISER HAS BEEN RESERVED FOR A FUREVER HOME. Gill

I had just spent a month with my sister, who lives in Spain, talking about stray dogs amongst other things when she sent me the above picture of Kaiser, as she felt he looked so like Cully, our six-year-old Labrador. We were actually in our caravan on the way home, but I contacted the charity and asked about him. We were told he was a two-year-old Labrador and got on well with other dogs and cats. That's all we needed to know, and we went ahead and applied to adopt him. Kaiser arrived on Sunday 2 August 2015, having travelled by van for three days, organised by the charity. He got on with Cully straight away and Millie (the cat) put him in his place immediately by giving him a slap when he got too close. He was very nervous of David (my husband) to begin with, but he soon settled into his new home and slept on the floor in our bedroom on his first night.

He was a lovely dog with us, but we soon found out, on our first walk, that he was dominant and aggressive with other dogs. Owners would shout at me, and I would come home in tears. It was fairly early on that we decided the name Kaiser wasn't suited to an aggressive dog and, from then on, we shortened it to Kai.

It took about 18 months of training to teach Kai that he no longer needed to be aggressive with other dogs and that he had a permanent, loving home. The training was gradual and involved giving him a treat every time he passed a dog and there was no aggression.

When he failed to pass the dog quietly (which was more often than not), I would make him lie down, read him the riot act and make him walk behind me for five minutes.

Eventually, once when he attacked the same docile dog on our walk, there and back, I 'lost it'. I shouted at him, pretended to hit him, made him lie down, told him to 'stay' and began to walk off. I turned and saw the look of fear in his eyes – it was the thought of losing his loving home and, from then until now, he has become the perfect dog. David and I call it his 'epiphany'. To this day I find it amazing the change in him after that one walk. However, he's never forgotten the treat training and still expects to get a treat after he's passed a dog.

Kai with his 'look alike' sister, Cully.

Ziggy (Part 1)
By Paul Rane

HELLO, MY NAME IS ZIGGY, and I know stuff!

I didn't always know stuff, but I do now!

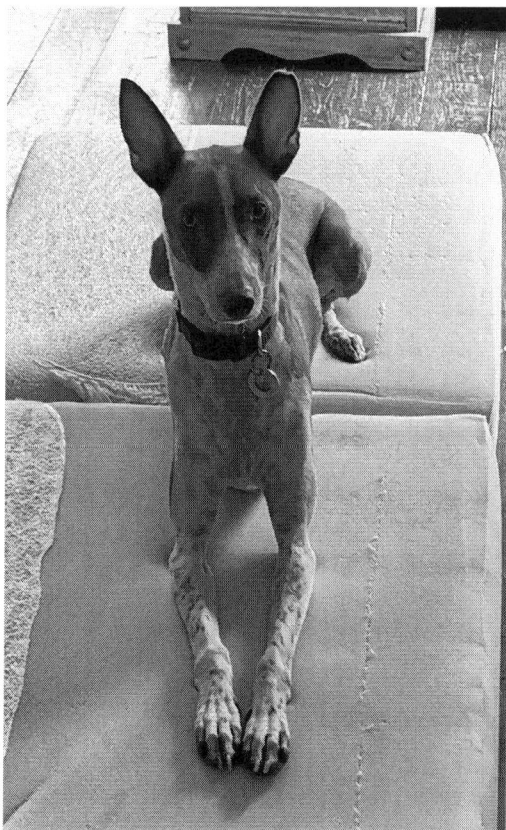

I know that the 2-leggers are called humans and that I am called a dog. We dogs come in different shapes and sizes.

My forever human dad, says I'm a funny looking thing and when he says so my forever mum tells him off and fusses me and says words I don't understand, like handsome, and gorgeous boy.

I came to my forever home from Spain, but I don't think it's because my forever dad felt sorry for me. He says he likes my name and talks a lot about some human called David Bowie.

I'll tell you how it all started from my early memories when I didn't know stuff.

My first memory is of my 4-legger food mother being kicked by a very angry two-legger. He made a lot of noise from his face; I don't know why the two-legger was angry but my brothers and sisters and I were very scared and trembled while hiding behind our food mother. Eventually he went away, and we all ran around to feed from mother's teats for comfort and of course milk. I was the smallest of all of us. I got pushed and shoved out of the way and only managed to suckle when one of my brothers and sisters had had enough. My tummy always made rumbling sounds in those days.

Our food mother found a new hiding hole for us and began to take us there one at a time. Again I was the last to be taken to the new hole. Maybe this time it was a blessing being so small as two 2-leggers saw me being carried. They followed us and saw all of us. When they saw us water came out of their eyes.

The 2-leggers made a lot of noises in soft voices. I didn't understand them, except by the tone of their voices, nothing like the shouty 2-legger earlier. They seemed nice, so we all wagged our handles.

There were more sounds that I can only describe as, "aw" and "so tiny".

I remember being picked up by the shorter of the 2-leggers. I never saw my brothers and sisters after that, I think the other 2-legger looked after them, but I was cleaned, fed and rubbed. I was taken to a place where there were a couple of bigger 4-leggers, but they didn't look like me. The only likeness was their handles, which they wagged frantically when they saw the short 2-legger and me.

I think this is where I realised that I am a dog and 2-leggers are humans. I think the humans that make softer loving sounds are girl humans and the gruff sounds come from boy humans. These human sounds were, "another little dog to join you big dogs." The dogs made lots of noise from their mouths, I now know that it's what humans call barking. I tried this but it didn't sound the same. The human laughed at me. Her mouth sounds were, "You sound like a baby Baskerville hound with that high-pitched noise." I didn't understand her, but she patted and fussed me so that was okay.

I decided it would be best to do what the other dogs were doing. The human put shiny round things on the floor, they had some stuff in them that made my mouth fill with water, and it leaked a bit.

Her mouth made sounds, "Wait," and the dogs sat down. I did the same. Her mouth made more sounds after we had been sitting a bit, "Okay," she said. The big dogs attacked the shiny things. I followed. I had never tasted anything like the stuff in the shiny things, it tasted so good, I ate very slowly as I didn't want it to end; but it did end because the other dogs finished theirs, pushed me away and ate mine. I tried to get some more but one of them bit my ear. I yelped and ran. At this time, you see, my ears stood upright and pointy and were bigger than my head, so it was easy to bite them.

In spite of having a chunk bitten out of one of my very large ears, we all became friends, and I learnt a lot from them. When it was time to do our business, they sat by the door and barked, I did the same. (Still a bit of a howl from me.) Anyway the human came and opened the door for us. The big dogs ran out and just lifted their legs against a tree, I wasn't used to that, but tried anyway. I couldn't seem to stand on 3 legs, so I just squatted. After we had done our business we raced around the garden chasing each other. I liked that; I now know humans call this "a mad half hour". I still do the mad half hour these days, but more about that later.

When it became dark we all went back inside, we sat with the human and put our heads on her lap. She always patted and fussed us. All this was very different for me, but it was nice, and it was warm, and my belly didn't rumble any more.

So you see, thanks to this human and her dogs, I've learnt to sit, play, and wee by squatting.

A Street dog called Lucy
By Fran Scott

SOMETIMES IN LIFE YOUR PATH crosses with a person with whom you become a friend, a partner or perhaps just a passing acquaintance. That meeting opens up new horizons, new paths, and new friends. Then, just sometimes, it's a four-legged that crosses your path and brings a similar result.

We found out about Lucy's history from a vet in Almunecar who had treated her prior to her rescue. She had lived on the streets with a drunken lady, and we think that's where she was taught her little dance which might have brought forth cash. The last the vet had heard about her was that she had been taken away after biting a policeman! (She is a very small dog so I can't imagine it would have been too serious.) However, the vet had assumed the worst, so was very pleased to find out differently when we turned up with her. Valle Verde had found four dogs held at a Spanish veterinary practice – not I would add in particularly wonderful conditions. There were photos of said four dogs on the Valle Verde site all of whom needed a home or foster care. We were 'between dogs' and the little black and white one appealed to me. "We'll have the little black and white one!"

We met Linda's husband and picked up a terrified, shaking little girl. I fell in love with her immediately and I named her Lucy. She had a bad skin condition and not much fur left around her neck where it looked red and sore. It wasn't leishmaniasis thankfully, so we set about trying different natural remedies to cure her problem. When we had looked after Lucy for a few weeks Linda said they wanted to send her to Holland to the rescue centre there, where she stood a chance of being adopted. I am so thankful that I said no because her skin wasn't one hundred percent cured and that we would keep her until an adoption could be organised.

After about ten months in our care, we were told that an English gentleman was interested in Lucy. We arranged to meet up and he arrived with a French lady friend. It all seemed to go well, so since they lived in the Alpujarras we offered to do the home check. It took forever to reach their home in Pitres because we got stuck behind a bus, but eventually we arrived. Lucy made herself at home straight away. I had told her this would be her new home and she seemed happy with that. I should introduce her new family – Bernard – a famous cellist and Thérèse, a French therapist. Little did I know then that we would become friends. Bernard drove us to a plot of land where he and Thérèse were planting trees and making a lovely garden.

The area is quite beautiful- in the mountains with very old houses and very old pathways and it has quite a special atmosphere. Bernard had a shelter on the land where he was able to sit and write. So it was just the perfect place for Lucy to play.

When we returned from our visit to the land we gathered Lucy's belongings from our car, only to see her trotting into the house without a backward glance! I admit to crying the whole way back down to Pampaniera. What a huge wrench it was to let her go. I had told Bernard that if they ever wanted to go on holiday then we would have Lucy to stay. I had previously put her in kennels for two nights and no way could I let her go through that again.

I hadn't realised then that far from losing Lucy, we were gaining a couple of special friends and that we would still be a part of Lucy's life – she often came for holidays or on visits. It was at a small fundraising event at a local bar when Bernard and Thérèse had come to support me, that Bernard told me that he and Thérèse were getting married. By then they had moved to Cañar and that is where the wedding took place. Since both of them are big in the music scene of the Alpujarras we were treated to a very special event – a classical concert in Cañar church. We were quite overwhelmed. Among the performers

Bernard played his cello and Thérèse sang 'Non, je regrette ríen'. How could that not be special. Bernard, Thérèse, and Lucy have become part of the Alpujarran life and known to many of the local people. Apparently on one occasion someone asked Bernard what breed of dog she was. "She's a Lucy," he replied. Sometimes she goes to the beach where Thérèse puts her in the sea and sometimes she goes to the mountains for walks among the pine trees.

We think Lucy is about 8 years old now, but she still looks as young as when we first met her. She has been on holiday with us for the past few weeks and although we now live in a flat in town, we have taken her for a couple of walks back to the Lecrin Valley where she had lived with us in the beginning. She was overjoyed to return to campo land.

Sadly, Thérèse passed away at the end of 2022. She was a special 'mummy' to Lucy and a special friend to me. So this week Lucy will be back in the Alpujarras living with Bernard in a house with land where she can play and relax in the sun; she particularly loves sunbathing. We will still be part of her life I'm sure, for she is the sweetest little dog.

A postscript to Lucy's story… Sometimes life throws a curved ball, and since I wrote Lucy's story her life has totally changed. It became quite difficult for Bernard to look after her, and so once again she ended up living with us. Now I'd always thought that if anything happened, then she would become my dog on a permanent basis, and in fact that would have been my dream. Sadly, however, it turned out that this was not possible for several reasons. So back in the early summer we took Lucy to live with a new mummy where she has become part of a new family with other animals. During the changeover and continuing on from it, Lucy has been undergoing treatment for leishmaniasis. She has been the same brave little dog she has always been, and we are all hoping for a successful outcome.

Carla's story
By Adelene Chinnick

THAT HUMAN SMELLED LIKE A good human. I liked the smell of him. He was on two wheels going up the hill, I ran after him, would he stop for me? No. I returned to my leaf nest by the side of the road. Dang! I was so hungry!

It had been many, many nights now that I'd been without my pack. They weren't much of a gang and I was always last for getting to the meagre food thrown at us, but we were a group at least. Here, well, I was on my own. Good things, bad things. Good, in that I wasn't bullied by the alpha males anymore or by the human that came and hit us sometimes. Bad, in that I was hungry, lost and frightened. Oh well. At least it was springtime, and I wasn't too cold. I'd made a cosy patch in the dried grass and leaves where I could nestle down and sleep. But I could really do with some food, so perhaps a kind human would take pity on me and give me something, anything.

When a car drove past I chased after it, hoping that the humans would notice me, desperate, in the road. It was a busy day and the road to Pampaneira was full of cars going fast. It was dangerous chasing them, but I had no option if I wanted them to stop. Then I smelled that same good human again. He was coming back down the hill, faster on his wheels. I ran after him again, dodging traffic, the shrieking car horns hurt my ears, but he didn't even slow down despite seeing me. Soon his bright yellow shape disappeared and then his scent was lost. I could have howled with disappointment.

After a while I decided to rest up. I dreamed of the pack, how we'd gone out hunting and how I got left behind. In my dream I was running, running, trying to keep up. A bit like real life, me always falling short, not even being a full blood Podenco. If I'd been a real Podenco, bigger and more fearless, perhaps there would have been more care for me. Or maybe not.

The sun was moving down the sky when I began waking up to a good smell. A foody-human aroma – perhaps I was still dreaming? When I opened my eyes I saw a REAL pile of biscuits a little way from my nest. Woohoo, I gobbled them down but there weren't enough. There was another pile, but they were further away. I needed that food, so I left the safety of my nest to get at them. I ate those and looked around for more. There was more food, but it was right next to a human, the good human who now had a car close by. Would he trick me? Trusting dog commandment number 3 "Scents don't lie" his kind scent tempted me to get closer, slowly.

"Don't hit me, don't hit me…" I made myself as small and humble as I could, creeping on my belly, keeping my eyes on him and the biscuits. He stayed very still, letting me do the moving forward. I felt I could trust this one not to hurt me because he gave off a calm stink, his regular breathing made me feel relaxed and gradually not so afraid.

Bit by bit I was close enough to reach his hand. I touched him first, with my outstretched paw. He waited and then stroked my foot very gently, then my leg, then my head. His touch was as good as his smell – respectful and kind. I was at ease accepting more food from this one. I wasn't even concerned when he tried to put something around my neck, but it was too small, so he picked up my whole body and put me in the car. I could have bitten him or run away, but you know what? I was so tired of running, so tired of being hungry that I chose to go with what I knew: here was a good one and I should trust my luck.

***

"What am I looking at exactly?"

"Look in the car, look closely!"

"I can see a pair of white eyes swivelling around… oh no, don't tell me. It's a dog, what've you gone and done?"

"I spotted her when I was on my bike going up to Pampaneira. She was in a dangerous situation, chasing cars, but there was nothing I could do on my bike, so I came back for the car to get her. I was going to talk to you about it, but I saw you were on the phone, so I had to make a decision. We were only discussing yesterday what to do about getting another dog and so it's a bit freaky that she showed up today. I just really like the look of her and want to keep her."

"She does seem very sweet. But you know she may have a chip, so it might be that she's got an owner."

"I know. But we'll take her to the vet tomorrow to get her properly checked out."

***

I spent my first night in this strange place not knowing what to do with myself.

It was all so new. I had never been in a human house before and hesitated before going in. I was comforted a little to smell that another dog lived here, a gentle dog albeit old and sick. He was not too big, and even better he was black with a white bib, just like me. At first he wasn't bothered by my presence, a gruff, "Who the hell are you? Just keep off my blanket," and then he wandered off to said blanket in the corner. He seemed OK if a bit grumpy. I found out that this dog was called Blackie and soon he mellowed to me being part of the team.

"Listen, kiddo, this is a good pack to be part of. They took me in as a pup from an old neighbour man, otherwise I would've got the chop, know what I mean? Alpha male human is a softie, always up for fun and games, cuddles and sometimes ham. You've landed on your paws here."

"But what do I do? How should I be? There are no goats, no other gang mates. I'm not used to this type of corral. Are beatings part of the life here? I don't want that, but I can't be abandoned again, I just can't."

"Relaaax, there's no hitting here, but there are a few small rules – easy enough to pick up. I'm old now and my time's nearly up, I can feel it, even though the humans don't want to believe it. So you'll be on your own soon. The humans want you to love them. They need you to make them play, humans don't play or run around nearly enough as they should and it's up to you to put that in their life. That's your pack role. So do it well for them."

The next day I was put in the car again. Was I going to be left on a road somewhere? I tried to squash myself into the floor of the car when we stopped, but it didn't help because they pulled me out. Both good human and his female came on this journey to see this vet human. She kept touching me all over, looking at my teeth (she was complimentary at how clean they were and said I was young – true!) pulling out nasty ticks (a lot), jabbing me with 'vacunas' and saying I was healthy and not pregnant – (also true!). There was no trace of my previous life, so vet human gave me a 'chip' somewhere and it was some sort of magic because now I had a real home. Just like that.

As the days went on, I tried my best to do what I thought would make this pack accept me. Sometimes I got it wrong, and Blackie would have to put me straight. "No pee in this corral, kiddo. It's a big no no, you have to learn to wait until you're outside. But let the humans know you want to go, and they'll take you. You can go on the roof if you're really bustin', I've never understood why they don't like our pee perfuming their mats, but it's just how it is, they don't appreciate it so don't, OK?"

One day I saw good human get out a small stick, the same small stick I lived in fear of in my other life, the whippy stick that went 'thwack, thwack' stinging my back and face. How could I have got him so wrong, surely he couldn't be like the mean human the pack used to know? Fear got the better of me and I curled up small, crying and shaking. Good human used the stick to swat a fly! Then he saw how frightened I was, and he put the stick away and cuddled me. It took me a while to be brave enough to ignore that stick, but over time I've realised it's not going to be used on me, I can trust this human and that's a good feeling.

Although Blackie was very old, he seemed to enjoy my company when we went for walks, making an effort to run and play with me. He said I made him feel like a pup again. With all the good food I was given I now had so much energy I could hardly contain my springy steps and bounciness.

Sometimes he couldn't keep up, his legs were stiff, and his breathing sounded funny. But we both enjoyed sharing 'sniffs' around the village, that was something we could do slowly together. A short time after I arrived in this new place Blackie left. His empty collar was on the kitchen wall and the humans had a sad smell. He'd made a space for me in this pack though, so I took over his role and his sleeping blanket. I had his job to continue: to make my humans laugh, play, run around and sometimes just to sit quietly with them and give them the same love they give me.

My favourite place though is on the roof. There I can watch what's going on from my vantage point, being a sight hound it's in my character. I can smell a neighbour man's goats in the campo, their tinkling bells is a comfort to me, reminding me of my puppyhood. And on a warm night I sometimes like to sleep up there, looking at the moon, listening to the night creatures and other dogs calling from far away, stirring my blood. I'm reminded of my old pack and the different life I had back then.

I didn't have a name in that life, but I'm called Carla now and all in all it's worked out pretty well.

Bink, Charlie and Inge
By Inge Lugthart

INGE LUGTHART HAS FOUR CATS. Two are still very young, but she has had the other two for a number of years. Before the two little ones came, she had cat Charlie. Charlie and Bink came with a past. That past is not completely known, but it is clear that it was not fun. She tells how it went when both cats came to her home.

Seven years ago I decided to adopt a new family member, cat Bink. Unfortunately, everything turned out differently than what I had hoped. Bink had to leave on Wednesday because his owner became demented and blind and could no longer care for him. I only got back from Turkey on Friday, so Bink stayed with other people in a flat for two nights. He was supposed to be brought to me on Friday, but instead the phone rang. I was informed that Bink got through an open window at night (I may not equate it, but grrrr anyway), and jumped down from six floors. His head landed on the return floor of the third floor gallery. Bink was taken to a vet in Woudenberg by animal ambulance, more dead than alive. No one wanted to pay the costs for medical care and Bink was taken to the shelter. They would then pay the costs, or he would get an injection if it all became too expensive.

When I heard this, I immediately called the vet and told him that he was absolutely not allowed to go to the shelter. I told them that they had everything they needed for him and that I would pay the costs. The vet completely agreed with me that it was absolutely unnecessary to put Bink to sleep. They patched up Bink as much as possible and I was able to pick him up from the vet on Saturday. I took him home, but he was still very sick. I wanted to cry when I saw his head covered in blood on the couch. It was all so unnecessary. He had a severe concussion, a broken nose and little strength left in his body. I mainly gave him a lot of rest; he really needed it. Above all, he was so terribly tired. Obviously I showered him with all the love he needed and that I had within me.

After two nights he seemed to be a bit more alert in the morning than during the two previous days. He even protested when he was given his medication and he also protested when I picked him up to take him downstairs. I took that as a good sign. It turns out that the strength had returned to his body a bit. He ate like a construction worker that night. That was good news. There was a little more life in it.

This story is now seven years old. Everything turned out fine with Bink. Bink is a real cuddler and likes to be outside to enjoy the sun. He is now almost eight years old and still lives with me with the cat Joep and two little cat brothers Guus and Bram. Everything turned out fine with his injuries. He got nothing out of it.

When Bink came to live with me, I already had a cat named Charlie. Charlie experienced too many bad things in the first year of his life and was severely traumatized when he came to live with me. I wrote him a letter back then in which I promised him that he had a safe place with me.

My dear Charlie (look at his moustache and you'll understand why I named him that).

Four years ago you came to live with me as a severely traumatized and abused cat. I don't know exactly what happened to you. I only know a little bit, but the little bit I know is bad enough. You no longer trusted the world and certainly not people.

As a great animal lover, I took you in without a doubt. I thought very optimistically, I'll fix that in no time. Nothing could be further from the truth. For three months I tried to become your friend and win your trust, but it didn't work. I couldn't get near you without you completely panicking.

For weeks I lay on a mattress in the living room, because my bed was already occupied by the other cats, and you also found them scary. I was lying on a mattress in the living room, because sleeping people are not threatening, I thought.

But that didn't work either. Treats, toys or leave you alone? I tried everything, but you still found it very scary. I felt so sorry for you, but I realized I had to leave it to you. You would come to me when you were ready, but that didn't happen either. You were already two and had to be castrated before you could go outside. But yes, you were scared and there was no way I could approach you.

Veterinarian Evert from Veterinary Clinic De Arker advised me to put pills in your food that would put you to sleep, so that I could then take you to the clinic to have you neutered. The food went well, but you didn't go to sleep.

You were swinging around the house like a drunk and strangely enough, at that moment a switch went off in you. You suddenly thought I was sweet and started rubbing your head against me! Geez, how bad is it to put a cat in a cage, when you finally have earned his trust and then have him neutered?

In any case, I couldn't bring myself to do it. So no vet and no castration. But to this day I have your trust. It's been four years now and we're still great friends. Castration took place a few weeks later. No hassle, no pills, just go to the vet in peace and confidence.

You're still a loner and afraid of the world, but we are inseparable buddies now. When I get home, you'll come running. I don't even have to pick you up because you jump into my arms. So sweet, so vulnerable and so beautiful! Tonight you will lie wonderfully close to me on the couch. Grunting loudly and shaking heads. When I get up, you're in my way. My dear Charlie, you are safe here, here you will never want for anything and always receive all the love. No one will ever hurt you again, but you know that. If that isn't friendship and love!

CHARLIE

ONE DAY IN 2019, CHARLIE SUDDENLY acted very strangely with his head. He turned his head all the way to his hips and if he didn't he walked with his chin on his chest. Of course I didn't trust that and took him to the vet to get him better. Unfortunately, the vet found that his kidneys were no longer functioning. One kidney had already failed completely, and the other kidney was only functioning at about 20%. There was nothing more that could be done, and I had to put Charlie to sleep. How this bothered me for a long time afterwards, he was only 10 years old. The great thing is that Charlie was able to enjoy all the love in the world for another 8.5 years after we met, and we adored each other for 8.5 years. He didn't fear me anymore, in fact there were only hugs. Even though things don't always turn out as you hope, a loving and stable life means so much to animal.

Jeroen's story
By Jeroen Hooglan

AND THEN IT WAS JANUARY 14, 2012

This was the day that Mona and I (your Ed) took a short trip to Spain to take a look behind the scenes of our Spanish colleagues from Paws for Thought. After their visit to Holland to see how our foundation "HzH" works it was now time "to return the favour". The difference being that here it was "freezing" and there we were to be blessed with three warm days. After a pleasant evening full of chatting with our "babysitter" and a forgotten night's sleep, the car was loaded at around 3am ready for departure via P3 smart-parking. A rendezvous was planned here with Larry and his adopter for a special reason.

Larry was a placement from a few months ago, with the farewell between his caretaker in Spain and Larry being quite intense at the time. During two reunions in the Netherlands the love between the two was ever present and a discussion was had that if something was to ever happen that would require Larry to be relocated, Larry would have to come back to Spain. Unfortunately the unpredictable happened and due to circumstances Larry had to be rehomed. Ordinarily we do NOT fly dogs back to Spain, but this was an exceptional case. It was up to Mona and me to arrange for Larry to go back to Spain. After goodbyes between Larry and his adoptee, Mona and I checked in and headed towards the Transavia check-in.

Here we were rightly told that the weight of our bag had exceeded the allowed limits by as much as one whole kilo! But too much is too much, and after paying overweight (of course at another counter) we were allowed to continue to the next stop which was "unusual luggage and pets". Since the relevant customs official was not yet present at Schiphol International Airport we had a half an hour wait. Luckily we were prepared and had plenty of time. After Larry's check-in we left for customs. Here it turned out that me, your editor once again did not have the correct appearance and was once again called back by control. After first having had a body check, because the scan continued to beep, even after passing twice, there was also something wrong with my hand luggage. An object seen by the scanner was labelled as dangerous and had to be removed from the bag for further investigation. It turned out to be the small change pouch (purse) I had with me because my wallet broke the previous day, the coins had fallen out and were all over the place. Anyway, after overcoming these obstacles it was time for a quick coffee and a sandwich.

After this it was time to make our way to the plane and boarding was done quickly. After an uneventful flight, baggage collection and a quick reunion with Larry (Larry was reunited with us within fifteen minutes of arrival, Viva España), we hurried outside, towards the Spanish sun. A little later Jo called to say that she was there and that she would come to the place where we were.

I must tell you it was a wonderful sight to see how happy Larry was to see Jo and jump from the ground into her arms with all his agility. A wonderful reunion of a couple in love, who would be inseparable from now on. After this we walked towards the car and we met Richard, Jo's other half, and we drove towards Nerja where I enjoyed a good old English breakfast, for Mona a sandwich and a large cup of coffee were enough. After a lot of fun and eating this breakfast, we drove to Seacrest kennels. We regularly do business with these kennels because they also take care of the foundations we work with in Spain. They also take care of the storage of all travel crates when Grayvis transports them to Spain for us.

We also picked up Trixie from Seacrest. Trixie would fly with us on January 16 on our return trip to the Netherlands and stay with Linda until then. After our visit to Seacrest, we drove to "the roundabout" in Nerja to drop off the dog Sarah. Sarah had Jo and Richard with her all the time and went into "foster" with the lady they had agreed to meet. After dropping off Sarah we drove to Salobreña and took a look at Jo's house.

A short-term stay there was somewhat extended because the key that had to go to Linda from the storage was already on its way by Richard and he did not realize that we were also going to Linda's. After Richard's return we also got in and drove towards Almuñécar where we took a look at the house and kennels of Linda and Pete. After meeting the dogs and chatting together whilst enjoying a coffee, we were taken to Torremolinos by Pete, and we looked up our hotel for that night.

We were shocked when we saw the hotel's signs hanging large against the facade on the main square, with large, lowered shutters underneath. Well, what do you think, internet booking, nice and cheap, what bad luck, pennies gone. But yes, we can't be caught for one hole (a Dutch saying) and after some research the entrance of the hotel turned out to be around the corner and voila this hotel was a winner. After settling in to the hotel room we finally entered Torremolinos and went for a bite to eat. After a good (yes in Spain you can still eat good and hearty food for little cost) piece of meat, salad and fries, we went to the coast to see the sea. After this we left for the hotel, but not without succumbing to a cappuccino and a large slice of chocolate cake. Full and satisfied, we sunk into a deep rest that night. And then it was January 15, 2012, And just like last year, I was back in Spain this day (my birthday) and received the best present you can imagine that day, the SUN. Mona and I were due to be picked up by Pete and Linda at 1pm, until then we were in Torremolinos enjoying a small breakfast and coffee.

By now dear readers, you know that eating and drinking in Spain is one of my favourite pastimes. The good thing is Mona and I share this hobby. I can hear you thinking, but no, you can't see it in my size. After a nice breakfast we went to a local jeweller to browse and I received a nice gift from Mona, namely a new watch, which I had needed for a long time. This watch would provide a fun anecdote later in the day. Around one o'clock Linda and Pete were waiting for us at the agreed place, and we drove to Torrox. Here we were reunited with Jo and Rich and surprise - Dawn and Bill were also present. Dawn and Bill also regularly rescue Spanish dogs and several of our readers have adopted a dog from their home. We were treated to something (yes) to eat by the six mentioned above. A Brazilian BBQ. I deliberately write this in capital letters because boy oh boy, was this good!

In the Netherlands we know this under the name Rodizio, only the pace, the quality, the fried bananas, supplemented with the location on the beach, fresh Mojitos and fresh Sangria made this an unforgettable meal. After this extensive meal we drove to Torrox with Jo and Rich to a place where they had agreed to meet with a Spanish and Belgian lady as they would help her mediate for two rescued dogs.

Because we probably knew adopters for one of these dogs in the Netherlands, it was quickly decided that we would take one of the dogs with us. The Belgian lady then capsized like a ship at the Italian island of Giglio (changed her mind) and said that she had fallen in love with the puppy. Jo was angry, and the ladies started arguing, because she had spent time for nothing, and this was the end of cooperation. This too is dog rescue in Spain. After a drink on a terrace we got back into the car towards Torrox because we would also visit a couple of stray dogs who lived in an abandoned building on a steep rock slope and had 7 mix Staffordshire puppies roaming freely around there, which may be adoptable in the Netherlands. After Richard had dropped us at a junction in Torrox we continued with Linda, Lisa and Jo and drove back towards the coast of Granada.

After descending the somewhat steep mountain we came upon the up vagrants/junkies/alcoholics and soon the relationship became grim and there were words between Lisa and the two gentlemen who were there. Finally they said; "We just had to take all those f*ck*ng dogs with us!" After some consultation between Lisa, Jo, Linda and Mona it was then we decided to take the females with us in order to reduce the chances of reproduction.

There also appeared to be a bitch scurrying around that the vagrants had said previously had "disappeared". After picking up this bitch, a third man came storming out of the house and started yelling, "Mi perro," and getting louder and louder. Jo, who had this puppy in her hands, had to dive to avoid a swing of the arms. The puppy was pushed into Mona's arms while the conversation started to take a nasty turn. The whole thing progressed into a situation where I initially tried to calm down the man and tried to make it clear to him that this had been agreed with his "friends". Because the situation was getting more and more grimmer and the idiot tried to hit the ladies and me, it was decided to quickly take two more puppies that were in the vicinity. The idiot kept shouting, "Mi perro, mi perro," and after he even tried to bite me, I grabbed him by the throat and didn't let go until the ladies could go uphill.

They were in possession of, yes, two males and the female that started the trouble. On the way back up the steep slope Mona thought for a moment that she could play "slide" with two dogs in her hands and fell down another metre. After this we had to avoid a herd of goats that were out on their daily walk about. We arrived at the car full of adrenaline. When I got to the car, Lisa, Jo and Linda asked me if I was okay because that weirdo tried to hit me a few times. Mona was also interested and asked me if I still had my new watch…? For the sake of fairness, I must tell you that I had owned a watch from her a few years before. I then went to a pre-sale of football tickets with my newly acquired watch, in the crowd my watch was stolen from my arm and to make matters worse, the football tickets were also sold out before I got there... Well, she had the right to speak! And I still had my watch.

With three rescued puppies in our possession we then drove to Jo's house with Jo and Linda. Two coronas later realisation dawned that shelter had to be arranged for a while. After acting quickly and a few phone calls to the Netherlands it was decided that we would try to book another bag at the airport the next day and get two of the three puppies to the Netherlands. This was when the exportation of puppies was more lenient.

Good news, the bitch and one of her brothers could go to the Netherlands. The female was named Ezra while her brother was named Bentley for now. After the stress had subsided we went home with Linda and after a delicious cup of coffee we spent the night there in the guest house. And then it was January 16, 2012, at about 6 o'clock in the morning, while it was still quite cold in Spain and especially in the mountains, the alarm went off for us. Today was the day of our return to the Netherlands. After being greeted by Linda's numerous dogs (she had about twelve at that time) and a good strong cup of coffee, we loaded up Trixie, Bentley and Ezra and drove with Linda at about 7 o'clock from Almuñécar to Salobrena where we had arranged to meet the foster parents of Satur and Brownie at the now famous parking lot at Lidl. Richard also came to us here because we needed help transporting dogs and cages to the airport. After saying goodbye to the foster families we drove to the airport. After an hour's drive and while it was daylight between the mountains of Andalusia, we arrived at Malaga airport. Here we unloaded the dogs and put them in the transport crates. We said goodbye to Richard and started the airport run together with Linda.

Due to the sudden events of the day before we were still dealing with the hassle of the two extra puppies, without going into too much detail, I can tell you we succeeded. It was a bit of a run between the various counters of flight care, Transavia and check-in, but an extra bag could be booked. Mona and I would be sitting in the same row with an empty seat in between. We gave a friendly smile to the airport staff on duty, thanking them very much for all their efforts and above all to let them know that this would have not been successful without their efforts. Oh, and so it was. What helped was the sight of two very cute puppy faces. It's nice to see that the sight of Ezra and Bentley made even the tough customs ladies melt. One of them almost begged Mona and me that if we didn't want to join them in line (because when the bags are scanned the puppies have to be taken out of the bag for a short time) that she could help to hold the dog while we go through the body scanner.

Despite the hectic pace of this airport run we were still right on time for boarding, and we boarded the plane well in time. Everything according to plan and was well arranged, we thought… Trixie had different ideas. While we thought that all bags were properly secured Trixie had found an escape hatch in her bag and went to relax three rows in front of us, to take a shit. When we were alerted to this by the stewardess we put Trixie back in the travel bag which we immediately secured with the tie-wraps we brought with us. I cleaned up Trixie mess then freshened up the air with the help of the crew and a can of air freshener. Fortunately, the ladies who were settled in the row where this happened accepted our sincere apologies and could laugh about it. Thank God! After a successful flight, we arrived at Schiphol airport at around 2 o'clock. While waiting for the dogs in the travel crates to be brought to us we showed off the smaller dogs through the window that were to be collected by Ed. An hour later, Brownie and Satur were also brought to us, and we headed for the exit. After the handover of the dogs, the many hugs and the shooting of photos, we finally took a group photo.

After coffee I picked up the car and after loading Bentley and Ezra and the transport boxes we said goodbye to Ed and went home. Here Bentley met his foster mother and went home with her later that day. All in all a busy weekend, which went completely differently than we could have imagined in our wildest dreams, but we are glad that we have now also seen and experienced first-hand what our colleagues and volunteers in Spain endure. And we are grateful to them for their unbridled efforts with which they are committed to the stray dogs there. On their behalf, we also had to thank everyone in the Netherlands who is committed to making the lives of Spanish stray dogs more pleasant. Because hope is needed there, the hope that stray dogs will be rescued, the hope that eventually understanding will come from the local population for the treatment of animals, the hope that the volunteers there can continue to work, the hope that with our support to care for these neglected dogs. I would therefore like to convey these thanks to everyone and to add our thanks because we at HzH also know that we cannot make it without the support of our volunteers and everyone who cares about us, as well as all the adopters.

A life with dune and house rabbits
By Louis Ringnalda

THE AUTHOR OF THIS STORY was taken by his parents to the beautiful Dutch Wadden island of Ameland at a very young age. He soon became acquainted with the dune rabbit because the tent house where they were camping was located directly on the North Sea dunes.

There were many holes in these dunes. It was made clear to me that these were rabbit holes. During the day they were not actually there, but towards the evening they showed up in large numbers. We were playing and running in the open areas of the campsite while my mother gave me a white sandwich with peanut butter. What later became clear to me is that the females have the upper hand in the rabbit world. A rabbit can make noise, but only if the female lets the buck, the male, know that she is in charge. A kind of growling sound comes from her throat. The other sound that is made is what every rabbit wants to avoid, namely that of being terrified by, for example, being grabbed by a stone marten. As a boy on the island, I was confronted with a completely different cause of death, namely the consequences of the imported disease myxomatosis. Many important organs are affected, such as the senses and muscles. The sense of orientation is gone. A poignant example of this happened to us in the autumn of yet another stay on the beach on Ameland. During our walk, a bunny with this terrible disease ran straight from the dunes into the surf... a kind of suicide attempt. We couldn't find him again in the turbulent waves. The reproductive organs continue to function, which unfortunately causes the disease to spread.

"Why are rabbits with that scary disease always sitting nearby or lying dead next to the shell paths, Dad?" Because the sun warms the path during the day, and they can still feel it when they can no longer see. In the evening before going to sleep I was taken to the mysterious hare meadows in the forest. There were two. I was allowed to take the big flashlight, financed with the deposit on empty bottles, into the dark forest. No hares gathered in these hare meadows, but... yes, rabbits. On the way back to the campsite we shone the flashlight in the eyes of the many long-eared owls that were making themselves heard while screeching. After such a rabbit evening, from my bed in the tent house, I saw the lighthouse light up three times through a small window, something it still does to this day.

Over the years I slowly but surely developed a soft spot for rabbits. While in my childhood there were also black mice and canaries as pets. Interest in rabbits received a considerable boost from the film Watership Down with the title song Bright Eyes by the duo Simon and Garfunkel. A tear-jerking film and a book about rabbit families that have to survive in a world that is increasingly being taken over by humans.

My brother, eight years older, had a poster with a then American actress holding a rabbit in her arms. A beautiful picture. He also said that one of his girlfriends had a pet rabbit that ran loose on the floor of her apartment. And it was even allowed in bed. I thought that was strange, after all a rabbit must have space and be able to be outside. During my studies there was no time for keeping a rabbit. Dogs were there in my partner's life. I had to watch out for a very small dog…. the pincher Tippie! He regularly showed his teeth. Then we got Meta, a beagle who was more interested in a blade of grass, than a wild rabbit on the business park next to the parental home.

And then, finally a big wish came true. A holiday home on Ameland. During those years, the associated garden was regularly visited by rabbits of various colours. Some house rabbits brought from the mainland had remained on the island and the dune rabbits also liked them very much. Our twins also wanted rabbits, which for me meant the fulfilment of a cherished wish. Flipje and Timmy came to enrich our family. Both black in colour. They were even taken to Ameland during holidays. Unfortunately, Timmy was soon confronted with death at home due to stress due to a loose sheepdog. Flipje was 9 years old and had problems with her molars. A natural death for her. A rabbit alone is not recommended because it is a group animal. Therefore, soon a visit was made to the De Wissel animal shelter in Leeuwarden. Strangers had left four rabbits in a cardboard box on the sidewalk. The long-eared gray Pip and the bearded rabbit, also gray, named Saartje, were taken home. They turned out to be big huggers for the children.

Pip was very fat, which increased the chance of a visit from a maggot-carrying blue fly. So that happened. Pip did not survive. Saar was left. A new rabbit would and had to be brought in to provide the required company for Saar. Benny, a real dune rabbit whose colour resembled a real dune rabbit came into Saar's world. A very sweet and submissive and somewhat skittish bunny who found our couch in the living room quite a challenge. Saar had less trouble with that. Unfortunately, Benny suffered a broken hind leg, which manifested itself in a grinding sound. The advice was to put him to sleep. And with the rest of the family, this now sixty-year-old also had tears in his eyes. I saw the little one's life disappear from the little body. So defenceless. It's tough that we can make the decision about life and death for such a beautiful creature.

The result was that Saar, a real lady, was alone again. That was not possible, so the castrated Bram, black with a brown glow, entered Saar's enclosure. A very sweet rabbit and immediately submissive. Saar had also visited the vet because she suddenly stopped eating and drinking. That will be fatal within a few days.

She came back every time. But in June of this year (2023), disaster struck after a fantastic life of nine years. A large growth on a molar at the back of Saar's mouth caused brackets on the molars because she could no longer eat. Food and drink were no longer available. An injection to end her life was the result after about two weeks of force feeding and medication. When I close my eyes, I can still see the look in her eyes, looking at me from the carrier on our way to the vet. It was as if she wanted to ask me to help her get rid of the pain. That was the end for her. The burial in the garden was a dignified farewell.

Now Bram couldn't stay alone. It was striking that Bram suddenly became very accessible without Saar. So sweet and proof that another partner was needed. It was our daughter in particular who started looking for a suitable partner for Bram. That turned out not to be so easy because of stricter rules. The outdoor enclosure for two rabbits turned out to be a bit too small, even though they could regularly play in the grass in the run. A shelter lady who was very fond of rabbits told us about Daisy, brown and white, who had been in a hamster cage measuring 30 x 30 x 30cm all her life, and was around the age of 5. Terrible. She now has Bram as a partner, and he immediately returned to the submissive role. Together in a nice large loft with a large outdoor area.

Holidays mean being babysat by others. A burden for someone else. Open up the night cage in the morning, give them pellets and plenty of fresh hay and water, an occasional pea flake or a small piece of bread or apple and fresh vegetables in the evening and back into the night cage to prevent a visit from the dreaded stone marten.

I am still happy with Bram and Daisy, but I try not to get attached anymore. This is difficult but it has to be done. Now that the children have moved out of the house, a babysitter must always be found for the rabbits. We have an agreement with the said shelter lady that if Bram leaves, Daisy can return to another owner through the shelter. Still, that will be a difficult decision for us, because my rabbit heart continues to beat.

The Guinea Pig Foundation
By Isabel Ringnalda

IF YOU HAVE HAD A love for animals from an early age and are crazy about guinea pigs and rabbits, among other things, then you cannot ignore the vacancy for a volunteer at the guinea pig shelter.

It was also a fun and valuable activity during the corona pandemic, to which even after the pandemic you can no longer say goodbye. The guinea pig shelter was founded 26 years ago with the aim of taking in guinea pigs and giving them a good home through rehoming. Of course, its purpose is also to give out the right information to increase the well-being of the animals. Because that is often not the goal of breeders, unfortunately.

For example, the Guinea Pig Foundation has taken in groups of hundreds of guinea pigs several times. Large groups that were not properly cared for. Fungus and scabies are common and highly contagious conditions. This is often caused by a deficiency of vitamin C, as guinea pigs do not produce this themselves. For example, if you, as a volunteer, can feed the 300 guinea pigs their peppers with lots of vitamin C, this will make you very happy. Partly because of the thank yous that they give: the nice and cheerful sounds they make.

When people come by because they are looking for a new buddy for their guinea pig, you visit all the cages to find the best match. Of course, people always have a preference. No red eyes, no long hair or a certain colour. You've found the lucky one and then you see how they react to each other. The castrated male has to show what he can do, so he quickly seeks out the lady. He spins around her and makes a certain sound. The lady is interested, and also finds it exciting. She also makes certain sounds. In the meantime, something tasty is ready, so a short break to eat something is a must, but then the party continues straight away.

Experienced people often know the behaviour; otherwise it is well explained to them, because this behaviour can continue at home. Ultimately you can tell that it is a match if they leave each other alone, but also visit each other every now and then without getting at each other's throats. Happy people, happy guinea pigs and a happy volunteer who was able to find the animal a new good home.

Of course, there are also people who give up their guinea pig(s). This is, for example, because the children no longer care about it, or they can no longer take care of it. A waiver form is completed, and the guinea pig is given its own place in one of the many cages in the guinea pig shelter. First the guinea pig relaxes for a while and then is paired with a friend in the guinea pig shelter. Guinea pigs are group animals, and you immediately notice loneliness in their behaviour when the guinea pig is alone. They often stop eating or sit quietly in a corner. You'd rather hear the nice sounds they make together.

What people also make great use of is the holiday care that the foundation offers. For a few Euros a day they can bring their guinea pigs and they will be well taken care of. The period often varies from a week to a month. The guinea pig shelter also has a large enclosure for guinea pigs that stay in the shelter forever. People can adopt a guinea pig for a certain amount per year. These are animals that are difficult to rehome, such as guinea pigs with a condition such as a chronic respiratory infection or guinea pigs that are very old. This group of about 40 guinea pigs are having a great time together. In the summer they can go outside and walk through the grass. Although grass is also something that is very tasty to eat.

Food is something that should certainly not be missing for a happy guinea pig. Whenever the chicory or endive bag cracks, a loud cheer can be heard in the form of squeaking. Vegetables are something they need to eat every day and luckily there is a greengrocer that donates vegetables to the shelter that cannot be sold for human consumption anymore. This has helped the foundation a lot.

In addition, guinea pigs eat pellets from which they obtain nutrients, but also with which they keep their teeth in length. One thing guinea pigs can never get enough of is hay. Fortunately, the foundation has a large area available where many bales of hay can be harvested so that they can last a whole year. Fresh water is also important, although guinea pigs can also get enough fluid from the vegetables they eat. Naturally, what comes in will also have to go out again. Fortunately, there are several volunteers who help with the cleaning every week.

Of course, I also have guinea pigs myself, because you just can't resist those cute faces. I started with two guinea pigs, now there are five. Pien is the oldest of the group. She has short hair with brown, white and red colours in the coat. She is about five years old and high in the pecking order. The other ladies really go out of their way for her. In addition, Gijs is the boss because he is the (castrated) male. If there is a discussion between the ladies, he is often there to put them in their place. He has many crowns in his coat and mainly has red hair. Then you have Mollie, a stubborn lady who does what she wants. She hates clipping nails; she shows that by biting your sweater. She is a beautiful long-haired lady with a white and cream coloured coat. Bibi is also part of the group. Just like Gijs, she has many crowns and a gray coat colour. Bibi is very submissive, but is the first to scream for attention when she thinks she will get food. Finally we have Kaatje. She joined the group last. It took a while to make friends, but in the end it all worked out fine.

Kaatje is a feisty girl who is not easily discouraged. Just like Bibi, she will do anything for food. With her brown face, ears and paws and cream-coloured smooth-haired coat, this beauty is a nice addition to the group. Guinea pigs are sociable; you are never alone at home. They all have their own character and that makes it so much fun. I would recommend it to everyone.

The Process from Rescue to Adoption
By Linda Rane

WE HOPE THIS WILL ENLIGHTEN people on how the process works from the minute an abandoned dog or cat is found through to when they eventually find their forever loving adoptive home. Initially we get a phone call, an email, a text message, or a whatsapp message from concerned people who have found an abused or abandoned cat or dog. Once caught we first need to ascertain if the animal is microchipped. This can be checked by a vet or the police. (Or we also have our own chip reader which we can loan out.)

If chipped then the police or the vet will call the owner to come and collect their pet. Sometimes though this doesn't work as the owners may have moved house and not changed the details on the microchip database. Or they may say that they don't want their pet anymore (for various reasons!). In this case, we ask them to sign documents to put the animal into our name. If the owner can't be traced, the police have to send them a letter to the address registered against the chip. After 10 days if no response, then we have to go through the lengthy process to get the animal chipped into our name.

If no chip is found then we can legally take the animal immediately and get him or her prepared for travel and new ownership. The very first thing to be done is to worm and deflea the cat or dog. Then get them fully vaccinated against parvovirus and distemper and rabies. In Andalucía it is the law for them to have two rabies vaccinations one month apart. Also the polyvalente vaccination (against distemper and parvovirus) needs two vaccinations, also one month apart.

If it is an adult dog, we then get them blood tested for the 5 Mediterranean diseases. For cats we test them for Feline aids and Feline leukaemia. If they are old enough (that is over 6 or 7 months old) we get them neutered.

We then spend two to three weeks with the dog or cat to assess their behaviour and character so we can inform potential adopters exactly what they are like. Also so that we know which would be the best home and environment for them. The advertising of the animal can now be started.

We mainly use Facebook and also they are listed onto our website (www.valleverdeanimalrescue.org).

Once we start to get enquiries, we send out our initial adoption application form. If the potential adopters seem suitable from this initial form, we then organise a home check and visit them at their house when another lengthy form is completed. Once we are satisfied that the home is right for the dog or cat, we can start to organise transport.

We do home some dogs within Spain (so transport is fairly simple for this) but most of our dogs and cats travel overseas to Holland, Germany and the UK. All three countries use over land transport which is not cheap. We also charge an adoption fee for cats and dogs which goes towards the expenses that we have already paid out to get them neutered and ready for travel.

The adopters sign a contract which states that if anything goes "wrong" they must immediately contact us so that we can advise them or in worst cases scenarios rehome the animal.

Alba
By Linda Rane

WE GOT A CALL A few years ago to tell us about a Podenco dog wandering the streets of Almunecar. She appeared to be pregnant and was scavenging for food near the bins. We agreed that we would try to catch her so we could get her spayed and rehomed. This was, I think, about 2020.

Anyway, we posted on Facebook and asked people to look out for her and tell us if they saw her and where she was located. We got a lot of replies and people tried their best to catch her, but she was very clever and always evaded them.

In the meantime she gave birth to pups (we don't know how many but more than 5 we guessed!). This meant that she was even more difficult to catch as she hid the pups and protected them fiercely. She went into total hiding and there were no more sightings of her or very few.

We did see her once more, on the main road between Almunecar and La Herradura and together with two friends we searched that area for over two hours but no sign. In the end we decided that she was just going to be one of those dogs who would permanently be "wild".

My last post said that if anyone caught her then Valle Verde would take her into our shelter and care for her. A year passed by, and I had forgotten all about that last post. Then one day Gema from SOS Salobrena called me and said that they had caught her! She was at Gema's house in foster and was very

very scared, but Gema was working with her to gain her trust. There was no sign of her pups who by then must all have been grown up and also wandering the streets somewhere.

We honoured our promise and Gema brought her to our new shelter (by that time we had moved from Cantalobos up to our smaller one above Otivar). She hadn't been spayed yet as she was in bad condition, so the vet wanted to wait until she had put more weight on.

She arrived at our shelter, but disaster struck two days after she was there! SHE ESCAPED! Oh no, after all that time trying to find her (over a year to 18 months) she got out! I thought, well that's it then, she's off back to Almunecar to have more pups and live on the streets again.

Two days later, Ingo our caretaker at the shelter called and said that she had come back for food, but he couldn't catch her! So he kept putting food and water outside the gate for her. It took over a week before he managed to entice her inside his house! Once inside, we managed to catch her, and I got her straight to the vets for spaying (we definitely didn't want more pups!) then she came to my house as I thought she would be safer here and couldn't escape.

I initially kept her inside the house and only took her out on a lead to do her business because although my grounds are fully fenced, she is a Podenco, and they find any escape routes. This went on for over a month until I felt confident to let her off the lead inside my grounds with me watching her to make sure she didn't escape.

She was still quite nervous but improving day by day and I was gaining her trust very slowly. I then started to take her on walks with my dogs but kept her on an extendable lead. She hated being on a lead while the other dogs were off, so I relented and let her off. She does tend to run off but always comes back in her own time.

Of course, I fell in love with her and decided to adopt her. She has since been to Ireland, Isle of Man, Scotland, UK and France with us and one of our other dogs in our camper van. We kept both dogs on the lead during our travels as Podencos are hunting dogs and not trusted as they go off hunting. I didn't want to lose her. Our other dog, Tommy is a border collie, so he was also kept on a lead during the holiday as he tends to chase sheep!

So now I was back up to owning 5 dogs plus one foster! Never ending! But I love them all.

Lucy and her pups
By Linda Rane

"DON'T COME BACK WITH ANY dogs," my husband said when I told him I was going to "look at and feed" a mum dog and her pups which had been found on a rubbish tip near Salobrena.

"Of course I won't," I replied. "I just want to make sure that they have food and water."

Two hours later I arrived home with a tricoloured scruffy Podenco mum dog and her two black pups. I named her Lucy and the two pups Jack and Jill.

This was way back in 2009, two years after we had moved to Spain to retire and relax! It was a new experience for me to foster dogs. I had always been a cat person and fostered cats and kittens when I lived in the UK for the PDSA and the RSPCA.

I was at a complete loss on what to do with the dogs, how to find them homes or where to advertise them. Black dogs especially were not a popular colour in Spain, and I had no idea of how to advertise outside of Spain. Jack and Jill and Lucy their mum stayed with us for a year or two.

Jack and Jill were not very easy to look after, as they tended to get up to all sorts of mischief. Although my grounds are fully fenced in, they could leap over the fence like gazelles and one day they chased and growled at a runner, who threatened to denounce me to the police.

This grew to be a problem before we found an organisation in Holland who could help us rehome dogs. HzH (Hond zoek Huis) was run by Mona Koopman and her partner Jeroen Hoogland.

Another problem was, I was very ignorant of the typical Mediterranean diseases that dogs could catch, leishmaniosis being one of them, so I hadn't protected the dogs against this by using scalibor collars. Jill contracted leish but Mona still managed to find a good home for her in Holland.

I am still in contact with Jill's (now called Luna) owner in Holland and although she is now getting to be an old girl she is still going strong. Her leish disappeared after about a year of living in a colder climate.

Jack continued to live with us for another few months before I found a lovely home for him, in the UK, in Milton Keynes. Jen adopted him and totally adored him even with all his naughtiness! Like chasing deer near her home and disappearing for hours on end giving her so much worry!

In 2018, I received a message while I was on holiday in South Africa that Jack had suffered some sort of stroke and although Jen and the vets tried their best to save him, unfortunately he died. Such a heartbreak for both Jen and I as she always kept me up to date with all his escapades and adventures.

Lucy, their mum stayed with us. My husband kept saying, "I can't understand why she hasn't been rehomed as she's such a lovely dog!" The reason was because I hadn't advertised her as I had fallen in love with her and was not going to let her go.

Lucy lived with us until her old age and died at home 18 months ago from, we think, a stroke. I still miss her dreadfully but hope that I gave her a good life away from the rubbish tip that we found her on.

The ephemerally of rodent existence
By Mirjam van der Veen

I HAVE HAD SMALL PETS all my life. By this I mean the caged variant. A mouse, hamsters, a rat, rabbits, guinea pigs and the lost goldfish. As a little girl I always had to control myself not to crush them, because I thought they were, 'Soooooooo sweet, Mommy!'. I have a story about every animal. I would like to share the most memorable ones. I got the first furry friends as an 8-year-old girl. My mother sang in a choir and one of the choir members had a litter of hamsters. So one evening after singing she came home with a cage and two hamsters in it; Speedy and Thumper. We were woken up to experience the spectacle. They were running wildly on their own wheels. They had to take turns at the wheel, because they couldn't fit in together. I still remember the adrenaline of the little ones combined with my intense happiness that these little animals were ours. I also remember that we had a small round ashtray in the cage, it looked like a small hole, which they used as a toilet. They were potty trained!

The sad thing about hamsters is that they don't live long. And so after two years Speedy, or Thumper, had died and a new hamster was added; Jopie. But, they couldn't share a cage, so there was a second one next to it. Jopie was a master at escaping from the cage. He was also fast. Barely holdable in my small childish hands. Probably also because walking freely is of course a hundred times more fun. And of course, he also got a new neighbour in his life because Thumper, like Speedy, disappeared to the eternal hunting grounds.

The local newspaper with the dozens of mini advertisements selling second-hand items also once featured a hamster. With a box I went on the back of my mother's bicycle on the way to the sales party. It turned out to be a gray, long-haired hamster. And of course it had to have an original name; Kali. (Kaal meaning bald in Dutch.) Because yes, she was of course anything but bald and so I thought this name was very funny. And in her life she also got another neighbour; a black and white mouse Pim. But my sister and I thought that was less successful. Pim was as quick as water, and we could not catch it. In short, we didn't bond with the mouse and so it remained with that one mouse.

Meanwhile, there was also a hutch with a rabbit in the garden; Punkie. In retrospect, this was a very sad affair. After all, rabbits shouldn't be alone. But I wasn't aware of that at the time. Perhaps Mother knew this, but she probably thought it was enough with all those little four-legged friends. Punkie outlived all the little ones living inside the house. Sadly enough, he died during my teenage years at the hands of the holiday babysitter. They had forgotten that an animal does not survive long if it is left in the sun and does not get anything to drink.

It wasn't until I was a student that I adopted a pet in a cage again. Previously, I and a housemate had given a good friend (also a housemate) a rat on her birthday. This went everywhere with her. Nestling comfortably in her neck. I also wanted this idyllic image of the furry friend sleeping in your pocket and so I bought Bodhi. A black and white male. He walked freely through my dorm room. Also, he peed in every spot, but that didn't spoil the fun. A fantastic friend. He died three years later from pneumonia. Incurred due to being in a draught. He was often taken in a travel basket from my room to my parents' house at weekends. In all weather conditions.

After that, there were no more animals in a cage. That was pathetic. Until my sister wanted to get rid of her daughter's hamster. She felt sorry that the animal no longer received attention. And so Cornelia came into my life. A lovely, fat golden hamster. Very tame and crazy about the yoghurt treats for rodents. Her ending was quite abrupt.

There were also four cats in the house. So Cornelia was high on the closet.

An interesting detail in this story is that she had the tendency to push open the door of her cage. And to keep her inside, there was a construction on the door so that it could not be opened from the inside. One morning I went into the living room and there was something indefinable on the floor. It was Cornelia, without a head. She had managed to open her cage (how is still a mystery to us), had made a smack from the cupboard and thus entered the domain of the cats; exit Cornelia.

There are many more of these unfortunate deaths in the history of small animal memories. For example, the goldfish that had a tendency to jump out of the bowl, so that there was a rack on the bowl to prevent this, yet it miraculously managed to get through the bars. After returning from a weekend at Mom's, the fish lay dehydrated on the carpet. Or the chick that 'disappeared' by (probably) falling into the rabbit tunnels. Or the complete 'disappearance' of two guinea pigs from their outdoor enclosure.

This last story can be described as memorable. They had become part of a real massacre. The marten had gotten them. We knew this because the neighbour's two rabbits had already disappeared. No trace. And so we should have known better and closed the cages in the outdoor enclosure. But because of our stupidity, ignorance, negligence, we had not done that. We didn't know then that a marten returns to the place where it managed to find a meal.

When the neighbour's garden turned out to be empty, he or she went to look a garden further away. There Kiki and Lola were sitting in a large outdoor enclosure, together with an elderly show rabbit (which we had also received from a very old breeder who had to get rid of his 'winners' due to his health). In the outdoor run there was a night cage with a small opening, without a door. The marten must have crawled in here and grabbed the guinea pigs from there. The next morning, all that was left of the guinea pigs was one drop of blood and a small tuft of hair. The elderly rabbit lay dead in the run. This one had probably run so fast or been in such shock that it was fatal.

My husband and I were shocked. Our daughters a little less. As if the harshness of rural life was taken for granted. In addition, the guinea pigs were not really cuddly. They had lived with a breeder for the first year and a half of their lives. In a dirty cage with no windows and little love. The children could not catch Kiki and Lola themselves, so if the children wanted to cuddle their guinea pig, my husband or I first had to make an effort to catch the fast running animals.

A year later new guinea pigs arrived. We unanimously agreed that they were no longer allowed outside in the cage. Caramel and Odette only came outside in a cage when the weather was nice. They were half-sisters, four days apart in age. They didn't look alike at all. Caramel was black and caramel coloured. A bit fatter than Odette, who was white with a gray nose and red eyes. They couldn't live without each other, but neither could they with each other. We regularly heard them grunting at each other to fight out who was the boss. Caramel always won this. She just had a few more grams below the belt.

For five years there was no problem. Until Caramel got a bald belly. Her hair on the back also became a bit wispy and after two weeks we went to the vet. There she received an injection; scabies. But, we had already bought some things for that at the specialty store. That did not provide any improvement, but the vet would know. We had to come back a week later with Odette, because she would also have it by then. Despite the fact that we said this was not the case, we dutifully took two guinea pigs to the vet.

He concluded that Odette was healthy. And because Caramel seemed to have improved slightly, she received a second injection, with the advice to come back a week later. Then she also received another shot of medication, but her body could no longer process the latter. The next day she was lying down in the country house. I put her in the cage inside, her sister was still licking her head and in the morning she died.

Then we only had Odette. The adolescent children had not been able to pay much attention to the guinea pigs over the last year. As a family we had decided that we would no longer have rabbits or guinea pigs in the house. But a guinea pig alone is not okay, so we had to come up with something for her.

After a search I discovered that there are real guinea pig shelters. Odette was able to go to one of those locations. The managers of the place provide accommodation, food and even relocation. But because Odette was already elderly with five years of life experience, she was allowed to spend her retirement there. The shelter has a large indoor and outdoor run called the 'guinea pig village'. The perfect place to spend her old age. To get used to her new environment and also for observation, she was placed in a cage with a castrated boar (the word for a male guinea pig) and a sow. Both were known to be very sweet to other guinea pigs. Odette was immediately in her place. The latest news is that she has been upgraded from the cage to the guinea pig village with thirty other guinea pigs and that she likes to walk around in the grass looking for the tenderest blades.

Lytse the tough girl
By Miriam van der veen

CATS COME IN ALL SHAPES and sizes. This story is about Lytse. Her name means 'little one' in Frisian. She compensated for her name in her great character and perseverance. We got Lytse when she was 7 years old. She was the victim of a divorce. The man had come out on top and was allowed to take Lytse with him after the divorce. But a new woman came and Lytse had to leave the field. She came to us through the grapevine; a 'traditional' family with father, mother and two children. We always had cats, one more was no problem, and we live in a place with a large garden and a lot of love for animals. At that time we only had male cats, so an additional female cat would provide a nice balance.

The night she was brought she was literally hanging in the curtains. Anxious and upset. Fortunately, she quickly felt at home and discovered the free environment around the house. Characteristic of Lytse was the complete love she gave when she came home after an afternoon in the sun at the back of the meadow. Every time she was so happy to see you, as if you hadn't seen each other for weeks. Then she made a sound that can best be described as 'Prrrrrww'. She had a very specific head with a pointed face and big, yellow eyes.

It was summer and we went on holiday to Terschelling. The neighbour looked after the animals. There was no problem until the neighbour sent a message two days before we left the island: 'Lytse hasn't been home for 10 days. I saw her running away very fast when she was almost run over by a tractor'. A message like that doesn't immediately mean the end of the world, but we still looked forward to the moment of coming home to be able to look for her. We made posters that we hung throughout the village. Lytse was 13 at the time and no longer the strongest. After all, it was not for nothing that she was called Lytse when she was found in the hayloft by the previous owners. The smallest of the litter.

After a few days of searching, we received a call from the farmer who runs an arable farm a kilometre away. 'That cat on that poster, it has been here on our land for some time.' Lytse had already been gone for almost three weeks. We quickly went to the farmer's land. Our search seemed somewhat impossible in the vastness of the plots. After half an hour of calling and shaking kibble, we heard a surprised meow coming from the reeds. She came up from the water's edge. Smelling like a ditch, somewhat haggard, but not emaciated. Frogs and mice were probably greatly reduced in numbers.

We were very happy and glad that she was back home! It always feels like a hole in your heart and a herd of bison in your stomach when an animal is sick or lost. Peace had returned to Sloddervos House. Lytse slept like a marmot on the couch. The next day she hung around in the garden for a bit, but then decided to walk towards the meadow behind the house. She didn't come home in the evening. The farmer's wife called the next morning: 'She is here again, but now she is locked in the marten cage.' This time it was less complicated to find her, and we picked her up immediately. She had a little blood on her nose, because the flap of the marten trap had hit it, but she seemed more indignant that we had picked her up than happy to be taken back to her warm home. This time we decided to keep her inside for a while. Despite the excellent temperatures, the door remained closed to prevent Lytse from going to the potato farmer again. After ten days she was calm, sweet, well fed and we let her outside again.

This time we saw her walk straight to the backyard and through the pasture to the 'back farmer' plots. We were perplexed. What was she thinking? Did she just decide to leave us right away? We didn't expect that. Apparently

Lytse no longer felt like having a spread out bed and a bowl full of kibble. We decided not to pick her up a third time and sent a message; 'Lytse is probably back on the land with you, this time she can bring herself home'.

And indeed, we received confirmation that she had decided to continue living her life on the land. We knew she was alive and that it was her choice, so we let it go. After all, we had done our best. A cat on a string is not an option for us.

The following days we continued to shout from home. We wouldn't reach the kilometre to the farm with our voice, but it was more about the idea. That she still knew where her house was and that she was more than welcome to come home to eat from her bowl. No reaction. Until it started raining. Who was standing at the door? Lytse. With this weather, her ladyship didn't feel like being outside anymore. And probably all the mice were gone. She was never seen on the farmer's land again. Six weeks of adventure were apparently enough for her.

We were full of admiration and amazement. That little cat had managed to feed herself for a month and a half and stay alive there in the field with the hares, martens and heavy agricultural equipment. What a cool lady! We could see that she was exhausted from being outside, having to feed herself and, by all accounts, never having had a really deep sleep in all those weeks. She slept a lot at first, but soon we noticed that she was walking a bit crooked with her front legs. Arthritis was the conclusion. Nothing could be done. It mostly looked worse than it was.

Every summer after that we said to each other, 'this will probably be her last', when winter comes her body won't be able to handle this. Heat was her thing. She preferred to sit right next to the fire pit at the campfire in the garden. When the fire pit was still warm the next morning, she literally sat in warm ashes. When the wood stove was on, she lay right against it. Just before the third summer after her farm adventure, we took Lytse to the vet for the umpteenth time. She had been having constant colds for the past year. She always recovered with a pill from the animal doctor, but as soon as the box was empty, the snot flew around her ears and on the furniture again after a week.

It was April. This time when the stethoscope was placed on her lungs he said, 'Her body is all used up. The stretch is gone from her lungs, she is short of breath and has a cold. This will only get worse.' We went home with the vet asking, 'How long do you want to stretch it out?' We didn't see this coming. We had witnessed the deterioration, but had been so close to it that we no longer saw how bad it actually was.

We were so surprised by the news that she was doing so badly that we did not want to euthanize her there at that moment. Lytse didn't deserve to die on the cold table. After all, she hated the cold. Of course, we also understood that it was mainly our human brain that could not yet say goodbye to this legendary sweet, tough and special cat. Two days later the vet came home to give the injection. She is also buried there in the garden, overlooking her beloved potato land and the associated farm.

Tales of doggy fostering
By Lesley Hart

IT WAS A HEART-STOPPING moment. Ramon slipped off the pillar at the edge of our terrace into the garden next door. It was blocked from view by a high wall, though we knew our neighbours' swimming pool was adjacent to this wall. Most of the year the property and the pool were empty as the Belgian owners only visited in August. We heard no sound from Ramon, imagining all sorts of dreadful injuries. We rushed to bring a ladder, propping it against the boundary wall, and the intrepid Faye climbed up and saw that a totally unharmed and unabashed Ramon was waiting on the other side. The climb over the wall was dangerous as it entailed negotiating not only the ascent and descent into our neighbours' garden, but it also had a drop of some 30 feet into our other neighbours' property which nestled at the bottom of the hill below us.

Our house, like many in Almuñecar, is built into the hills rising up from the various bays. The surrounding houses are terraced on the different levels, and ours resembles a crenulated castle protected by a high white wall, thirty steps leading up to large terraces and our house and pool. Along two sides we have 'battlements' looking out over the houses below.

Getting Ramon out of the neighbours' garden was a challenge. The house and its extensive gardens were securely fenced, and all gates were locked. Faye managed to climb over and drop down into the neighbours' garden avoiding the pool. She passed Ramon up to me and I deposited him safely on our terrace. Then came the realisation that there was nowhere to place a ladder and no easy route back up the neighbours' wall. The grounds were surrounded by a high linked fence and chained gates with no obvious way out. The only apparent solution was for me to carry stepladders down our hill and up our neighbours' hill, pass them over the security fence so Faye could get over and pull them up after and hope that the Guardia was not alerted to an ongoing burglary by two elderly women! Mission accomplished and Ramon avoided his battlement patrol thereafter.

Ramon had been handed in to Valle Verde by some kind person who had found him in the Baza area. A chestnut coloured cross between a staffie and a miniature ridgeback. He was a loving, protective and fun dog and we fostered him whilst all the formalities were finalised before his trip to his adopted family in the Netherlands.

Ramon was only supposed to be with us for two or three weeks before his emigration to the Netherlands, but this was March 2020, an auspicious time. Almost overnight the country was plunged into a stringent lockdown, his stay extended until rules were relaxed and flights resumed. We had him for five months and it was a huge wrench when the time came for him to go. When you foster in these circumstances there is always the knowledge that once the dog had its passport or has recovered from its medical treatment it will move on to its forever home.

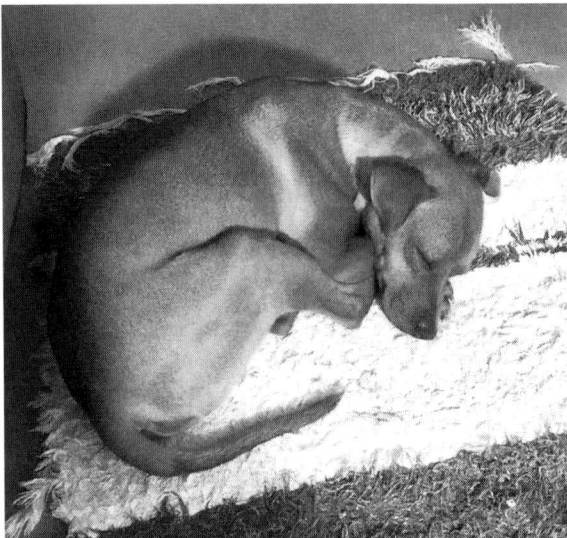

Covid meant that Ramon snuggled his way into our hearts and lives, and we developed the relationship and routines that knit lives together. Every night he would join us during the 'clap' for the medics, police and other service personnel, barking strenuously to accompany the clapping and whistling ringing out over the valley, across the Vega and from the old town. He stood proudly on one of the crenellated plinths of our boundary wall. Despite our constant efforts to discourage his mountaineering, this was clearly his sentry post. He was similarly on sentry duty and concerned about our welfare, running round and round our pool, barking anxiously whenever we got in. It took several weeks before he realised that we weren't drowning.

The following July we said a tearful farewell as he set off for his new life as Willem in the Netherlands. We still miss him and often speak of him. We never drive past the Cepsa garage in La Herradura without wistfully thinking of the farewells to our various dogs being collected by Krista in readiness for the next stage in their lives. We remember anxiously watching their progress en route to their new homes via GPS and the relief of seeing them safely arrived at their destination airport or new homes.

As we travel between the U.K. and Almuñécar it is difficult for us to have our own dog so fostering for Valle Verde has been a blessing for us. We have fostered twelve dogs; some simply awaiting their journey to their adopted home, some recovering from operations and needing a quiet environment in which to recover, and some, tragically, in their last days of life. We fondly remember each of them, following the fortunes of those now living in Ireland, Finland, the U.K., Germany, and the Netherlands.

Once the dogs relaxed and learned to trust us they have all been affectionate and loyal, quick to become protective of us. We have been amazed by the way even those who have suffered heartbreaking cruelty learn to love and trust humans again and how stoically they face the distress and discomfort of the necessary medical interventions.

All our foster dogs have been special, some more demanding than others, but all lovable. We'll never know their stories or the names they had before they came to Valle Verde, but what is clear is that there is a continuing need for people who can take animals into their hearts and homes, get them ready for their onward journeys and be able to let them walk away in the knowledge that their future lives will be safer and happier. They have all given us so much in our brief time together and we will never forget them. Our lives have been enriched by Rocco and Roxie, Lara, Pepper, Sigge, Pepo, Rosie, Angel, Max, Paco, Ramon and Lula.

Co the travelling tomcat
By Marjanne Meijer

WHEN I MET PATRICK, NOW my husband, he had a cat, Heste. I had a rat, Julius. Heste was pregnant and gave birth to 5 healthy kittens. Those kittens were all adopted, except one. After a few months we decided to keep him and we called him Co. Heste en Co means horse and cow in Danish, that's why. After a few months we adopted a dog from the local shelter, called Sam and our little family was complete.

Co was always a special cat, but something happened that made him even more special. Something went wrong with Tom Poes' cat food during that period. A toxic substance has ended up in it, causing the death of many cats in the Netherlands. We only heard that afterwards. Co and his mother both ate from the same bowl, but one piece was poisonous and the other was not. Only Co became ill and there was nothing wrong with Heste. Co became paralyzed from the neck down. He couldn't do anything anymore, he couldn't walk, he couldn't eat, and he couldn't go to the litter box. He lay in a basket all day with a very grumpy head. I often took him with me in that basket when I went to hang up the laundry or make the bed, for example, so that he occasionally had a different view. I gave him liquid food in a syringe, and we hung him over the litter box and pushed his faeces out. You do all that for your animals.

It lasted about three months, then he started moving again. Slowly but surely he became his old self again. The only thing he was left with was that his hind legs remained x-legged, and he could no longer purr. He sounded like a cooing dove. What we got in return was a cat that trusted us completely. We'd been carrying it around for three months without dropping it, so you couldn't drop it from eight inches high anymore. Then he was in splits.

We later heard from the manufacturer of the poisonous cat food, who came to see how things were going and to pay the veterinary costs, that more than ninety percent of the cats did not survive. Co grew up as an inveterate bachelor, who always lived at home with his mother. His ears were washed, and he happily snuggled up to Mom for a nap. There was great drama when his mother died in a car accident at the age of five. Co spent nights crying through the house looking for Heste.

Mother and son always slept in each other's arms and when Heste died, Co sought body heat from Sam. He missed that and regularly tried to lie in the basket with Sam. At first Sam didn't want that, but persistence wins.

From then on, we took Co with us to visit friends as much as possible so as not to leave him alone at home. He was very easy about that. We always said he was a dog in a cat's body. We transported him loose in the car, next to Sam in the backseat. Whenever we tried to put him in a carrier, he went crazy. Just sitting on my lap was much better. Even in the waiting room at the vet he just sat on my lap. When we went to visit our friend Koen, we often spent the night there. Co enjoyed himself all evening and night in Koen's house and garden. When we went home in the morning, we would call once, and he would always be there within five minutes. Without exception.

We left for Belgium when Sam and Co were around seven years old. They were both from 1995. We had a Mexican restaurant there for two years in the village of Coo, namely Cantina Mexi-Coo. Sam and Co lay together in the basket in the restaurant, which was still possible at that time. En Co entertained the guests on the terrace by sitting at their table.

After two years we left Belgium and planned to travel through Europe by bus. We thought it necessary to buy a harness for Co. After all, when people travel with a cat you always see that they have it on a leash at the campsite. I bought the smallest dog harness; Co was a fairly sturdy tomcat of about eight kilos. We put that on him, and it made him walk backwards. He looked like Michael Jackson doing the moonwalk. We were laughing so hard that it took a while before we were able to get the harness off him again.

But as it turned out, that whole rig was unnecessary. Co just stayed near the bus and all we had to do was shout or start the engine and he came. It has only gone terribly wrong once. That was in Sicily.

We stopped at a car scrap yard because we needed a part for the bus. However, the company was closed and after we tried to look through the gate to see if our type of bus was there, we continued without any further action. We went to refuel first, because we planned to drive quite a distance. We drove about 150 kilometres that day. On the way we stopped for lunch at the beach and in the evening we did some shopping at a supermarket. It wasn't until we were putting away the groceries that we noticed we were missing someone. Co was nowhere to be seen. We were terrified, but there was no time to lose. Since we had no idea where Co had jumped off the bus, we decided that Patrick would stay where we were. I would ride the bus back to different places to look for him. We had one phone (2003), and Patrick kept it. I could then find a pay phone to call him.

I would first drive back the same way we drove that day. But along the way I became more and more convinced that he had to be at the demolition company. No idea why, but I decided to look there first. I also brought Sam along to help search. When I got there I started shouting. I let Sam run through the tall grass to search. It took a long time, at least half an hour, but then he appeared. At first he was happy to see me, but soon that changed and he was angry. Very angry. Rightly so. I drove to the nearest phone booth to scream into the receiver, 'I've got it! I got him!'

We felt terribly guilty of course and never drove again without counting heads. Co forgave us and lived in the bus with great pleasure for many years to come. When the money ran out and we had to work again, we ended up in Denia, Valencia. It was the end of June and already quite warm. Our Dutch dog and cat had to get used to the heat quite a bit. Just like us, by the way.

Every day when we came home from work the bottom door of the refrigerator was open, which was the freezer. Patrick and I blamed each other for not closing the door properly and we almost had a real argument, until one day I was in the kitchen making a sandwich and Co walked in. He walked to the refrigerator and pried the door ajar with his front paw. Then he turned around and planted his bottom in the nice cool air coming from the freezer. I immediately called Patrick and we laughed really hard about it. Relieved that we could stop blaming each other for that open freezer door. Fortunately, he got used to the heat later and the refrigerator door was no longer always open.

Unfortunately, he did not live to be very old. He developed gingivitis, a very painful inflammation of his gums. The vet gave me some ointment to rub on his sore gums, but I gave it back to him. No chance. Co took prednisone for years to control gingivitis so he could eat. All that prednisone gave him diabetes. We injected him with insulin before meals for a few more years, but diabetes is an assassin. He died in Denia, Valencia, almost twelve years old.

Famke and Bas
By Avelien Buiting

WHEN OUR DAUGHTER WAS THREE years old and it became clear that she would not have any brothers or sisters, we decided to buy a dog. The choice fell on a wire-haired dachshund. Small enough to carry under your arm, but with a distinct character of its own. As was the case in the era before the Internet and Marktplaats, we looked for an advertisement in the newspaper and travelled to a supplier of dachshund puppies. It turned out to be a rather dubious address with many stables with puppies in all shapes and sizes. We were given a dachshund puppy in our arms and, despite the fact that she peed on my coat, we were immediately sold. We called her Famke. It took many weeks for her to be potty trained. With those short dachshund legs it was difficult to see when she was peeing, and I was usually too late to intervene. The mop remained within reach for a long time. But when the penny finally dropped, it was resolved.

It turned out to be a cheerful, bright and active dog who especially liked to fetch tennis balls. All day. Until it drove us crazy. So a year later a playmate arrived, another dachshund, Bas. A completely different character. It took him even longer before he was potty trained. He turned out not to be very smart, maybe even a bit stupid. Sometimes he didn't seem to realize that behind his head there was a whole body that also belonged to him. But he was very sweet. He was gifted with an innate hunting instinct. This has cost the lives of several animals. A few free-range chickens from the neighbours made the mistake of foraging in our garden. When Bas noticed them, hell broke loose. Most of the chickens were able to find safety just in time, but one was too slow. I think the neighbours ate chicken soup that evening... A nephew's guinea pig also had to acknowledge Bas in an unguarded moment. Fortunately, we still have good contact with the nephew, although he still talks about it with some regularity...

When Bas was once allowed to walk freely, he discovered a herd of sheep in a nearby meadow. He took off running and so did the sheep. A few dozen metres behind that I arrived with Famke, whom I had now put on a leash again. It turned out to be quite a spectacle and we attracted quite a lot of attention from passing cyclists who stopped in front of it and chuckled to see how I was going to solve this. Fortunately, after some time a helpful neighbour appeared in the meadow and together we got hold of the dog. Afterwards, I was surprised at how skilfully this otherwise not so smart dog managed to isolate a single sheep from the rest of the herd. It was the last time he walked outside without a leash. The sheep was lame for a few days but fortunately escaped unscathed.

Famke and Bas got along well. There was no doubt whatsoever about the ranking in our little pack. Famke was the leader. When the doorbell rang, both dogs rushed to the front door, barking loudly. When Famke died first and then the doorbell rang, nothing happened. Apparently Bas always ran after her barking without understanding what was going on…. The neighbour later asked why I hadn't opened the door. So even I was completely used to her leadership… Famke lived to be over 14 years old. She has been healthy and happy all her life. On her last day we walked, throwing and retrieving tennis balls, towards the forest across the road. Once we arrived at the edge of the woods, she picked up the ball and instead of putting it down with me to throw it again, she turned back and headed home. I will never know why she did it that way, for the first time in her life. While crossing she was hit by a car.

We buried her in the backyard, along with her beloved ball. We never noticed that Bas missed her. His life continued as normal. The human qualities that we like to attribute to animals do not always appear to be there.

In his last year, Bas suffered from a heart condition for which he was given pills. He passed away peacefully in his sleep at the age of 15. When both dogs were no longer there and our daughter also left the parental nest, we enjoyed the freedom of closing the door behind us in the morning and coming home late in the evening without even being there, having to think. Yet…

Hooray, we have a puppy!

They always say that you should never look at puppies if you are not planning on getting a dog. For me, a photo of a litter of puppies was enough to make me decide again. It is a girl, her name is Jip, and her mother is a cross between a Tibetan terrier and a cocker spaniel. Her father is a poodle. This makes Jip a true mixed breed. A very cheerful bouncing ball! As I often heard from other people and actually knew myself, it is a lot of hard work and takes a lot of energy to raise a puppy. She is now potty trained.

She also has slightly longer legs than a dachshund puppy... Just like the dachshunds, she loves shoes and especially laces. And she doesn't shy away from a tasty chair leg either. But we trust that everything will turn out fine. We have skipped the puppy course; after all, we are tried and tested. And we look forward to another 15 years with a nice roommate!

Sam and the magic mushroom
By Marjanne Meijer

SAM WAS MY FIRST DOG after I left my parental home. We were told it was a Doberman/Malinois, but since I have lived in Spain I suspect he may have been part Podenco as well. I was twenty when I got him from the shelter. I lived in Utrecht at the time and Sam came from the shelter in Houten. Together with Patrick, now my husband, I picked him up and decided to go to the forest first. We wanted to see how he responded to us and how well he listened.

It all went so well that we even let him go. He immediately listened. There was an open field where he ran a few laps. When we called, he immediately came running. Or almost immediately. From across the open field it looked like he was eating something, but we couldn't be sure. We were too far away.

After an hour we went home to introduce Sam to our two cats and rat. Our cats were a mother and son. Mother Heste was not amused about her new housemate, but son Co liked it almost immediately and wanted to become friends with Sam. Sam thought it all happened a bit quickly, but at least they accepted each other and there was no arguing. We thought that was wonderful for a first day.

Julius, the rat, thought differently. When I put him on my hand and let Sam smell him, he chose the strategy: attack is the best defence. He jumped, bit Sam on the nose and hung there. Sam carried the scar on his nose for the rest of his life.

While we were cooking, we noticed that Sam started acting a little strange. He seemed a little uncoordinated and became unsteady on his legs. When he leaned against a kitchen cupboard with one leg crossed over the other, as if he were a human being comfortably leaning against the neighbour's fence, our roommate came in. He immediately said: "That animal is epileptic. He does exactly the same as my girlfriend's cat." We then decided to call the vet.

The first two weeks we were obliged to consult the shelter vet, so I called the vet in Houten. I told him that we strongly suspected that he had eaten something, possibly a mushroom. Or that he was epileptic. The vet told us that if we thought he had eaten a mushroom, he would have to puke it up. So give him a mouthful of salt and lots of water and he'll puke. He liked to eat salt, he liked it, but he did not drink water. Didn't throw up either.

After we called back, we went to Houten in the car. I was sitting in the back seat with Sam, and he saw all kinds of things moving in the black back of the driver's seat. Things I didn't see. The vet opened the door for us, it was now after closing time, and let us into his practice room. He took one look at Sam and burst out laughing. His exact words were: "Where did you find that mushroom? Let's go back. That dog is tripping."

By now it was too late to make him throw up. The mushroom was clearly already in his blood. We went back home and kept an eye on him. He had a fantastic evening, we a little less so. At the end of the evening when we went to bed, everything seemed to be fairly normal again. The next morning all three of us woke up in the bedroom. Sammie sat on the bed between us. He looked from me to Patrick and just as Patrick pulled back the blanket, Sam finally puked. Right over Patrick.

Patrick: "Hmm, I think I'll take a shower."

Me: "Hmm, I'll have to change the bed."

That was the first meeting with Sam. He was nine months old at the time and we were the fourth owners. He hadn't had a chance anywhere. After this first, less successful day, everything turned out fine. We were still studying and working on the weekends on one of the Wadden islands of Vlieland. Sam always came along. We lived with someone who had several dogs. Together with these dogs, Sam often went to the beach several times a day. Even when we were at work, Sam was constantly walked in a place that is nothing less than a true paradise for dogs. Sam was particularly fond of water and even swam between the ice floes in the sea in winter.

If we didn't go to Vlieland and we had a party in Utrecht, Sam would come too. I cycled through Utrecht with Sam without a leash next to the bike. He did that perfectly. He listened very well. I have never again had a dog that listened so well.

A few years later we left the Netherlands and started travelling around by bus. At that time we only had cat Co, the son, and Sam. Mother Heste and rat Julius had died. We first had a restaurant in the Belgian Ardennes for two years, a true outdoor sports paradise. Above us was a company that organized outdoor activities. The instructors often met with their groups on our terrace. They regularly asked if Sam could come along, so that he could entertain the people in the group who were waiting for their turn. They could then throw sticks in the water for Sam. Sam was happy to come along. He got excited when his favourite instructors entered the terrace.

We drove all over Europe with Sam and Co in our van. In Denia, Valencia, we parked the bus and moved back into a house. Co died there in 2007 from his diabetes. A few months later, Sam had a new brother, but this time it was a dog, Manu.

Sam has swum in all the seas of Europe and has even been to the African continent, in Morocco. That's where we almost lost him to his obsession with water and swimming. We drove over the Atlas Mountains and stayed halfway in a village. We parked the bus at a campsite, which is mandatory in Morocco. A stream flowed past the campsite. It wasn't wide, but a lot of water passed through it. That was melt water that flowed down to the sea from the top of the Atlas. So it was freezing. None of that mattered to Sammie. Sam went swimming.

Before we knew it, he had thrown himself off the rather high side and was in the water. The water was flowing very quickly, but he held on to some brush. We couldn't see him because of an overhanging wall and a lot of vegetation, but on the other side a farmer was working on his land. He could see Sam and gave us directions.

When Sam could no longer hold on and was swept away by the water, the farmer shouted to us and pointed out where he was floating. Patrick was therefore able to jump into the river at the right time to grab Sam by the scruff of the neck. Relieved, we hoisted Sam onto the shore, and I went looking for a towel to dry him off. His teeth were chattering from the cold. But when I turned around to get on the bus, Sammie immediately ran back to the river and nearly jumped back in. Near-death experience or not, Sammie goes swimming. I was just able to grab him by the scruff of the neck.

We lived in Barcelona for a year and then we moved to Andalucía. In Granada we ran a hostel where there were always two large dogs in the hallway. Manu liked it a little more than Sam, but Sam also quite liked all the extra attention from the guests. He eventually died in Granada at the ripe old age of fifteen.

The Story of Polly
By Maaike van Lunenburg

SO I'M ESTRELLA, THAT MEANS star in Spanish, but no human calls me that. The humans I live with call me Polly, little girl (at least, that's the translation. In their language it's meisje), Princess, Beauty etc. Fine by me, especially the Princess.

The people I lived with in Spain, decided to go back to the UK. They took some of the animals with them, but not me. I came to live in the shelter and that was a bit of a shock: so many dogs around and dogs are not my thing. The people at the shelter were nice, they looked after me well, gave me cuddles and nice food.

As time went on, I longed for a home with nice laps to sit on, no dogs, blankets, just for me, and humans of my own. Other cats were adopted, leaving me feeling lonely. The shelter did everything to get me adopted. I even was a calendar girl (April that is: the birthday month of my male human!).

But, you see, I'm a bit special. I'm white. I have a green and a blue eye. And no ears. My ears were removed after I developed cancer. And with that my chances of getting adopted. But then friendship and social media stepped in.

One of the volunteers at the shelter knew that a friend, living in the Netherlands was looking for a cat. The volunteer and the friend used to work together, 30 years ago. Before I knew it, I was in a small cage in a transporter lorry. There were a lot of other cats in there, and dogs. Damn.

And off we went; we drove and drove and drove. No idea where I was heading for. It seemed endless, but after many hours we stopped, and some animals were unloaded. Just my luck, I thought, I have to stay in the lorry. So I meowed my biggest meow. 'I hope that is my cat,' I heard a male voice say. And suddenly, somebody grabbed me, put me in another cage and carried me out of the lorry and into the hands of a man.

"Hello, Estrella,' he said. I recognized the voice: it was the man that responded to my miaow. After yet another drive (in a normal car), we arrived in this apartment. They opened the cage, and I ran off to the shower room and hid behind the washing machine. But I didn't travel all this way to hide behind a machine. I carefully sniffed my way around the house. I went looking for this nice man, found him in the living room and jumped on his lap, just after being ten minutes in.

This man had this weird thing hanging on his chin. I tried to knock it off. The humans laughed: She is trying to get rid of the beard they said. After lots more sniffing and walking I passed a dictionary English-Spanish. (I later found out that the male human bought it in case I felt homesick, and he could say something Spanish, to make me feel better.)

I jumped on the couch where the female was sitting. She had a blanket! All this happened more than a year ago. I feel at home here. They let me go my own way and I found lots of nice places to rest and hide. A cupboard, the windowsill, the bed, chairs, laps and my own special flowerpot lined with straw, so my fur doesn't get dirty. The humans say they love me and consider my previous owners stupid for not taking me with them. I'm glad they didn't.

Manu and the complications of being a Spanish husky
By Marjanne Meijer

WHEN OUR CAT CO DIED, we only had our dog Sam left. Since Sam and Co were the same age, it crossed my mind that if Sam also died, I would have an empty house. A house without animals is a nightmare for me. Because we move quite often, we thought it would be more convenient to get a dog instead of another cat. Besides, we would never get such a wonderful cat like Co again. It became Manu.

Manu's mother was a full husky. She had arrived pregnant at the home of an English couple. There she gave birth, and all the puppies and mother were adopted. Only Manu was left, his name was different by the way. But now, after two and a half years, they had decided they didn't want him anymore. We were told a vague story, but later it turned out that they wanted to adopt two children and Manu was definitely not a friend of children. He was very afraid of children with pricking fingers and grabbing hands. We only found out later.

We saw a note hanging in a pub with a photo of Manu. 'Free to a good home' it said. I looked around at the bar hangers and quickly grabbed the note. I thought, 'you better come home with me, doggie.' We called and made an appointment to meet him and especially to introduce Sam to him. Of course, they had to like each other a little. When we saw it, we immediately fell in love. He was beautiful. A lot bigger than Sam and immediately very sweet. Sam thought he was okay too.

Seeing our happy faces, they handed us his passport and lead and left. Suddenly there we were with two dogs. We hadn't counted on that. We thought we would just get acquainted and then make an appointment for when he would come to us. We had an appointment at a restaurant for our friend Omar's birthday. Fortunately, Willem the restaurant owner didn't think it was a problem and we went to lunch with two dogs under the table. Poor Manu had not expected anything either and was shivering under the table. After lunch we went to the beach. At the time we were living on the Costa Blanca, where they have beautiful beaches.

Just like with Sam, we thought we would first take a walk to see how he reacts to us and to Sam. And just like we did with Sam, we let him off the lead to see how well he listened. Pretty stupid, because he didn't listen at all. He looked at us once, turned and ran away. We spent the entire afternoon running after him with a number of people we had enjoyed Omar's birthday lunch with. He ran all around Denia and eventually found his old house again. He had run so fast and walked so far that he had broken the soles of his feet.

We received a call from the English couple, and they brought him back. We didn't dare let him off the lead for at least six months. It took a very long time before we actually got through to him. Actually made contact with him. His eyes remained empty. He thought we were quite nice, that wasn't it. But he just wanted to go home. Homesickness. We couldn't really leave him home alone. Then he tried everything to escape. He tried to dig through the wooden window frames. He crawled between the bars of a crate. He couldn't be contained. The funny thing was that as soon as he escaped he kept walking back and forth in front of the door. He didn't leave, but he didn't want to be inside the house all alone.

Fortunately for Manu, another move was coming. At first we went to Barcelona, but after a year we realized that that was not our Costa. Moreover, we were looking for our own business to run. We found that in Andalucía. We went to Granada to run a hostel. We also lived in the hostel ourselves and that was extremely good news for Manu. We were always at home. We lived at work and so did Manu. For ten years he was never alone.

But Granada has a different climate than the Costa Blanca. It can be below zero in Granada in winter. Manu was not used to that and even though he was half a husky, he was often cold. His teeth were literally chattering. So even though I had always said I would never walk a dog with a jacket, Manu and I went shopping together for a jacket. We went into a store and tried on all the jackets. It eventually became a coat, which was modelled on a horse blanket, because Manu was the size of a small horse.

Moving is always good to get more contact with your dog. That they realize that you are the constant factor and not the house. Plus a few months' trip through Morocco in a camper, that also helped. Manu and we had completely found each other, and he had changed from one extreme to the other. He had become the shadow type. Every step we took, he did too. All day long he followed us through the corridors of the hostel while cleaning. He also cooperated, because when we were at the back of the hallway, we didn't hear the telephone in the reception. Manu then started howling like a real husky, so that we knew the phone was ringing. He absolutely loved the hostel. He got attention from a lot of people all day long and could stick his nose in all kinds of suitcases. Every now and then someone came who was afraid of dogs. He thought that was so sad that he always wanted to comfort that person.

When I explained that to people, a large part of the fear was often gone. He has helped quite a few people get rid of their fear of dogs. It has often happened that a group of girls who came in screaming on Friday were on their knees around Manu on Sunday. And Manu on his back in the middle. Regularly. In October 2010, Sam, our first dog and Manu's big brother, passed away. Manu was an only child for a year, and he thought that was fantastic. Exactly one year later, October 2011, Oscar had a car accident in our street and Manu had a new brother. He didn't think that was necessary at all, but that's how things go.

Manu was about five years old when he developed a strange wart on the side of his rib cage. After the vet, Jose Carlos Cuerva Carvajal, removed it and examined it, it turned out to be a very aggressive form of skin cancer. Jose Carlos told us that he had about six months to live if we didn't do anything. So we started with treatment. And apparently the vet took exactly the right path, because Manu eventually died at the age of 15 in 2009 back on the Costa, the Costa Tropical this time. And I often tripped over the hole in the sky behind me, where he was no longer standing.

Sirius

By Jenny Skelton

FACEBOOK COULD BE DESCRIBED AS the good, the bad and the ugly. The Spanish rescue dog I was tagged in three years ago could certainly not be described as ugly. Indeed, he was beautiful. It must be said though that, although he is often good, if one were being unkind (or even truthful), one could also describe him as a little bit bad!

Sirius is a large dog (55kg) and, due to his size, the vet in Spain wrote Irish Wolfhound in his passport. Having had several rescue Irish Wolfhounds (and several injuries to show for it), I could see that he was no Irish Wolfhound – in fact, he looked just like a smallish, black bear. I had just lost an elderly dog, so a space had become available in my house – and my heart – for another rescue dog. I was intrigued by Sirius so, before I knew it, I had agreed to take him. I adore giant dogs and he had such a beautiful face; I just couldn't resist him. Here was the first problem – he was too big to travel in the normal pet transport vans. Suella, from Big Red's xxx, said that she would find a way to overcome that logistic hurdle and she took him to have his rabies vaccination, ready to be adopted. After a dog has had his rabies vaccination, there is a 21 day wait until he/she can leave the country. Having always been on the impulsive side, I decided that there was no way I could wait 21 days to meet Sirius, so I booked a flight and an apartment in Torrevieja to stay with him for a few days.

He was every bit as gorgeous as his photographs and we looked forward to a lovely break. Well, it would have been lovely, but the plane was diverted to a different airport because the original airport was on fire and then, a couple of days after we had arrived, Storm Gloria decided to pay a visit to Torrevieja. The 100km gales brought snow and torrential rain with her and destroyed many of the restaurants. We watched as tables, chairs, doors and windows were hauled across the closed beaches. It was like some kind of dystopian world. Our journey back to the UK was also delayed because the airport was shut but it opened just in time for our flight.

My disabled, adult daughter brought a teddy bear with her to Spain so that Sirius would not be the only bear in the apartment. Sirius was a perfect dog to spend a holiday with and we couldn't wait for him to be home with us. As good as her word, Suella arranged for her cousin to drive to Spain from the UK and then drive back to the UK with her, her teenage son and Sirius. She sent photos of their journey across the snow in France.

Sirius loved to spend his days lying outside in my garden. He still does, even when it is cold. I have a dog door so my dogs can just potter in and out of the garden whenever they wish. Sirius likes to lie just on the other side of the dog door so that the other dogs can't get in or out. He absolutely knows what he is doing – he just wants to be obstreperous. His first mischievous task was to teach one of my other rescue dogs, Milo, how to escape from the garden. My fence had been perfectly adequate before the black bear arrived from Spain. My garden backs on to five miles of countryside so, once they escaped, Sirius and Milo could run for hours. They had a brilliant time! They always came back home together – joyous, guilty, and completely out of breath. I live less than a mile from the sea and they were usually wet when they got home. I almost felt mean for curtailing their adventures. Sirius had arrived just as the world closed for Covid so there were no fencing companies available. I had to search my shed for anything which looked vaguely fence-like. I fastened anything I could to the existing fence panels. Along with wooden planks, there was an old iron bed, several baby gates, body boards and doors. Whatever makeshift repairs I made, Sirius found a way to get out, even chewing up bits of old iron. It was not until I eventually managed to get hold of a fencing expert that they stopped escaping.

I have had eleven rescue Irish Wolfhounds and, not long after Sirius arrived, one of them, Ben, died. Ben's passing opened up a space for a disabled, twelve-week-old Irish Wolfhound puppy, Logan. When Logan first arrived, Sirius very kindly showed him how to dig cavernous holes in my lawn, which is something Sirius had never done before. Cheers, Sirius!

Sirius is an unusual-looking dog, and I am constantly asked what breed he is. Shortly after he arrived, I had a DNA test carried out. He is actually a mixture of Czechoslovakian Wolf Dog, Great Dane, German Shepherd and Komondor but does not look like any of them. I suspect he is really a bear, but no one dare tell me.

Sirius is now four and, in the last year or so, he has decided he is not too keen on some other large dogs. He is not consistent with his dislike though, which makes things difficult. He has no problems with most of them and doesn't fight them but runs at them, barks, and then runs away. Understandably, other doggy people aren't exactly thrilled by this behaviour. I have sat him down and endlessly explained to him that the reason he has to wear a harness and be on a lead most of the time now is because of this non-endearing habit but he does not seem to be listening. If anyone is conversant with that illusive language 'Dog' or knows Dr Doolittle, please get in touch. I will be eternally grateful – and so will Sirius.

Raining cats and dogs Sunday, March 19, 2019

By Miriam Kooger

SCRATCH, SCRATCH, SCRATCH, SCRATCH, THE windshield wipers scrape across the car window. The downpour has stopped, and a pale sun is actually emerging. A beautiful sight, radiating through the trees of the narrow forest road. It is still quiet on this Sunday morning. I enjoy it.

In the distance I see the silhouette of the stable looming. As I approach the boarding stable I see the horses in the meadow. I turn into the yard and see that there are already 2 cars there. I think: 'They are early too.' Even though it's almost half past nine.

I get out of my car and walk into the stable. 'Hello,' I hear. The daughter of the stable owners has just come out of the indoor arena. Her mother is also present. A little further on I greet the old stable owner who is busy spreading the stables. I walk down the hall to the other exit and open the door. And there in the furthest meadow I can already see Carousse, my horse. I call her and she looks up. I walk over, but she has no intention of coming to me. I look thoughtfully at the meadow that has turned into a mud puddle. Of course I can't slip into the mud with my newly purchased riding shoes. Then get my rain boots.

Back in the stable, the old stable owner offers help and steps into the mud to get Carousse. Now she obediently follows behind him. What muddy legs, or actually feet. I give her a quick cleaning and saddle her up. I'm going to practice today; I'm looking forward to it. My horse gets a bit restless, but once in the saddle it disappears. I'm not alone, 2 other ladies have been riding for a while.

Drip, drip, I hear splashes on the roof. What unpredictable weather, a pale sun was just shining. Then the dripping starts to turn into a louder tapping, it sounds like hail. Carousse is getting restless, and I can feel the tension rising in her. The tapping now turns into a loud drumming sound. The other horses also become restless. I try to calm my horse down, but I feel the tension building even more. Maybe I should just get off for a while. But before I could do that it happened... a buck, another, and another. She is now so panicked by the crashing hailstones that she gives an explosion of punches one after the other. I don't stand a chance and fly through the air.

Thud, there I am, flat on my back. The pain shoots through me. I get cold and then I break out in a sweat. I feel like my lower back is on fire. I can no longer see what is happening around me. I feel something being placed under my head and the next moment I'm staring into the face of one of the 2 ladies who was riding just now. Shortly afterwards the stable owners are with me, and I also see the other person who was just riding bending down next to me.

Getting up is not an option and I hear the stable owner calling the ambulance. I feel like it will take forever for it to come. But then there it is, parking next to me in the courtyard. They immediately check whether I can still move everything and pffff, I can. I am lucky, I think, before they put in the IV with painkillers and everything becomes blurry. I barely feel them lift me up onto the stretcher and into the ambulance. Strapped up so I can't move my head.

The paramedics are talking to me. They tell me where we are driving and that we are going to the hospital, near my house. They don't care for horses and were glad there wasn't one around when they entered the arena. I try to put on a weak smile.

Before I know it, I'm in the hospital treatment room. The painkillers have done their work and I feel like I'm in some kind of twilight zone. My head is stuck and all I see is a boring hospital ceiling. Hospital staff introduce themselves left and right. I also know that the stable owner is there. A reassuring thought. My tight riding clothes are being tugged at and luckily they don't have to cut them. Photos are taken and we have to wait. Everything passes me by in a kind of daze.

Little by little I become clearer. A hospital employee comes to me and tells me it's not too bad. I have a stable fracture of my 3rd lumbar vertebra. A clean break so I don't have to have surgery. I do have to keep calm for the next 6 weeks. Do not bend or lift anything. Dressing and undressing myself is not an option. Pfff, I feel relief and sadness at the same time. 6 weeks... and what about my work and my horse I wonder. Well, let's get home first.

I try to get up, and my eyes go black. It is not easy with low blood pressure and having my head stuck for a long time. My neck feels like a tight cable that doesn't want to move to the right or left. Eventually I can lift myself into a wheelchair with help.

And now...? I have now been home for 2.5 weeks. Dependent and with nagging back pain, but with the house full of flowers and lots of visitors, phone calls and texts.

The reunion.

The days pass and flow silently into weeks. I miss Carousse. What she did was out of sheer stress, but with quite an impact. I don't blame her.

I let the car drive ahead and with help and some effort I manage to get into the passenger seat. The hustle and bustle of the passing cars full of crackling exhausts and loud music doesn't do me any good. I feel a migraine coming on.

We approach the stable and the tension rises. I slowly walk through the stable complex to the meadows. And then I see her. Her brown body shines in the sun, her white feet in the sand. I call her name and she turns around and raises her head. She neighs softly. I stumble towards her and melt. She presses her face against me, and I realize how special our bond still is

My name is Ziggy
and I know more stuff...
Part 2 by Paul Rane

ONE DAY THE OTHER NICE 2-legger who found us, came to visit. She was making sounds into a small flat thing she was holding in her paw. Then she pointed it at me a few times. I could see her paw tapping this flat thing.

When she had finished she made sounds to the other 2-legger. I didn't understand but it sounded like, "What are you going to call him?" Our 2-legger picked me up, looked into my eyes, looked at my sniffer and my big ears and sounded, "Ziggy is going to be his name, at least while he is here." The other 2-legger started tapping the flat thing again. The flat thing made a few funny pings. Her mouth moved, sounding like, "I think I've found you a Forever Home, Ziggy, in England."

I didn't understand but I thought it might be a good time to wag my handle and jump around for a bit. Both of the2 2-leggers made happy sounds.

After about 10 more feeds out of the shiny things, the bigger 2-legger came for me. She put some cloth around my neck and attached it to a long stringy thing. She then pulled, doing this made me follow her. So I had to trot along behind her. Her sounds were, "It's time to go on a long trip to meet your new mommy and daddy, say goodbye to foster mum Linda." Water came out of our 2-legger's eyes.

The tall 2-legger, also called Linda (why do humans have the same names?), took me to meet lots of dogs. Dogs crazier than me. They ran around me making loud dog noises, barking I think the 2-leggers call it. I started shaking a bit, I think I was scared.

It wasn't long before Tall Linda Human took me to a quieter area. There were only 2 dogs in this area and lots of other very furry small 4-leggers. They had pointy ears and handles that didn't wag and long whiskers. My sniffer was twitchy, and I thought I should run around them. The other two dogs just ignored these little creatures, so I thought I should also. So I ignored my sniffer and looked at Tall Linda Human blankly. Her sound was, "Ziggy, this is Blondie," pointing to the older looking of the 2 dogs, "and this is Tommy." Tommy pushed and shoved me and stuck his sniffer in my ear, Blondie just walked away.

I ran around and played with Tommy for a bit, when we did this, instead of running with us, those little furry things scattered in all directions. I don't know why they didn't want to play with Tommy and me.

When the shiny things were put down later that day, I didn't stand a chance. All the barking dogs and Tommy ate the food stuff so quickly. They slurped and licked and made lots of loud eaty sounds, I couldn't get near. I thought my tummy was going to rumble a lot now, and wanted to go home to Short Linda Human.

I had just started to make sad noises, when the crazy dogs were shoo'd out of the area. Two shiny things were put down for me and Blondie. I learnt that Blondie was too old to eat with the crazies and I was too small. So we had our food stuff together, just me and Blondie. This is how Blondie, and I became playmates. She was very old and didn't run as fast or as much as me and Tommy.

But she didn't chase the little furry things like the crazies did. So I didn't either. I think the furry things are called cats. I know this because Tall Linda Human often sounds at the crazies to, "Leave the cats alone!" I live with a furry cat thing now, but that story is for later.

Tommy and Blondie's Daddy Human is called Pete. He patted and stroked me when he saw me. He sounded about my big ears, like lots of humans I meet, "Oh look at those ears, I suppose he'll grow into them." I think this is because my ears are as long as my sniffer. Pete Human is kind and helps with the food stuff in the shiny things, he also cleans up the crazies and my toilet business. There are a lot of crazies, so this takes a long time. Pete Human has a lot of time for us and our doings.

The next day Tall Linda Human and Pete Human kept going from their shelter to a smaller shelter carrying all sorts of stuff. Then Tommy, Blondie and I were put into the small shelter. This small shelter had only two rooms, two seats at the front with a big round thing in front of one of them. It had a long seat and a food stuff maker. If all the crazies come in here, I thought, it would be very crowded.

I decided this was a new adventure and made a few high-pitched dog noises, I wagged my handle and bounced around. Pete Human strapped us in and climbed behind the big round thing at the front. Tall Linda Human sounded, "We are going to England now, Ziggy to your forever home. It will take about a week, so be a good boy and settle down like Tommy and Blondie." I had no idea what she meant but I was very happy and excited and wagged my handle a lot.

My excitement may have been because when the shelter started moving I could see that the crazies and the furry creatures weren't coming with us.

Borre the cat and other stories
By Doutzen Ouderkerken

INTRODUCTION

I AM BORRE THE CAT and I live with Bep in a house that is quite big. That's nice, then you can walk up and down the stairs. I also have a cat basket, but I don't really like it. I'd much rather lie on the couch. But Bep doesn't like that. Then I have to vacuum the couch every day, she says and sends me off the couch again. So annoying. And then she calls me a hairball. Ridiculous, I think cats should sleep on couches.

Well, there are more things that I find annoying about Bep. I love food. Nothing wrong with that, right? I get food in the morning and evening. And only drinking water, so strange. She doesn't just drink water, does she? I like a bowl of whipped cream every now and then. Or mayonnaise or chicken nuggets.

I'm going to tell you what I've been experiencing. These could also be stories from my family. Other cats have also lived with Bep, and they have experienced all kinds of things. Girls also come to Bep sometimes.

Their names are Freya and Elin, those are her grandchildren. It is always very nice when the grandchildren come because then I can play with them. Well, they play, and I lie down with them. Then I am regularly petted, and I am often allowed to sit on their lap. I like that. Cats and more animals also live with Freya and Elin. They experience lots of things.

BORRE TO THE DENTIST

You will never believe what I have experienced this week. It really happened.

As you know, we cats never go to the dentist. We also never brush our teeth. We don't have toothbrushes and we can't hold them. And how do we cats get toothpaste? Our humans don't take care of that. We cats have to see for ourselves how we take care of our teeth. That went completely wrong for me. I had often told Bep that I had a sore mouth. But she doesn't understand me and so I walked around with sore molars for months.

Until one day Bep scratched my head. I usually like that very much, but she touched my sore molars and I suddenly screamed loudly. It hurt so much.

"This is not good," said Bep, "I will call the vet tomorrow."

Oh dear, I thought, that's wrong. Do I have to go back into such a small basket and then a doctor will look in my ears again and listen to my heart and then they often also put a thermometer in my poop hole. And that feels so strange. And it doesn't matter whether I hiss hard or something, the doctor just does what he wants.

And yes, Bep put me in a basket that was much too small and put me in the car. I screamed with all my might that I didn't want to go to the doctor and that I wasn't sick at all and that my molars no longer hurt, and that Bep was being very annoying. "Shut up shouting," Bep said over and over again.

We got to the doctor and Bep put me on a chair and sat next to me. We had to wait a while. I started screaming again but Bep again told me to keep my mouth shut. Through the cracks of my basket I saw a dog. He looked so silly and did nothing at all. It was quite a big dog. If I were him I would run away. But no, that idiot just stayed put.

Then a voice shouted: "Borre!" Oh dear, that's me, I thought. This isn't going to go well. Bep picked up my basket and walked with the doctor. Bep put me on a high table and opened the basket door. I had to get out. Well, no, I said, first you put me in that basket and then I will definitely have to get out on my own. But Bep tilted the cage so much that I slipped out.

"There you are," said the doctor. "Hello, Borre." Hello, now I definitely have to act nice, no way, I'm going to scream, I said to the doctor, but he didn't understand me either. And he grabbed my ears, turned them inside out, looked into my eyes, pulled my tail, pushed the thermometer into my poop hole and said I had a little fever. What is that? "No fever," said Bep. The doctor listened to my heart, but I started purring very loudly and then he heard nothing. I liked it. But yes, I came for my toothache and now my mouth had to be opened. The doctor opened my mouth and said, "Oh dear, that doesn't look good. Watch." Bep also looked into my mouth pretending she knows anything about it. Not so.

"We have to do something about that," said the doctor, "he has a serious infection there. He should come back and then we will see under anaesthesia what is going on. We may have to pull out some molars."

Whoa, whoa, I meowed for a moment. Do I have anything else to say? They are my molars even though they hurt. But no matter how I raged, Bep made an appointment for the day I had to return and to make matters worse, I also had to take very nasty pills against the inflammation. And a painkiller, that was nice. My molars didn't hurt so much anymore.

The day came when I had to go to the doctor again. So a dentist. Freya and Elin also go to the dentist sometimes, but I never hear about anaesthesia and dirty pills or something for the pain. I do not understand. Bep didn't give me anything to eat either. "You have to be sober," she said. Being sober? Doesn't that have to do with alcohol? I don't drink alcohol and am always sober.

"Being sober means that you are not allowed to eat or drink on the day you have to go under anaesthesia," Bep said. What nonsense, I want to eat. And without food I was put back in that basket where I can't turn my butt and Bep put me back in the car. I was already expected at that dentist there. Bep spoke briefly with a doctor, and she said that if molars had to be extracted, then so be it. Well, I ask you, I would have to decide that about her. She would scream bloody murder if I said the dentist could pull molars. No matter how much I meowed and screamed, it didn't help. Bep said goodbye to me, good luck and she was gone. I was taken by a doctor and taken out of the basket. "There, Borre," said a very nice lady. She looked friendly. "We are going to take a look at your teeth and get them in order." I squeaked a little, because I didn't want to act like a baby. But I would have preferred to run away really fat.

I got an injection in the scruff of my neck and felt completely weird in my head. I thought what was happening, but the light went out, it was dark, and I was sleeping. I woke up in a cage again and I felt bad. Terrible, pain in my head and nauseous and my mouth hurt. And there were cats around me. And there is nothing worse in the world than other cats. How I hate cats. They want to play or fight with you and then they jump on your neck, and you have to like that. Well, not me, I don't like it, other cats. What posers. That's why I live alone with Bep. Bep wanted to have another cat, she said it was for fun, but I bullied her away. And so luckily I live alone with Bep again. And sometimes that's hard enough.

The people at the doctor were also very nice. Suddenly I was put back in that little basket and the nice doctor said that Bep was there to take me home. I was still so dizzy and sleepy that I thought it was fine. The doctor sat me on the counter and Bep pressed her face close to the basket.

"Hi, darling, how are you?" I didn't say anything back, I couldn't think. "He is still a bit drowsy from the anaesthesia," the doctor said. "We pulled two molars and removed tartar and brushed and polished the teeth. And the inflammation is already a lot less, the pills do help," said the doctor. Hey, hey,

I squeaked, what happened? I do not understand anything about it. It felt very strange in my mouth. But it also hurt less. Maybe I'd gotten rid of my toothache. But I didn't know that for sure at the time.

"He can have some soft food again tonight," the doctor said, "because he may still be very nauseous, and he may vomit. There may be some blood there, but that comes from his mouth." What is that person talking about? I thought. Horrible, vomit and blood? Is that me? Help, I want to go home and sleep. Bep, get me out of here, I squeaked. I didn't like it anymore. We went home and Bep put the basket in the room and opened the door. I couldn't even think of what to do. "Come out, Borre," said Bep. I stood up slowly and it felt strange. My legs were very wobbly. My ass felt very heavy. I carefully got out of the basket and tried to walk away, but I felt so strange that I fell over. The whole room spun around me. I saw Bep three times. That didn't get any better.

What was wrong with me? And I was nauseous, I didn't even want to eat. I tried to walk a bit, but my backside didn't cooperate, and I fell over again. I stood up again and now I stayed upright. I carefully walked through the room, but I was so tired that I stopped again after a few steps. This will never work out again, I thought. What a situation. It was so difficult to walk that I lay down.

"Poor, Borre," said Bep, "you are still suffering from the anaesthesia. Well, we just have to work that out first." And then suddenly I felt so nauseous and had to vomit. Damn, that smelled, and my mouth hurt. "Oh, oh, what the heck," said Bep and cleaned up the place. I didn't know what to do. I tried to jump on the couch, but I fell over onto my back. Now I ask you. And that happened twice. I felt terrible so I went to sleep. And after a few hours I woke up and felt a lot better. I could walk normally again without falling over and I was no longer nauseous.

And the best thing was that I almost no longer had a toothache. It still felt a bit strange in my mouth, but it was a lot better. And you know what else happened that day? Freya's loose tooth came out. This happens with human children when they are about six. Then the teeth fall out of their mouths, and they grow large human teeth. And the same day, Elin told Bep to brush my teeth with a small toothbrush. It was a day of teeth and teeth. I don't think that should happen too often. And I'd rather not have Bep brushing my teeth. She's crazy enough for it. I don't like that.

I'm doing well again now. Bep tells me to stay inside, that's what the doctor said. And the food should be soft. Now Bep has bought me some very tasty food, but she then puts that nasty pill in it. I don't get anything else, so I have no choice but to swallow it all. It's not that bad. The drink against the pain is tasty and that makes the food taste good again. It will be okay. We'll make it, Bep and me.

DIRK FALLS INTO THE WATER

I would like to introduce myself. I'm Dirk. I live with the little daughters, you know, Freya and Elin. Their mom and dad also live there, and Pelle, a very fat red cat, and Lytse, a thin cat who always screams for food, and Mopus, a very old cat of 18 years old who pees everywhere. But she can't help that she is really very old. I like her a lot, she sits still a lot and then you can jump on top of her, so much fun. She doesn't like that because when I jump on her, she screams hard. Unbelievable. And then she just falls over.

Mom and dad, as well as Freya and Elin, keep telling me not to tease Mopus, but that's not teasing, I just want to play. Bep, you know her, from Borre, also goes crazy when I want to play with Mopus. Then she hits me with a tea towel. Sends me outside even when it rains. You can't play with Pelle, he can be so grumpy, and that's no use to you. But he was in a car accident and now his backside hurts when you touch him there. So it's not nice to jump on top of him unexpectedly. And nothing can be done with Lytse. She just wants to eat all day. And she doesn't want to play, she hits me around the ears. That is not nice.

Fortunately, there are also chickens, and they sometimes walk in the garden. You can really chase after them nicely. But you shouldn't get too close to them, or they'll peck you in the head. I can sit quietly with the rabbit for a while. We sit next to each other and have a chat. Well, a chat, he sniffs a bit and I meow a bit. It's nice. He has a nice field of hay, and you can sleep wonderfully in it. The rabbit's food doesn't taste like anything, such strange hard chunks. I'll just let that pass me by.

Anyway, I'll tell you a story. Not that fun for me, but Bep laughed so hard when she heard it and she said she was going to write a story about it. She also wanted to do the same about Borre, but luckily Borre tells his stories himself. Because that Bep is a real piece of work. She looks after Freya and Elin every week, so I see her often. She often gives me food, which is nice. But I'm not allowed to sleep on the beds, they're for people, she says. And I can't tease Mopus. That's why I often sleep when she's there. We don't bother each other. She likes me because every week she says she wants to take me to her house. I can play nicely with Borre. I do not think so. There are no chickens there and there is no rabbit either. But she does pet me a lot and that's nice.

Where I live you can play outside very nicely. A large garden with many shrubs and trees. And lots of beautiful places to lie in the sun and take a nap. And then of course there are the chickens. At the end of the garden there's a kind of pond, it is actually a ditch. Dad made that. There are a lot of frogs in there. And all kinds of other strange aquatic animals. And lots of frogspawn. That's dirty stuff, thick green sludge.

Adults can easily walk across the pond, but Freya and Elin walk on a shelf. Pelle and Lytse also walk over that. You can jump over it, but you have to do it right, of course. And pay close attention in advance to how you jump and such. And that went completely wrong once. I was chasing something, a bird or a butterfly or a chicken or a cat, I forget. In any case, I ran really hard through the garden. I must say that I was still very young. About six months. Well then you are just a primary school child if you compare that with human children. So I was running after something and wasn't paying attention. You can't do two things at the same time, only girls, big and small, can do that. Men can't do that and I'm a man.

So I ran towards the ditch with a vengeance. Actually, I forgot there was a ditch. You have that when you are little, you still have to learn that you have to remember things. And what happens? I ran and ran and ran and then the grass ended, and the water started, and you can't walk on that. At least, I don't. And I went under. So I was just a young tomcat and I had never had a bath or shower.

Children sometimes do that with pets. Then they think that we as animals like to take a bath. So no, we pets, especially cats, don't like water! I just want to say that now, no cats in the shower or in the bath. We don't like it! I went under. And if I say I went under, I mean I went under. I was going so fast that I ended up at the bottom of that ditch. Cats always land on their feet and that's true. So I stood at the bottom under water, and I didn't know where I was. I thought this will never be okay again.

Because it's filthy there on that bottom under water. All kinds of dirty animals and plants that crawl around your head and frogs and frogspawn and flies and lice, what a mess. I thought, I have to get out, I have to get out. I started kicking and kicking with my feet and sure enough, my head surfaced again. I could see again. But what I saw wasn't nice. Frogspawn floated around my head and crawled up my nose and that dirty water was in my mouth. And I had all these strange plants hanging from my ears.

I have to climb out, I thought. Come on, Dirk, you can do it, I told myself. And with a lot of pain and effort I climbed onto the side. And wet I was. The water was running out of my fur and out of my ears and dripping down my tail. And then Freya and Elin came running. "Oh, Dirk, what have you done?" they shouted. "You're all wet." As if I didn't know that myself, I meowed, I fell into the water. But of course they didn't understand me. The mother arrived.

"What happened?"

"Dirk fell into the pond," said the little daughters.

"Wow," said the mother, "I can see that. And boy, does it stink. I don't want him in there like that. It just needs to dry out a bit first."

But I'm stone cold, I meowed, I need to sit down in front of the wood stove. My ears are freezing off. And I have frogspawn in my mouth and my tail is really wet. But the mom didn't want me to come in. "Go into the rabbit's hutch, there is nice hay there, you can dry a bit first," says the mother. The little daughters did not agree with the mother.

"You have to dry him," they said. "Bep always does that when Borre has been rained wet. Then he is completely dried, his legs and his head and his ears and his tail and the back otherwise he'll have a cold tomorrow."

"Cats don't catch colds," said the mom. "Anyway, I'll dry him off. But it smells terribly." Mom dried me off and I was allowed to sit in front of the stove. But no one wanted to pet me.

"He smells so bad," said Freya and Elin and Mom and Dad. But Elin said, "I'm a bit angry with Dirk." I understand that, but my dear, you still want to pet me! Well no, that was very stupid. Mom said, "You should have watched out; it was your own fault."

What kind of nonsense is that? It's the fault of that something or thing I was running after. The world isn't fair I had to stay inside the next day as punishment, which wasn't fun. I went to play with Mopus that day. She didn't like that very much. She screeched like a suckling pig and fell over. That is very irritating and that is why I went to Lytse. She wasn't paying attention because she was washing herself. I thought she might like a surprise attack. I just jumped on her back. Just like Mopus she screeched like a suckling pig. Wow, but instead of running away she fought back. I was much stronger, so I still won.

But my mother dragged me away from her and scolded me. The next day I was allowed to go outside again. This time I paid close attention, I thought that was smart. Then I took a nap in the hay with the rabbit. Then Freya called me, "It's time to eat, Dirk." I was immediately wide awake and sprinted towards her. I like food very much. I sometimes secretly push Mopus, Lytse or Pelle aside and then I eat their bowls. Now I'm going to take a nap like real men should do. Good night!

CAT ON THE ROOF

Have I ever told you the story of my Uncle Redje who kept walking on the roof? No? Well, that was a piece of work. Bep always says I'm a fat cat, but my Uncle Redje was really a fat cat. And I say that, while I think that cats can be a bit sturdy. Do you know why his name was Redje? Because it was a ginger cat. And redje means little ginger in Dutch. Uncle Redje passed away some time ago. I know his stories. He also lived with Bep.

Bep was still living in another house at the time. That house had a flat roof. The house was in a row of ten houses in a block. There were tall trees around it and as you know, we cats love to climb trees. You can then look around you very well. When we walk on the ground we only see the legs and wheels of bicycles and cars and small children who want to pull your tail or pet you wrong. And from the top of a tree you can have a good view of the street and the gardens.

Sometimes things go wrong when a cat climbs a tree. Especially if you don't know what to look for. Then you sit at the top of a tree on a thin branch, and you can't go back. That is very annoying. The fire brigade sometimes comes to get a cat out of a tree. Then you feel ashamed that as a cat you can't even get out of a tree yourself. You have to use your head when you climb a tree.

One day when the wind was blowing hard, Uncle Redje climbed a tree to take a look around. He climbed higher and higher, and the branches became thinner and thinner. He wasn't paying attention to where he was and at one point he couldn't get back. Now Uncle Redje couldn't meow. He had been very ill as a newborn kitten and his vocal cords no longer worked. Bep always liked that very much, she found it nice and quiet.

"Finally a cat that doesn't scream," she always said. But Uncle Redje was a bit scared there in that tree. He opened and closed his mouth, but no sound came out. So no one noticed that he was at the top of that tree. And what happened then? There came a strong gust of wind and the branch that Uncle Redje was sitting on swayed back and forth. Back and forth so hard that Uncle Redje had to hold on to the branch with all his might. But that wasn't enough. The wind started to blow even harder, and the branch swung back and forth so hard that Uncle Redje could no longer hold on. He flew through the air and in a large arc he landed on the flat roof of the corner house. He was a little dizzy and nauseous from fright and sat completely dazed at first. Of course he had landed on his feet because cats always do that.

Finally, he recovered from the shock. He looked around and walked carefully to the edge of the roof. He looked over the edge and saw the children playing. He knew all the children on the street. And all the children knew Uncle Redje. He also sometimes walked into other people's homes, but that's another story. Uncle Redje opened and closed his mouth again to meow, but no sound came out. He looked at the tree and saw that he had to make a very large jump to get back into the tree and to descend again. How did he get down again? Uncle Redje started walking further. He walked to the house in the middle where he lived with Bep. Bep had two daughters who also lived with her. Those daughters were very happy with Uncle Redje. They cuddled and petted him a lot and sometimes he also slept in their bed. But Bep didn't know that. Bep says cats are not allowed to sleep in your bed.

"Cats belong in baskets," she says.

So Uncle Redje walked back and forth on the roof and kept looking over the edge of the roof at the children. Suddenly one of the children saw Uncle Redje walking back and forth on the roof.

"Look, Redje is walking on the roof! Look! How does he get there?" All the children looked up, including Bep's daughters. They were very shocked. "Red, come down, what are you doing there?" What a situation, Uncle Red just walked back and forth along the edge of the roof and didn't know what to do. And neither did the children on the street.

"We're going to get Mommy," the daughters shouted, because Bep was of course their mommy.

"Mom, Mom, Redje is on the roof and can't get off! You have to take him off."

"What is going on?" Bep asked. "What a commotion here, what happened?"

"Redje walks on the roof, and he can't get off. You have to get him off with the ladder!"

Bep walked outside and the children pointed to the roof where Uncle Redje was just looking down over the edge.

"Fool," Bep shouted, "what are you doing there? Come down. How can you possibly end up on the roof?"

Uncle Redje said that he had climbed the tree and that the wind had thrown him onto the roof, but Bep did not understand that. She doesn't understand how cats talk and besides, Uncle Redje didn't make a sound.

"Mommy, you have to climb to the roof with the ladder and pick him up," the daughters said.

"I'm afraid of heights," said Bep, "I get nauseous when I stand on a ladder. I can't even hang up party streamers, I get dizzy."

"Mom, we have to, Red can't stay there."

Bep sighed deeply and they all walked to the ladder to lean it against the house. Luckily it was a ladder that you could extend and so it reached the edge of the roof. And then Bep had to climb the ladder.

"I think it's so scary," said Bep and she looked white around her nose.

"We are holding the ladder," said all the children and Bep slowly started to climb up the ladder.

The children shouted, "Red, Red, come over here."

For the first time in his life, Uncle Redje listened and walked to the edge and saw Bep carefully climbing the ladder. Suddenly Bep's head came over the edge of the roof and she said in a trembling voice, "Come here, Red, and I will get you off the roof." Uncle Redje didn't like it. If Bep didn't hold him properly he could fall down. Uncle Redje carefully walked to Bep's head, and she grabbed him by his flea collar. Uncle Redje braced himself and tried to walk backwards. "Stupid cat, this way, come on, we're going down," Bep shouted.

She pulled and pulled and finally she had pulled Uncle Redje over the edge of the roof by his flea collar and Uncle Redje was dangling back and forth like a dishcloth. Bep swung Uncle Redje back and forth and then hugged him under one arm and carefully started to climb down the ladder. The children were constantly shouting over each other. Then Bep stood back on the ground and handed Redje to the eldest daughter.

"I'm shaking all over," said Bep, "what an idiot that cat is. This was once, but never again. I find it so scary on that ladder."

Uncle Redje was completely upset. He wanted to be released as quickly as possible and get his coat in order. He jumped out of the eldest daughter's arms and took off like a hare. He ran out of the garden and down the alley and hid in the bushes. The children ran after him and kept shouting. I'm going to stay here, Uncle Redje thought, and only come out when everyone has left. But yes, cats love food and Uncle Redje got hungry. He emerged carefully and walked home, looking around. The daughters and Bep were eating there, and they were happy that Uncle Redje was back. Bep said nothing and just looked angrily at Uncle Redje.

And if you now think the story is over, you are wrong. The next day, Uncle Redje thought it was quite nice on top of the roof and that it wasn't too bad how Bep had gotten him off. She hadn't dropped him. What did Uncle Redje do the next week? He climbed the same tree again, waited until he swung back and forth on the same branch as the first time and landed on the roof again in a nice arc. He paced back and forth, occasionally looking over the edge of the roof. The weather was nice, and the sun shone brightly. Until of course he wanted to get off the roof again. Then he started walking back and forth along the edge again until the children playing below saw him. And again Bep climbed the ladder grumbling and again the children were shouting among themselves and again Uncle Redje was pulled over the edge of the roof by his flea collar and Bep brought him down. This happened again the following week. Then Bep had had enough.

"That's it," she said. "As far as I'm concerned, he'll be there for the rest of his life. I'm not climbing that ladder again." The children got angry and shouted all kinds of things again. Animal cruelty, and they threatened to call the fire brigade and the police, and they wouldn't go in until Redje was off the roof.

"I don't mind," said Bep and she went to drink tea and read the newspaper.

Do you know how Uncle Redje got off the roof? He walked back and forth for a long time until he realized that Bep would not take him off the roof this time. He took a very long run and jumped into the tree with a gigantic leap. The children saw him fly through the air and with cheering, Uncle Redje landed correctly and sank down neatly on his legs.

"See?" said Bep. "A cat always lands on its feet."

BORRE IN THE CONCRETE

I'm having a bit of a problem the past few weeks. They renovated the street. All the asphalt was removed, and the sidewalks turned upside down. A lot of workmen and big cars and smell and noise, you don't want to know. I couldn't even just cross the street to go to my regular poop bush. Men were busy everywhere and dangerous things stood in my way everywhere.

Bep also grumbled that it was a disgrace. They had just closed the street and she couldn't leave in the car. She had to babysit Freya and Elin and she couldn't leave. She called the gentleman who arranged the work and told him she was very angry. She should have had a letter in the mailbox, but she didn't get it. And if Bep is angry, just brace yourself. She's been stewing all day. I just kept calm, before you know it you'll get the full brunt.

Until one day I sank into the concrete. Then Bep grumbled again that it was a disgrace. I'm a cat, what do I know about concrete? It went like this. The streets were finished and now those workers were going to renovate the pavement. They first removed the old asphalt with a lot of noise and din. It stank and there was nowhere I could go for a walk. Bep had said that it was not wise to go outside.

"You'll soon be run over by those big trucks," she said. "Just stay inside and use the litter box."

Not great, I still want to go outside every day and get some fresh air. And actually I also wanted to know what was happening in the street. Before you know it you have nowhere to go. You have to keep an eye on things. Moreover, there were large piles of sand everywhere. And what could be more beautiful than a mountain of sand in which you can dig and take a pee. But the men who restored the sidewalks didn't like that at all. Once, while I was digging again, a shovel of sand fell over me. "Get out," shouted a road worker. I was very shocked. You don't do that with a cat. The asphalt had been removed from the walking path and I went to see what happened next. There was some gray stuff on the path, and it looked neat.

I'll take a walk on that, I thought. I stepped on that gray stuff and then I sank. You don't want to know what that felt like, I was scared shitless. I meowed, get me out of here, I'm drowning! No one came to help me. My legs sank further and further. I was already in that mess up to my stomach. I meowed and screamed and squeaked that I wanted to get out.

Finally, I managed to get to the side, into the grass. I looked at my legs and my belly, I was completely gray. That wasn't the worst. That stuff got hard and dry and it was very, very heavy. I could hardly walk anymore. I tried to wash but it was impossible. And it tasted bad, really bad. It made me feel sick. I decided to go home. Maybe Bep has a solution, I thought. When Bep saw me her eyes became as big as saucers.

"Borre, what have you done? Where have you been? My goodness, this is concrete."

"Did you sink into something?"

Yes, Bep, I meowed, cleverly observed. Isn't that how you see it? I don't have gray legs or a gray belly, do I? And it is so hard and also very heavy. Do something about it.

"You should take a shower," Bep said. I didn't think so, I meowed and tried to run away. Bep was faster, I couldn't run as fast anymore with all that heavy stuff on my body. Bep picked me up and walked me to the shower. And no matter how much I screamed and meowed, Bep turned on the shower and water poured over me. And as you know, we cats don't like water. Bep tried with all her might to clean my legs and my belly. I struggled and growled and bit Bep in the hands and arms. And then she got angry.

"I just want to help you, you wimp, stop it," she shouted. I didn't stop. And I won this time.

"Then you better get yourself clean, you silly cat!"

Bep sounded very angry. I was wrapped in a towel, and she dried me off. The concrete stayed on my legs and my stomach. When I was reasonably dry, Bep took me downstairs and put me in the room.

"You stay inside for now," she said, still angry. "Look what you did!"

She held her hands out for me to see. I didn't see anything special.

"I'm bleeding," Bep said indignantly. "I just wanted to help you."

I walked to my food bowl. Let's eat first. Then let's see again. And Bep fussed and grumbled and said she was leaving. She still sounded angry. As long as I get something to eat, I thought. If I'm not allowed to go outside, I have to get enough food from Bep. You have to plan ahead. It took a week before the concrete was somewhat off my body. I've been washing all day.

It's not easy being a cat.

BORRE AND THE GUINEA PIGS

The little daughters Freya and Elin go on holiday. What does that mean for me, Borre? I'll tell you. Bep has two small stools ready, and something will be placed on them. I'm not happy with that. After all, I live in this house with Bep, and I think I help decide who walks in and out. Well not so. When people come here, it's sort of acceptable, but when other animals come, I'm not happy.

"Caramel and Odette are coming to stay," says Bep. "Those are Elin and Freya's guinea pigs. And their cage will be right here." Bep points to the stools.

I don't like it and walk outside. When I come back inside, there is a huge cage on the stools. I meow at Bep and ask what this has been like. "Look, there are the guinea pigs," says Bep, "they will stay for a week." Now we will see what happens. For sure I am not allowed in the room anymore, I have to stay outside all week and that kind of nonsense. I walk to the cage and try to look inside.

"Oh no, Borre, don't do that, be careful!" says Bep in her stern voice. Okay, I know I can't do that again because Bep is going crazy, and you don't want that. Then I stay outside for a whole day and only come out when she has calmed down again. Usually late at night when I have to come in. There isn't much to those animals, they eat all day and run around in that cage. In the evening, Bep takes them out and then she strokes first one guinea pig and then the other. "Otherwise they go wild," says Bep. I guess, I don't know anything about guinea pigs. That food is what we want to talk about. You know that Bep keeps telling me that I am getting too fat and that I am not getting more food than necessary. Those guinea pigs eat a lot!

A mountain of hay in the morning and evening, vegetables twice a day, a bowl of chunks and another bottle of water. And do you know how small they are? I'm ten times bigger and do you think I get that much food? Well, I don't like vegetables and those chunks are also hard to chew. What I have also noticed is that one guinea pig is calmer than the other. There's a white one with red eyes, so weird. Her name is Odette, and it belongs to Freya. The other is brown and black and is called Caramel and belongs to Elin. That white one is a weird one. He always wants to sit in the same corner of the cage. And when Caramel is there, Odette jumps on top of Caramel and squeaks and screams and makes noise as if the world is ending. Caramel then goes back to sit in the other corner. Well, I wouldn't have done that. I would have started fighting a bit. I wouldn't let myself be sent away.

I was sleeping on the couch and there was a racket in that cage again. It woke me up. I'll just have to see what's going on, I thought. I stood in front of the cage and asked what was going on. Fortunately, the guinea pigs understand me, that's convenient. Bep doesn't understand me, or she doesn't try.

"I'm not allowed to sleep in that corner," said Caramel, "then she always jumps on me," and she pointed to Odette.

"I just want to sit in that corner, I like that," Odette replied.

"What nonsense," I said, "there are still three corners, why exactly in that corner?"

"Because I like that angle, that's why," Odette said and turned to the wall.

"You see, there's no reasoning with her." Caramel looked at me and if she could have shrugged, she would have. I meowed for a moment that I thought it was ridiculous and went back to my pillow on the couch. Caramel went to sleep in the other corner. I also asked how they felt about me.

"We are used to cats, we have five: Pelle, Lytse, Skrebbel, Nemo and Leon," says Caramel. I almost fell over in surprise. What a lot of cats together, I don't like cats.

"And do they bother you too?" I ask.

"No. They leave us alone and we leave them alone," Odette replies. "It's just that sometimes we don't get caressed enough. Because Freya and Elin also have to pet those cats. And they have to go to school and pony rides and pole sports and plays. And then they have to play on the computer and on the phone, sometimes we have to scream loudly for attention. Because a hug from time to time is very nice." Caramel says, "Yes, we need cuddles twice a day, at least. Those cats could use a little less attention."

"Ho ho," I say, "I don't agree with you. Cats have just as much right to attention as you do. After all, we are a lot bigger, and you need more attention."

I don't think I should have said that because those two guinea pigs stand against the cage and start talking and squeaking and screaming at the same time. Bep comes in and sees me standing by the cage. She doesn't understand that I'm talking to Odette and Caramel and that we don't agree about petting and cuddling and such. She probably thinks Odette and Caramel are afraid of me.

"Borre, what did I tell you, don't come near the guinea pigs. Go away you!" Bep sounds strict and sends me away. See, that's what I mean. I didn't do anything, and I'm being sent away again... That's great. I see Caramel and

Odette grinning and sticking their tongues out at me. At least that's how it looks. Then they both go to sleep in their corner, and I have to go outside.

A STORY ABOUT THE CAT THAT WAS LOCKED UP

Every now and then the little children, Freya and Elin, come to stay with Bep. That is always very pleasant. Then I get a lot of petting and cuddles and I can always sit on a lap. Especially with Elin, who really likes that. Only Elin's lap is not very big. My butt always dangles next to it or there is no room for my head. After a while I've had enough.

Bep doesn't want me to sit on her lap all day. Weird, right? I try again and again, but Bep puts me back on the floor after a while. I'm not allowed on the couch either, it's new and Bep doesn't want all my hair coming off. And she also says I'm so heavy on her lap. Always complaining about my weight.

Cats should actually be outside at night. We are nocturnal animals. Personally, I don't like being outside at night. It is often cold and when it rains you cannot lie down under a bush. It then drips onto your head or back. Nothing to it. I like sleeping inside at night. I would prefer to be in bed with Bep, but that is not allowed. Beds are for people and not for cats, Bep always says. Cats have baskets, people don't. So you sleep in your basket in your own room at night. And do you know what my own room is? The hall. Now I ask you. My basket is also in the hall where the coat rack is. And the litter box. Anyway, I'm not complaining, otherwise Bep will just put me outside at night, even when it rains. I'm not looking forward to that. Because no matter how loud I scream, she won't get out of bed to let me in. There are often other cats outside at night and they want to fight. Or they come into my garden, and I don't want that. Then we start shouting at each other and then people start getting out of bed in the middle of the night and shouting, "Shhh, shhhh," out the bedroom window. That's no fun either.

Now Bep had put me back in the hall that evening. The next morning I heard the little children and Bep coming downstairs. I thought, they'll open the door and then I can go eat again. Bep never leaves food and drinks in my hall at night. So weird. I could starve to death, right? I sat there waiting and waiting, no one came to open the door. I heard Bep ask what the little children wanted to eat. And that they had to hurry because Freya had to do a dressage test on a pony. I don't know what that is, but I think it was exciting.

I screamed and meowed very loudly: I'm sitting here, let me out. I want to eat as well. Nobody heard me. I also really needed to poop, and I prefer to do that under my own bushes near the parking lot. I couldn't hold it anymore, so I went into the litter box. If I make a lot of noise and start to stink, I thought, they will come and open the door. I started digging very hard in the litter box and it started to smell really bad. Bep has food that doesn't make me stink, but as you know, I sometimes eat out and that's food that does make you stink. I dig and smell - nothing. No one came and the door remained closed.

Now I meowed loudly again. I started hitting the door. I always do that when I'm outside and I want to go inside. Sometimes Bep just leaves me outside. Yes, I often walk back and forth. If I've been outside for five minutes, I often want to go back inside. That happens regularly. I like walking back and forth, out the front door, around the block, and back in through the back door. Nothing wrong with that, right? Bep says she is not my servant. Then she leaves the door open, right? I don't burn the heater for the tulips, she says. What she means by that, I don't know. And how did this end? When they had to leave for the pony exam they heard me. Elin anyway. "Bep, Borre is still inside. You forgot him!" "My goodness," said Bep, "that poor animal." Never thought about it again. Now I ask you. Have you lived together for ten years and then they forget about you? I'm not even allowed to eat with the neighbours, and she forgets about me. "We have to leave now," Bep said. "But he still has to eat," Freya says. "I'll put it outside," Bep said. She put out my food and drinks and they left. Of course I wasn't allowed to come along again. I ate everything immediately, you never know. Other cats also come into my garden, and you will see that when I walk around the block they eat my food.

Bep was still complaining that I had smelled bad again. "I'll clean up when we get home," she said. What a stench. Freya and Elin had a lot of laughs about it. "You should have let him out of the hall sooner," they said. "Then he could have pooped outside." They were absolutely right, don't you think?

Oscar, How a rescue became a saviour
By Marjanne Meijer

OSCAR CAME INTO OUR LIVES on a weeknight in October. At that time we lived in the centre of Granada, where we had a hostel. From our living room on the first floor of the building, I looked out the window at the cars passing by on the street below. On the sidewalk across the street was a man with a dog, a long-haired shepherd-like dog with a very long tail. They were playing. The dog jumped up and landed awkwardly next to the kerb on the street. At that moment a white bus passed by. The dog's tail ended up in the wheel arch and turned all the way around with the wheel. The dog's howling went through my marrow and bone. The van continued driving as if nothing had happened. The man who was with the dog stood next to him and seemed unsure of what to do with the situation.

As I called my husband Patrick to tell him what had happened, Arturo, our neighbour from the sweet shop, came running out. We also went outside to see what we could do. Arturo called just about every vet in Granada, but since it was past 9 o'clock no one was willing to come and have a look.

The man with the dog kept grabbing the dog's bleeding tail and banging it back and forth against the sidewalk tiles. I couldn't stand it and suggested I take the dog inside. Arturo first tried to pick up the dog, but it ran off with a limp. He didn't get very far, because he soon realized that he needed help. He stopped and allowed Patrick to pick him up.

We took him inside. The man with him also walked in. We tried to make it clear to the man that the dog needed a vet. He agreed, but admitted he wasn't going to pay. When we suggested to him that we wanted to pay for it, but that the dog would stay with us, he immediately agreed and disappeared within seconds. We called our own vet Clinica Mallo from Otura, and he came with his ambulance service.

It turned out that the dog's tail had been completely pulverized by being rotated in the wheel arch of the car. His pelvis was also broken. After staying at the vet for a few days, he came back to us. His tail was amputated, but nothing could be done about his pelvis. That had to heal itself. We named him Oscar and he became the new brother of Manu, the dog we already had.

A few months later I saw a photo of a dog on a poster that looked a lot like Oscar. The text read that someone was looking for a lost dog named May. We called the number to check if it was the same dog, and to ask where the name May came from. Was he perhaps born in May or is May a Thai word for friendship? After conversations between our vet Jose Carlos and Paco's vet, the man who had put up the photo, it turned out that it was indeed the same dog. We met up with Paco in a café in Calle Elvira.

Paco had been very happy with our call, because he was convinced that May/Oscar had been stolen from his garden as training material for fighting dogs. Unfortunately, this happened regularly in his neighbourhood, which was not very far away from Haza Grande, a part of Granada where family dogs are regularly stolen for that purpose. When he understood that Oscar was alive and well with us, he was very happy. But it turned out he wanted Oscar back to give him a life on a chain in the garden, whereas we wanted to give Oscar a place in a house with his own basket and no chain. When the vet bill arrived, Paco quickly agreed that Oscar would have a better life with us.

He had been called May after Mike Tyson. I met Paco a few more times while walking. Oscar always enjoyed seeing him, but quickly lost interest when I had a chat with Paco.

We got to know Oscar as a sweet and modest dog. The only major drawback was that he hunted cats, since Paco had taught him to catch and kill them. We didn't have cats, so that wasn't a problem for us, but I have seen a near collision with a stray. Fortunately, I never experienced him actually grabbing a cat, but he remained unruly when he saw one. When walking in the city, we always put Oscar and his brother Manu on a leash and so the cat problem was manageable.

About ten years later we moved from Granada city to the Costa and Manu, Oscar's brother, passed away. I was forced to go back to the Netherlands for a few months since my father had passed away and my mother was in a wheelchair, having had a brain haemorrhage a year earlier. Therefore, she could not live alone. I took Oscar with me as a mental support and refuge for myself. There was one small problem for which there was no solution for a while. In addition to four sheep, my parents' farm also had a cat, Rhea.

Rhea lived in the attic for the first few weeks. She was safe there, because Oscar couldn't climb the steep stairs. After about six weeks, Rhea came down one evening. She walked into the living room, stood in the doorway, and looked at Oscar as if to say, this is my house. Oscar sprinted towards her. Rhea didn't run, she just stood there. Oscar didn't know what to do with that. He sniffed her a little and then looked at me, as if to say, this one isn't running away, I think this one is broken.

From that day on, Rhea and Oscar lived together on the ground floor. When something scared Rhea, she shot under Oscar's belly. And Oscar behaved like a big brother should and protected her from the angry outside world.

After four months my mother also died. The sheep had now found another pasture, but Rhea had been supposed to go with my mother to a nursing home. That wasn't going to happen anymore, so it was clear that Rhea would come to Spain with me. After all, it was possible as far as Oscar was concerned.

Oscar and I went back home by car. I had placed Rhea with a friend. She had now had her vaccinations for the flight to Spain, but she still needed a booster shot. A few weeks later I flew back to pick her up. That was quite a journey. From Friesland to the airport in Eindhoven by car and train over two nights, but Rhea bravely endured it. Then came the plane and at the end she was in a completely different climate in a different country.

I thought it would be a bit unsettling, but she soon adapted very quickly to her new environment and loved the warm climate. Oscar remained the big brother, who protected her from the big bad world. After a few months, Paula, a Mastin, joined us and Rhea immediately got along well with her. The neighbour's dog, a black Labrador named Django, visited regularly and that was no problem at all.

One evening about a year after Rhea had come to Spain, we heard a little kitten screaming. It was dark and we couldn't find him. The next morning we searched again and found him — or to be precise, Oscar did, fishing a little ginger kitten out of a ditch which I then pulled out of his mouth. Johan was about four weeks old, and he continued to live with us. Thanks to Rhea, who had decided to confront Oscar in the Netherlands, this little kitten was able to stay with us. Oscar is still interested in running after stray cats, but he protects his own cats Johan and Rhea like a big brother. This is how our Oscar, who we scraped up from the street, became the saviour and protector of two other homeless animals.

Postscript: We moved last year and took the neighbours' dog Django with us, after it became clear that he too would be homeless after we left!

The stories of: Fiona, Red, Rosa And Bibi. Fiona

By Lars and Anne Gethe Moller

FIONA WAS FOUND AT THE campo of Fuente de Piedra, when she was around 4 months old, alone, scared and hungry. She had been living at a shelter for around one year, when she came to us in October 2017. She is a Galgo, probably left to die as she was (and still is) very afraid of shooting, fireworks, thunder and high sounds. She is an expert at escaping, if she sees something exciting she can burrow under the fence in 2 minutes. Though she settled in quickly and is very satisfied with the sofa. When Fiona turned 5, she started to have problems with her eyes, at first we thought she had a splinter in her eye, because she had a blood extraction in one eye. A trip to the vet took a turn we didn't expect. She suffered from an eye disease that comes from inbreeding. They could do nothing but keep the eyes free of bacteria, so we were given cream to treat her with. As time went by she had bigger and bigger problems to see. She changed her behaviour; she became capricious and aggressive towards our other dogs when they wanted to play with her. We moved to another part of Spain, where another trip to the vet was necessary because she had a wound on her leg that wouldn't heal because she wouldn't stop licking it. At the vet's, we told her about her vision problems, and it turned out that an eye operation would give her most of her vision back. An expensive treatment. After the operation the "old", happy and lively dog returned. It is now half a year ago. She is now 7.5 years old, and everything indicates that she has many good years ahead of her.

RED

Red has had a long journey. Red has had both a rough and long journey until he moved in with us. He had been walking the streets of Almunecar for many months, and although many tried to catch him, they did not succeed until he was hit by a car and broke his hip. After treatment at the vet's, he came to a dog shelter where he had problems partly with the after effects of the collision, partly with stress. Some dogs get very stressed and simply cannot live in shelters, despite the fact that everyone has of course tried to help him. He had difficulty healing and became very very thin. A Swedish lady sent him special food. In the end, he went home with an employee to see if he got better. This is where we got to know him and he ended up visiting us, and a few days later he moved in. He slowly began to gain weight, but was still scared, so seriously that he was shaking all over his body and had difficulty breathing properly, he was breathing very shallowly. It has taken more than 4 years to get to the point where he can withstand thunderstorms if he is put under a blanket and one of us stays in the same room as him. When he had been living with us for a few weeks, a woman from the shelter came to see him. You could see that he loved living with us, because he hid behind us, and didn't let her near him as he thought that she had come to take him back. He still has a lot of difficulty with new situations. A move from one place in Spain to another made him stressed, despite the fact that the whole canine and human family was there. He didn't want to go out with us, he ONLY wanted to be inside the house, and when he had to go out, he ran out the dog door, did what he had to do, and quickly came back in. He stays far away from strangers who come to visit, only a few times he has very carefully sniffed at guests. With the exception of one, the lady from Sweden, she visited Red at our place, he was glad to see her, it seems that he must have a mysterious feeling that she had helped him.

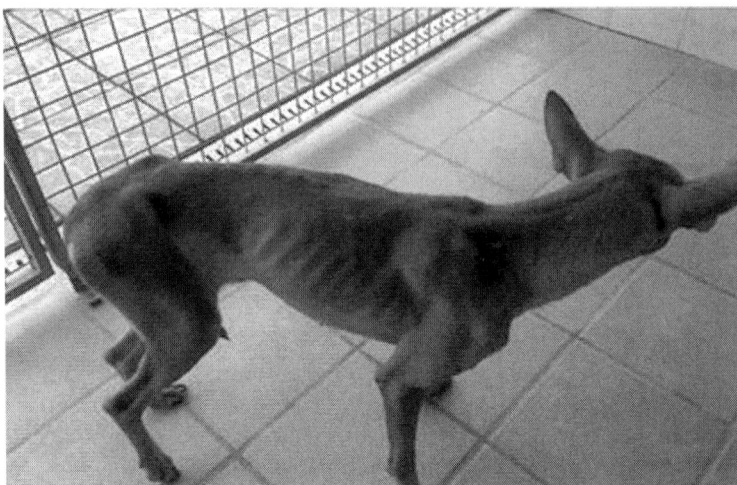

ROSA

Rosa had a short but rough history before she came to us. She was found lying on the side of the road at La Herradura, the lady who found her thought that she was dead and wanted to take her to the vet. But Rosa was not dead, and bit the lady in the arm. She was operated on and treated at the vet's. After a week she was paralyzed in the back and needed 24/7 care. We agreed that we could take Rosa home urgently until a permanent arrangement could be found for her. At the time she was about 7 months old, and the only experience she had with people was the treatment at the animal hospital. She was very scared but accepted us touching her, cleaning her cage and training with her. After a week we had her outside to do her business... and she ran away from us. We worked more intensively with her and slowly she started to be able to walk a little, but she walked with the soles of her feet upwards... Slowly, very slowly it has gotten better, she still drags her hind legs, but it doesn't seem to bother

her anymore. When she had been with us for a while, she had to be checked by the vet, but when we had to get her into the car, she got so scared that she attacked the "man of the house" and bit him seriously in the arm. We threw a blanket over her and managed to get her in the car. We just had to treat the bite wounds before they drove. At the vet's everything looked okay, even though she was very scared. It was actually more than a year before she trusted us 100% again and it is not possible to get her into a car without her being very sedated. When she was 14 months old she had to be sterilized. It went okay, we brought her home, but she had bled heavily during the night and was very weak, so she had to go back and have another operation, this time with an overnight stay. Another breach in the trust between us and her. Finally she could rest. But she never becomes completely calm and safe, the slightest change in the routine takes many weeks for her to get used to. She is very angry when we have guests, and with several episodes she has been threatening to strangers who have come to stay with us. We simply ask guests to ignore Rosa and not look directly at her, it makes her feel less threatened, and thus more calm. In the end Rosa will have a happy life with us, as we live on a farm, where we both work.

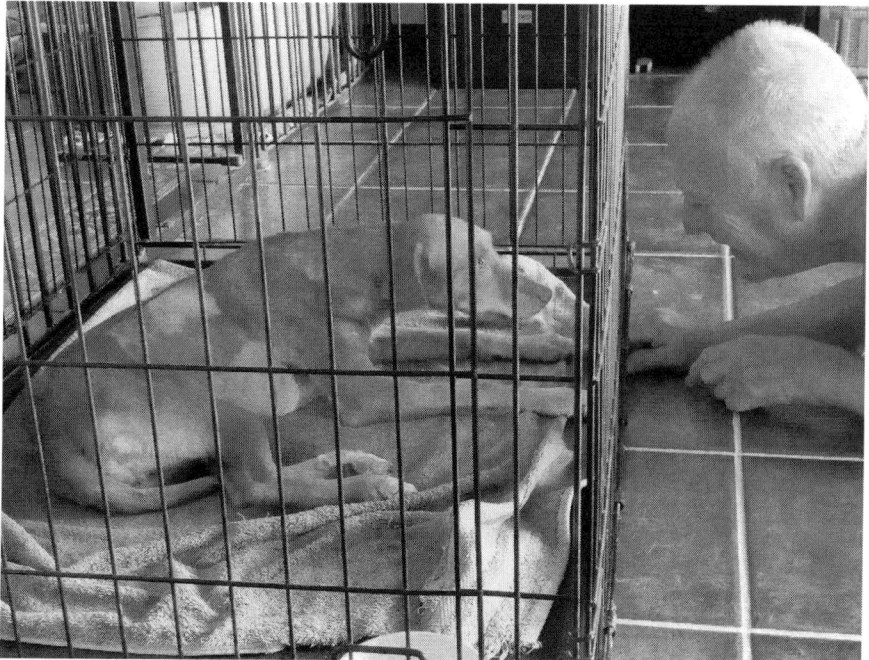

BIBI

Bibi was found in the campo, and was very simple to catch. The car door was opened, and Bibi jumped in and got ready to sleep. Therefore, everyone thought she belonged to a family, but she was not chipped and was not reported missing, not even by sharing photos and calling for the owner. She lived at the shelter for about 5 months. We thought Rosa needed someone to play with. Bibi moved in, and sometimes things don't quite go as expected, because Rosa and Bibi didn't become friends, almost enemies, who easily came to the top, as they both were and still are "determined" ladies. We were just about to give up, but with the help of the shelter, we got them to accept each other. Bibi is very independent and prefers to stay outside around 24/7. She is very fond of people and is not afraid of anything. She is a very good friend of our donkeys, with whom she spends many hours a day, especially she is good friends with the donkey foal Odin, who is 2 months old at the time of writing. All in all, Bibi is an easy, sweet, noisy and loving dog that everyone falls in love with. She would never be able to live in a city, or close to other people, because she barks at a car that drives by, a bird, a fox, or a gust of wind. Every once in a while she comes to us and says hello, gets a cuddle, then she's out again.

My name is Ziggy and now I know even more stuff part 3
By Paul Rane

(Ziggy this is England)

THE TRIP SEEMED TO GO on and on. The small one roomed shelter on wheels just kept going and going. One day there was no ground, everywhere we looked there was water, and I'd never seen so much. I was very shivery and kept close to Blondie and Tommy to stay warm. When there was more land we stopped every day, foodstuff was put in the shiny things, and we ate and played for a bit. The cloth around my neck had never been taken off and everyday Linda Human attached the stringy thing to it and dragged me off for what she sounded as, "a walk". Walking sent my sniffer wild with twitching and soon I was dragging her! There were lots of new senses that my sniffer hadn't experienced before. I liked a walk. I became very good friends with Tommy and Blondie. Tommy knocked me over a lot when we were playing but I didn't have to yelp. After "a walk" Tall Linda Human and Pete Human sounded a lot about "heading back" to something called a campervan. Think they meant the small shelter we all lived in now.

As the trip went on, it started to get colder and colder, and my body shook a lot. Linda Human put a cover on me when it was sleep time. She would often sound to Pete Human, "Have you seen Ziggy's blanket?" When she covered me I stopped shaking after a while. In the mornings I didn't want to follow Blondie and Tommy out of the shelter to do our toilet business. As soon as Ziggy's blanket fell off me I was cold and started to shake. Also, water came from the sky all the time, I didn't like it! I would shake my head, and my ears would flap around but the water kept coming down. I tried to get back in the shelter, but wasn't allowed to until I had eaten my food stuff and done my business. Linda Human and Pete Human made happy sounds and sounded, "Get used to it, Ziggy, this is England." I was not a happy dog.

Eventually, Pete Human sounded, "Finally, we are here," as he stopped the small shelter in a narrow lane surrounded by bigger shelters. Humans came out of the nearest big shelter. They were sounding, "They are here," and, "Where is Ziggy?" I thought they wanted my cover, Ziggy's Blanket, but then remembered that Foster Mum Linda had named me Ziggy, a long time ago. I suppose that must be my name.

Anyway, the new humans were looking for me, so I came out of the campervan slowly as I was a bit unsure what all this was about. When the new humans saw me all I heard were sounds like, "Aw, look, he is so small," and

"He's gorgeous," and, "His ears are bigger than his head," and, "Hello, Ziggy." I thought this all sounded okay so decided it was time to wag my handle and bounce around.

So I did, and the humans made lots of happy sounds and became very excited. I bounced and jumped and wagged my handle for a long time, I even leaked a bit of wee! It was all very new, my sniffer was going wild, my handle was going wild, the new humans were going wild, Tommy was going wild, and Blondie just shook her head and trotted into the big shelter.

Eventually the humans went into the big shelter, so Tommy and I followed. I was picked up by a lady human and I was stroked and squeezed a little bit. The lady human told me I was cute and lovely, and she sounded very kind. So I stretched up to her face and licked her sniffer. "Ooh," she sounded, "he gave me a kiss."

Linda Human sounded that this lady human was going to be my Forever Mum Human. There was a man human here also, Linda Human told me he was going to be my Forever Dad Human. He didn't sound as nice as the lady human;, his sounds were gruff, and he didn't seem as excited to meet me as the lady human. Oh well, I thought, if he was to be my Dad Human I better make an effort. I jumped away from the kind lady human and bounced around the gruff human. The gruff human laughed and sounded to Linda Human, "I suppose he'll do." If this human was going to be my Forever Dad, I better try and lick his sniffer also.

So now, there are 5 humans and 3 dogs in this shelter. Linda and Pete Human, Forever Mum and Dad Human and two elderly humans. It seems the elders are Linda Human and Forever Dad Human's mum and dad. Oh this was so confusing for a little fella like me, so I just wagged my handle and bounced around some more. Then Forever Mum sounded, "Come on, Ziggy, let's go home."

I remember Linda Human sounding about taking me to my "Forever Home". I didn't understand at the time; was I finally going to have a shelter I could call My Forever Home?

My name is Ziggy, and I am told I'm going home, whatever that means?

Read more about Ziggy's travels and adventures on: www.undermywheels.com

The cat that wanted to smell nice
By Tea van Lingen

CATS ARE CLEAN ANIMALS. THEY wash and brush extensively several times a day. Every cat owner knows the image of the paw being thoroughly pulled over the ears. However, a cat does not smell particularly nice. Not dirty either, but neutral: like a cat. This also applies to my Felicity, who smelled exactly like any normal cat.

I was very surprised when I noticed a fresh floral scent every time Felicity crawled onto my lap. Where did that scent come from? That wasn't my cat, was it? I stuck my nose in her fur just to be sure. And yes, it was indeed Felicity's fur. Wonderfully scented of a fresh alpine meadow full of spring flowers. How was this possible? I searched my house looking for the source, but couldn't find anything. And Felicity? From that moment on she smelled like the spring sun, and she looked as if this was what she had always wanted.

Felicity and I lived above an insurance office at the time. A neat office, where time had stood still since the 1970s. Deep pile carpet, many shades of brown, decent desks, a printer, a fax and lots of filing cabinets. I even thought I saw an original typewriter somewhere on one of the desks. The owner of the insurance office was also my landlord. A great landlord, we never had any problems. There was only one small detail... Because pets? They were actually banned. But hey, he never came upstairs to my house. And I just had a very sweet cat that I didn't want to miss. So I took a chance and kept Felicity hidden from the outside world as best I could.

One Friday afternoon I walked down to the insurance office with a question about the mail. The lady from the administration opened the office door and spoke to me kindly. "Come along, I believe a letter was indeed delivered incorrectly." I followed her, but almost choked on my words when I entered. Because who was sitting there, on top of this lady's desk, next to the keyboard, as if this were the most normal thing in the world?

Indeed. Felicity. How did my cat get in here? I knew she sometimes went out through the window and balcony, so she must have slipped into the office outside. Did I have to admit that this was my cat? Or pretend I didn't know her? Fortunately this was not necessary. "Such a sweet cat! And so cosy! When I sit here alone on Fridays working on the administration, she always comes to keep me company," the lady told me enthusiastically. "She's yours, right? She always comes down from the balcony. Don't be afraid, I won't say anything to your landlord. I find it way too much fun."

That little bastard of mine! I had tried so hard to hide her, and then she happily sits in the lion's den every Friday afternoon. "She also smells so good, especially for a cat." "Yes, I don't know how that happens either. She doesn't get it from me." And, I thought to myself, luckily my cat doesn't smell like this musty office either. Or the heavy feminine perfume that hung in the air. This was definitely not the source of my cat's fresh scent!

I was still a student and shared my home with an aspiring photographer. We each had our own part of the house, and occasionally spoke to each other in the hallway. She was specializing in food photography. I never thought about it that way, but it's not that easy to capture a plate of food in such a way that it makes your mouth water! Especially if you also want to give it your own creative twist. Before you have a good photo, a whole thought process has already gone through.

"Come over sometime and I'll show you how it works!" my neighbour invited me. No sooner said than done. When I stood in front of her door one Thursday evening with a bottle of wine, I didn't notice that Felicity had sneaked up behind me. Before I knew it, the cat crawled between my legs and ran ahead of me into my neighbour's room. She had clearly been here before...

Before I could properly apologize, my neighbour said, "Yes, she is welcome too! Whenever I'm fiddling around here and I can't figure out what to do with my work, Felicity is scratching at the door. When I let her in, she wanders all over the room. Creeps under the bed, messes up my things. And that helps!" "Don't you mind her coming into your room? Because that is of course not my intention!" "No, really, it actually helps me when I'm stuck and looking for inspiration. And you know what's funny, she smells so good too!" "Yes I know! It's a mystery how she got that wonderful scent, she didn't get it from me!" "Well, not from me either," my neighbour laughed. "But if you ever need a cat sitter, you know where to find me."

Felicity is a real people friend. Not just my friend, but everyone's. She chats with everyone she meets and makes contact with. I regularly see her on the street talking to complete strangers. "Is this your cat? What a sweetie! And she chats so pleasantly." And during that time also regularly hears, "She smells so good!"

In the house adjacent to our home, there was an empty, small apartment. This was used as storage by the insurance office. Until suddenly, a few months earlier, there was a lot of work and moving. I hadn't spoken to the new resident yet, but on a beautiful spring day we saw each other sitting on our balconies and started talking. Her relationship had ended, and she had been urgently looking for affordable housing, she said.

She had come into contact with the owner of the insurance office through her uncle, who had offered the storage space of his office for rent. A great solution! It was a tiny apartment, much smaller than what she was used to, but she enjoyed living there. Only one thing was a shame: she had to leave her cat with her ex. Because the landlord had been very clear: no pets allowed. And the ex had continued to live in the big house, with a garden. Every now and then she would visit her Kitty; but when a relationship has broken down, it becomes increasingly difficult. Fortunately, she had now found a neighbour's cat. A very sweet tabby cat, which had already crawled in through her window on the first day... Just at the moment when she felt a bit sad about it all, so alone in her new home. "A tabby? Who meows a lot? And smells really nice?"

Tabby and meows, yes she recognized that. But smell nice? She didn't actually know that.

She invited me over for a cup of tea sometime. And as soon as I walked into her house a few days later, I smelled it. Subtly, but clearly present, I smelled the fresh alpine meadow, with 1000 flowers in bloom. This was Felicity's new breath of fresh air! Felicity seemed to like to get into the basket with clean laundry, the new neighbour said. And so that smell lingered on the cat in some strange way.

Of course, I told the neighbour that Felicity was my illegal roommate. And that the employees of the insurance office were part of the plot to hide the presence of the cat. So it didn't take long before Kitty also moved to the apartment. And although Felicity did not crawl into the apartment as often after Kitty's arrival, she would occasionally sleep in the basket with the clean laundry.

Felicity and I have now moved, and the days of clean laundry are far behind us. But sometimes, when the weather is gloomy, and I press my nose into her fur, I think I can still smell a whiff. A little bit of spring sun, a fresh breeze, an alpine meadow with 1000 flowers. In the fur of cat Felicity, the cat who wanted to smell nice.

Lottie's Diary
Day 6

HEY GUYS, LOTTIE HERE AGAIN. As you know, I live with my Master and my mates Angel Holly and Good Boy Benson, but I'm the favourite because Master says my name the most.

Great, it's walk time. I'm so excited! I can't wait so I'm bouncing up and down, thrilled to be going out with my mates. Master is coming out and I want to be the first to get my harness on, so I'll give him a few licks on his arm. Master's not amused.

I'm smiling, I'm so excited. Me, me, me. But Angel Holly gets her harness on first. So I have to jump again higher and higher. Me next! Me, me, me. Master has put the harness on Good Boy Benson next, probably because he's so calm and puts his head through the loop on his own. Sycophant. Can't see why he should be before me. Yippee I'm next. I can dive straight into the loop myself. Oops missed. Never mind, Master can always refill the water bowl. Master's not amused.

Harness is on and we are good to go! I'm whizzing down the steps! Who cares who I knock over! Master's not amused.

Soooo excited to get out the gate! And we're off! Ah, no we're not. Got to be on the leads. None of us like it but apparently we are "uncontrollable" whatever that means. I want to be first out of the gate. Hmmm maybe I'll just take a bite out of Angel Holly's leg. That should slow her down!

Master approves 'cos he shouts my name!

We're through the gate and on our way! I'll use my adorable puppy-dog eyes with Master, it always works, and – "Yay!" I'm off the lead! Let's see how fast I can super speed it down the hill. Phew – 5 seconds – new record. Where are the others? Looking back I can see Angel Holly and Good Boy Benson moseying down the hill. Better just hurry them up. "Come on, guys! No time for a poo, let's go!" I'll just nip Angel Holly's legs to get her to chase me. We're racing back and forth across the terraces not looking where we're going. Master's not amused.

Good Boy Benson is finally joining in the game. He's a clumsy bastard and has just barrelled into a baby tree and broken it. Hee hee hee. He's getting a right bollocking now. I'll make sure to tell Master that it wasn't me that did it. A big lick on the hand should do it. Master's not amused.

New game, I'm gonna find a fallen avocado, a really scrummy squishy one, and get the other two to try and take it off me by chasing me across the neighbour's terraces. Ha ha, I love this game. I really like it when I manage to give the others the slip and sneak back to Master and give him a big lick on the hand to let him know I'm the winner. The other two idiots just keep looking for me and don't come back. Ha ha ha. Master's not amused.

Angel Holly and Good Boy Benson still haven't come back, but it's time to go home. Master is trudging up the hill using language I don't understand but I trot along beside him. I'm happy and smiling. Back through the gate. I get the doggy treat and the others don't. Hee hee hee. Master's not amused.

Finally, Angel Holly and Good Boy Benson have come back to the gate, but I won't tell Master until he's inside having a cup of tea. Then I'll tell him. They're in so much trouble. What a pity. Ha ha.

Told Master and he's walking back down to the gate cursing at Angel Holly and Good Boy Benson. Hee hee hee. I'll just give Angel Holly a quick nip on the leg to hurry her along. Master's not amused.

I love my Master and I lick his hand again as he says my name, "Fucking Lottie."

How I learned to love dogs!
By Gina Watson

I ARRIVED IN SPAIN FROM England, December 2003 with my three cats, to join my eldest son and his wife who had already been here just over a year. I had no expectations of owning a dog, as I have been a "cat" person all my life. However, on my first day, I was asked by my son to take in a stray dog they had adopted but did not have the proper accommodation to care for him. He had been found, injured, hungry and unwell wandering in the campo, and was thus named Campo. He was a lovely boy, golden retriever type, very docile and obedient. We kept him for several weeks until he was able to return to my son, after this, I just carried on with my three cats.

Sometime later, we had moved to accommodation in Tijola. On one of our walks, we came across two small puppies that were obviously abandoned. With his soft heart, my husband insisted we took them home with us, as they were friendly and following us. Despite the fact that our new accommodation came with a fourth cat, they came with us! I have never been sure of their breed, they were one male – Sam – and one female – Layla. We had them checked out at the vet's, they were healthy enough, though under nourished, and were duly vaccinated and neutered. Taking them for walks was difficult at first, they were growing quickly and trying to train them on a lead was a tough task! But they loved going out and finding the freedom to chase each other on our walks.

Soon we were able to buy our own property near Almegijar village. A small piece of land in the campo. By this time, both dogs had grown to their full size and Sam in particular, was huge! But he was a gentle giant, though the locals from the village, who farmed around us, were a little cautious about them! They loved their time here, had so much space to run around and so many lovely walks. We often loaded them into the car to drive to the river; they loved splashing about in the water, two very happy dogs.

We soon became the owner of a third dog – Lucy – a beautiful border collie cross. I have always admired the talent of the border collies with the sheep, and when a friend said she was looking for a home for one of her dog's pups, I couldn't resist! She settled in well, Sam and Layla welcomed her, and they became good friends. It was always amusing to watch Lucy herd them both when we were out for long walks. She just had the natural instinct of the collie and would chase them up easily!

So having acquired another cat – Olivia, whose story is also in this book, we now have a menagerie of four cats, three dogs and on odd occasions a horse that comes to graze on our land!

Walking down to the village one day for bread and a quick coffee, I noticed a small dog I had not seen before. It was very friendly and enjoyed a bit of attention from me. Over the next few days, I saw him frequently and he always came running up to me. I told myself we had enough dogs; don't want more, but this day, he decided to follow me! Each time I "shooed" him back, he just came forward again, eventually running ahead of me when he heard the other dogs welcoming me home! They were all chasing each other around having great fun, so suddenly, we now have four dogs! He was named Foxy, partly for his colouring but mostly for his slyness in finding a new home! Unfortunately, we only had him for a few months, he disappeared one day, and I thought maybe he did have another home to go to, as despite searching, we were unable to find him. After a few days, one of the villagers called me over to her land and showed me Foxy lying deep under a bush. He had either been unwell or attacked and had hidden himself away to die.

But life goes on, and we carried on as usual, despite some problems with boars coming and digging on the land. I was concerned about the dogs when the boars were around and tried to keep them inside. We had no major problems as we kept out of their way as we knew they had young ones, but it was fascinating to watch their behaviour.

This was an idyllic time for us all, we had created a vegetable garden, had almond, orange, fig and olive trees to care for and all our lovely animals. But sometimes things go wrong and have sad endings. One of my English cats was, I think, attacked, and we found her broken body in the morning.

Because of family problems, we took Campo back into our care; he's getting older now and slower and can't always keep up with the other dogs. But this does not stop him wandering into the village and fighting for lady friends, often coming home the worse for wear!

Soon after this, Lucy went missing, frequent searching and calling was fruitless, and after a couple of weeks, my son told me he had seen her on the roadside, she had been run over and died alone at the side of the road. Sad as this was, worse was to come sometime later. Sam and Layla had gone out early to attend to business but were gone a longer time than usual. Layla returned, but she was very unwell, shaking and unsteady on her feet. I quickly loaded her into the car and dashed to Orgiva for the vet.

By the time I arrived, she had died. The vet suspected strychnine poisoning, and I discovered when I returned home, that Sam too had died. We reported to the Junta, who came with dogs to check surrounding areas for poison but found none and concluded the dogs had been deliberately poisoned. We were devastated. So now we just had Campo and the cats.

But wait! A trip into town for quiz night and there was a lady with a puppy needing a home! We fell for him immediately, and he came back with us that same night. A trip to the vet's, a healthy pup, in due time he was vaccinated, neutered and chipped. We named him Dylan (after Bob!). He settled easily with Campo who was getting elderly now and easy to live with. But once more we had a lively pet who wanted lots of walks! Dylan was such a good dog, so obedient, easy on or off a lead and never a moment of trouble.

This was about the year 2010, everything carried on as normal until 2013, when my husband's illness developed into life threatening acute leukemia. He was admitted to hospital in Granada for chemotherapy, and after every day's visit I returned to an empty, sad house but had the comfort of Campo and Dylan.

My husband passed in November and life was never going to be the same.

After struggling for two years in Almegijar, I decided to sell my house and move to town. Campo had also passed, so it was just me, the cats and Dylan that moved on. Dylan was such a comfort to me; we went on long walks every day, mostly because my accommodation was not really suitable for a dog, as there was no outside space. I really enjoyed watching Dylan and one of the cats playing together, and Dylan seemed to be able to sense when I was feeling down. I considered trying to find an alternative home, but before this could happen, Dylan became very unwell, and spent some time in Durcal vet clinic being treated for kidney disorder.

He came home after three days with medicine and special food, but continued to deteriorate until one night he had a fit and could barely move. I rushed him to the vet's the next morning but could see that I had a big decision to make. The vet could see how bad he was, she had to carry him from the car as he could not move. So, she agreed with me that the time had come to let him go. Having had such bad luck with all these wonderful animals really upset me, and I decided, partly because my flat was not suitable, partly because I did not want any more loss, that I would not get another dog.

So back to being a cat lady, but still admire and try to help other dogs when I see them, often buying food for strays and dogs belonging to homeless people. I continue to try and support Valle Verde in their excellent work, and just try to cling to the good times we had with our dogs.

Matthew's Memories
By Matthew Allen

OUR HOUSE IN SPAIN IS small and rather quaint. In the quiet countryside of southern Spain atop a mountain we should have had all the peace and quiet we could ever ask for. It would have housed my family and I quite easily if that was all who lived there. But it wasn't. In fact, we would end up living in that small and quaint house with up to twenty-three guests at a time! Bilbo and his dwarves have nothing on us…

However, these guests were no ordinary visitors. To tell the truth, these guests might have been the messiest, loudest, smelliest, and most misbehaved companions I have ever come across! You might have guessed by now that these friends of ours are no regular humans, they are dogs. And now you might wonder why we would decide to house these four-legged (mostly) furry animals. There are two main reasons (well three if you include: because Mum said so). The first is that they simply have nowhere else to go, they are homeless. You see, in the late 2000s when we moved to Spain, dogs had very little rights or laws to protect them from ignorant or uneducated owners, nor is there anything like an RSPCA to look out for them. So dogs would often end up cast away or perhaps worse, left in extremely poor conditions for months, sometimes years, on end. My mother had a big problem with this and took it into her own hands to rescue as many dogs as she could.

The second reason we housed so many dogs is that, put simply, we love them. Did you know that just by looking your dog in the eyes releases a chemical in your brain that naturally boosts your mood and makes you feel happier? Not to mention hugging them! Dogs love you for you. There is no ulterior motive to their love, making them the perfect companion. They may not be able to speak but that doesn't stop them from saying 'I love you' in so many other ways! Just think about your furry friend waiting for you as you come home through the door, tail wagging, jumping up, that is their 'I love you!' Or late in the evening when they snuggle up next to you, 'I love you!'

I have countless stories from over the years about these lovable friends but there is one that stands out to me which I'd like to recount for you...

This is the story of Canijo, or as we liked to call him, Wobble. A smallish, light brown Podenco. Before Canijo was brought to Valle Verde he lived with a family who struggled to cope with him. The reasons for these struggles were obvious when we took him into our care. You see, Canijo was partially blind and clearly had some brain impairments making him shake and wobble uncontrollably (hence the nickname).

Rehabilitating a rescue can be hard enough, let alone when they are blind, and wobble for a living... It was clear from the many scars and nicks on him that he had been in a lot of scrapes in the past. Whether it was owing to abuse or just his general condition, he was extremely timid and any interaction, even the most gentle and friendly kind, led to him lashing out and biting wildly around him out of fear and panic. This meant it was extremely difficult to integrate him into an atmosphere with other dogs. Whilst he was living up at the shelter my mother told me about how it took him weeks to come around to people and they would have to spend half an hour a day with him every day to slowly show him we meant no harm.

I met Wobble after my mother decided it was best that he came to live at our house where he would have more opportunity to get used to human interaction. I tried my best to stroke him, but I was only met with bared teeth and growls followed shortly by biting.

He did, however, discover how comfortable the sofas were and like most of the dogs there had picked 'his spot' as we called it. Unfortunately 'his spot' was a popular one and he would often be rudely awoken by other dogs looking for a comfortable place to snooze. We always knew this had happened from the noises that ensued... In fact on many occasions this commotion would happen even when he wasn't rudely awoken by another dog. He would suddenly wake up crying and snapping at the air around him all completely out of the blue... bad dreams perhaps?

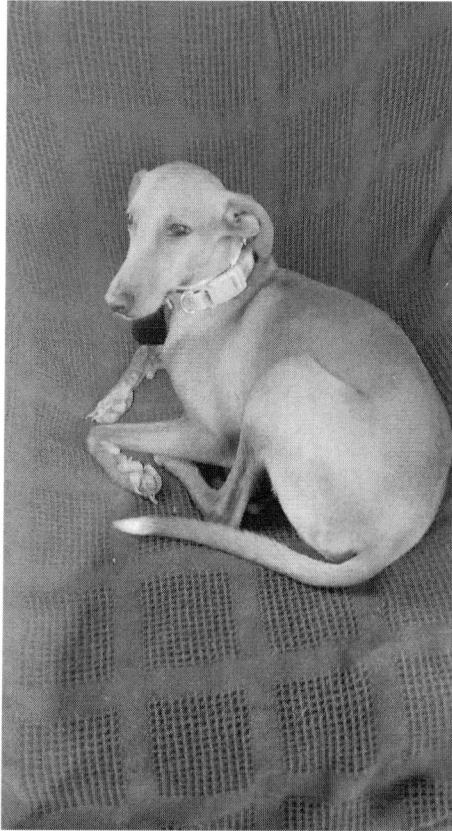

I tried my hardest with Wobble and he slowly got a bit more comfortable with me and I was able to stroke him, but all it took was another dog to run past and he was back into defence mode snapping at anything close to him. Until one day, completely out of nowhere, Wobble actually wanted to play with me! I was sat just on the doorstep of our house and beckoned him over to me (like I had done plenty of times before without success) and he came right up and practically tried to sit on my lap! I noticed he was leaning into my chest a lot; I assume this was owing to the blindness and perhaps also the wobble it meant he was secure and in a safe and comfortable position. He would lick my hands after I stroked him and for a while was ever so lightly biting my hands as if he was playing! After that day I never once came this close to Wobble again. I sometimes wonder if he thought I was my mum and that's why he allowed me to get that close. Either way I'm just happy he opened up to me and allowed us to bond the way we did. It was a bizarre experience and one I hope to never to forget.

Unfortunately after two severe seizures in a short period of time, my mother decided it would be best to have Wobble put down. Wobble was a troubled boy that's for sure, but he was also extremely special. I will cherish my memories of him. RIP Wobble.

Caspar
By Emma Stromberg

WE'D ALL WANTED A DOG for so long. My beautiful dog Caspar had died a couple of years before we moved from the UK to Spain, aged about 15. He'd been a rescue pup and had gone through a wedding, a baby, a divorce, another wedding and two more babies with me. He left a huge hole in all our lives, but as we then went on to spend the next few years travelling between the UK and Spain, home educating our children, we simply weren't able to fill the space that we carried with us.

After a couple of years of travels, the imminent consequences of Brexit (boo, hiss) meant that we had to decide where to lay our hats – and La Herradura was it. But, we were in a flat, so again, we didn't feel that a dog was a great option. We got ourselves a hamster. Then, as is the way with hamsters, after a couple of years he went over the rainbow bridge, so we rescued another that was on his way to being snake food. Luna Joyblossom Cappuchino, as my children unexpectedly named our boy hammie, is a delight, but he still didn't quite fill up that yawning gap.

Years had gone by since Caspar had died, and the kids weren't all still kids – even the little ones weren't little anymore. We realised that we were waiting for a time that might just be too late – a time where we could have a house and a garden for the kids to have their dog. Well, that's just not likely when life meant that we really needed to be in La Herradura village. So all this time the kids were growing up and missing out on what they really wanted – a dog or cat. As our oldest is extremely allergic to cats, that limited our options! Luckily, our lovely landlady agreed to "a small dog", so I decided that we would have to somehow manage a dog in a flat, and I went on the hunt.

I was open to any age – from puppy to elderly. But I had some very strict requirements. I wanted short hair (to minimise fur drop in a small space), a pointy nose (not flat faced with this heat), and not a bearded breed as I personally really dislike being "brushed" with water when they rub your leg after just having a drink! And they had to be smart, because what I really want is a border collie!

I searched all the local animal rescues for months. Most dogs were just too big for us. Others just didn't "feel" right.

Then I saw Jenni. I just knew immediately that she was "the one". She ticked all my stroppy boxes, but there was just something about her that I saw through my phone screen that told me that she was our dog, and I was right.

Jenni had been found at 8 weeks old. We don't know where she came from, but we guess that she was thrown out by a farmer for being too wimpy to hunt – she's the wimpiest dog I've even known! She was thought at the time to be a Podenco/Chihuahua cross, which does make one wonder (…) but as she's grown up I think she's more likely to be Podenco Maneto/Bodeguero. She'd had two lovely foster homes before she joined our family, which had given her a great start. She was about 12 weeks old when we took her in.

For the first few days Jenni would simply not be put down. She was like a newborn baby; she just got really distressed if I didn't carry her everywhere. Yes, including when I went to the bathroom. By week two she was okay going between a bed on the floor and lying on my knee, but at around 3 kilos this was no hardship. She slowly got more confident, and right now she's watching me type from across the room – thank goodness as she's now a lot bigger and heavier!

Jenni has been with us for about 6 months now. My husband and I work from home so although we're still in the flat she's always got someone around, and we can take her for regular trips out during the day. It's a great way for us to remember to stop typing for a while! We go north for the summer each year, and she travelled in the car for thousands of miles through northern Europe with us, for hours at a time, without a peep. She just loves to look out of the window, or snooze, and then gets all bouncy when we stop, only to relax again when the engine starts up.

She's the friendliest pup; she loves people, loves other dogs, and is amazing – AMAZING with the children. She relishes dog training, so my youngest son and I are following the Do More with Your Dog website and she's learning vast numbers of tricks. She gets us out to exercise, but she's equally happy to chill at home and just enjoy the doggy highlife.

We often think of what dog rescue charities do for the dogs. Less often do we think about what they've done for the new owners? I love, love, love how animal rescue charities save the lives of so many wonderful creatures. I want them to know how much happier they've made the lives of those who take on their charges as well as the dogs that they've saved. Thank you.

The power of birds
By Miriam Kooger

FLYING HIGH

There it is, in the middle of the aisle of the stable. Either she's invested or she's not feeling well. I pick her up and she softly closes her eyes. I ask someone for help, but he indicates that she is just very tired and that there is nothing else to worry about. I am complimented for my motherly feelings. And to think I don't have children.

I then put her on a chair and turn around.

Thud... A soft thud behind me. I turn around and there she is. Her wings spread with one last convulsion. Goodbye little one.

LOUD CALLING

It's warm in the house and I walk outside, followed by Candy, my cat. I'm eating my sandwich and hear a loud calling. I see a little one sitting near me. When I walk in I decide to leave the door open for a moment longer because Candy is outside. One moment of doubt... but I realize she is only interested in flies and other insects. But the noise doesn't stop. I walk to the attic to get to work. Less than fifteen minutes later I walk downstairs. And then I see it. A small pile on the doormat. How sad... I made a wrong assessment and instinct failed. Goodbye little one.

A BLACK SHADOW

There is a commotion on the street, I walk to my car and see a few people standing around something. Once closer I see you, you are crouched and motionless, perhaps you are injured. At that moment I see a dark shadow taking a dive towards you. I look up and see in surprise that it is a jackdaw. I lash out angrily; the jackdaw cannot be chased away and takes another dive, this time very quickly. You are being pecked and I look desperate and now run after the jackdaw. Bizarrely enough, the black shadow is not impressed and has only one goal in mind, to get this little one. A car in the street, a man in a suit parks his car neatly in front of the door. I run to him and ask him for help. He walks into his house and comes to us with his daughter and a cardboard box. Come on little one. The man picks you up and I see you are bleeding. And then you disappear into the box on the way to the bird sanctuary. I just hope you make it. Bye little goose.

ATTACK

It's a beautiful summer day. I walk across the yard with a friend, my horse by my side. The sky is clear blue, and we enjoy the sultry evening. Suddenly we are surprised by an unexpected appearance. Out of nowhere, something comes rushing towards us from the sky. We cower in shock. It feels like an inexplicable threat. But to our great relief we see that it is a small swallow flying through the air with unprecedented speed. Still, it's pretty scary. The little creature is clearly targeting us and apparently wants to chase us away. We quickly get away, followed by my graceful four-legged friend. Although she is very sensitive, she remains very cool about it, which also makes us feel a little protected. Why does the creature want to drive us away now? And then I see it. Two little ones near her, a beautiful realization that even such a small creature gives everything to protect loved ones.

BREADCRUMBS

I am sitting relaxed on the terrace of a cosy beach bar, looking out at the sea with my partner. I enjoy the sound of the breaking waves and the seagulls, and it always calms me down. In front of me on the table is my just-ordered sandwich, topped with fresh vegetables and goat cheese. Just as I reach out for the sandwich, out of nowhere a large seagull with outstretched wings comes straight towards my sandwich. Before I could even react, the cheeky bird had already grabbed my sandwich and flew away with it. And I've got it checked. I look at my plate in amazement, where there are only a few breadcrumbs left on it. The other guests at the beach bar start laughing and I can't help but join in.

Paula, the Mastín from the Sierra Nevada
By Marjanne Meijer

I HAD RETURNED FROM THE Netherlands just in time with my sweet, but sometimes slightly grumpy inheritance, cat Rhea, when Covid broke out and the whole country went into quarantine. Because Oscar had changed his mind about the purpose of cats, we were suddenly able to have a cat after all.

There were originally three dogs running around on the grounds of the house where we lived at the time. Two of them were a couple. One was called Pepi, the other we called Anne Marietje (little Anne Marie). The third dog was Django, a black Labrador. The three of them were friends, but it was clearly a married couple and their distant cousin.

When I was in the Netherlands with my mother, Pepi disappeared one night. We never found him again and we suspect he was shot dead by hunters. Anne Marietje was inconsolable.

Oscar came with us to the Netherlands and when he came back after a few months, Anne Marietje briefly hoped that Pepi would also get out of that car. So actually she lost him twice. A great tragedy. My heart broke, but I was powerless. Pepi had disappeared.

From then on, Anne Marietje lived entirely with us. But she found life without Pepi difficult and lonely. She tried to make something of it, and she loved us all, but she had lost her great love. In August I was looking at Facebook when I suddenly saw a photo of a Mastín with four puppies. We were not looking for a new dog, but Patrick had always wanted a Mastin. This one looked straight into the camera and therefore straight into our eyes. We were sold. We let it be known that if someone else would take the puppies, we would take the mother. So it happened and a few days later Oscar and Rhea had a new sister, Paula.

Paula's story, which we heard from the people who fed her and her pups, was that she had been declared unusable by the local shepherd. She had been wandering around the garbage bins in a village for some time. The puppies she had at that time were the second litter. When we picked her up, she had a wound on her foot. That made it extra difficult for her to find enough food and feed her puppies.

When Paula came to us, she immediately loved everyone. That was probably why she was not useful to the shepherd. She loved Oscar and Rhea, but Anne Marietje also got kisses for a change instead of just giving them. In the meantime, Paula's puppies had been shipped to Germany from Cantalobos, where Valle Verde Animal Rescue was still located at that time.

Paula had to be sterilized, because we don't want any more puppies. The adoption had gone through Valle Verde, at least the puppies, therefore Paula's sterilization took place in Cantalobos. Mariela, the vet came there once a week. I brought Paula and stayed on site to help a little. That was actually the first day of my Valle Verde career. After the operation, Paula was taken to a kennel to wake up from the anaesthesia, which would take an hour. After an hour I went to see if she was awake and if I could take her home. I found her unconscious with a bloated stomach. Mariela, the vet, was quickly called back. She had already left, but returned as quickly as possible.

It turned out that Paula's stomach had twisted, which can happen during an operation and especially with a large dog. Mariela came running back onto the property, grabbed a garden hose and shoved it down Paula's throat all the way to the stomach. This allowed the air to escape, and the stomach was turned back. I was warned that it could happen again. If so, surgery would be required to attach the stomach to the inside of the rib cage. As a precaution, before I went home I went to the DIY store in the village to get a tube.

Just when I was explaining to Patrick in the evening what exactly had happened, we see Paula's stomach inflate again before our eyes. I managed to get the tube down her throat and let out a little air while Patrick got to the car. We went to Nerja, where the Expedito practice is located, where Mariela worked. Paula had surgery there that same evening and her stomach was attached to her rib cage, so that it cannot happen again.

After we recovered from the shock, we could finally enjoy our new dog. She is a fifty kilo lump of love. This was our family for a few months, but it was not to last long. Anne Marietje's body turned against her, an autoimmune disease. We tried to treat it with our own vet Jose Carlos from Clinica Mallo in Otura. Anne Marietje got to enjoy a few car rides in her old age, but she didn't make it. The loss of Pepi must also have played a role. She never recovered from the mental blow she suffered. About a year and a half after Pepi's death, we buried Anne Marietje. We were glad that at the end of her long life she knew that some people cared for her.

Another year later we moved. That meant that Django would be left alone, because Pepi and Anne Marietje were both no longer there. We knew what that meant, because Django's owner, who also lived on the property, didn't want him anymore. On the last day of the move, when the house was empty and the full car was waiting with the engine running, I called the man. I said we were about to leave, and I asked what would happen to Django. His response was, 'Do you want him?'

'Yes, if you don't want him, we'll take him with us.'

'Fine by me. Take him with you.'

And we did that. We couldn't leave him to his fate. I went back a few days later to pick up Django's passport. Unfortunately, it turned out that he was not registered to the alleged owner's name. He did have a chip, but it contained no information. Without a signature from the previous owner, it is quite a hassle to get a dog registered in your name. It is possible and it works as follows in Andalucía. You will need a letter from your vet stating that the dog has been abandoned and how long you have been caring for the dog in question. In our case that was three years. You take that letter to the municipality and after a while you will receive a declaration of abandonment (Acta de abandono) from the municipality, which states that as far as they are concerned the dog is now yours. Then you go back to the vet with the certificate from the municipality. The vet can then register the dog to your name at Raia (Registro Andaluz de Identificacion Animal). It took a while, but it all worked out. Django has been officially adopted by us and is officially the brother of Oscar, Paula, Rhea and Johan. He finally belongs to a family.

Molly
By Fran Scott

WE WERE STAYING AT BAB'S and Dave's looking after their dogs and a cat. From their house near to the Padul Laguna, it is possible to walk into Padul town and during our stay there we decided that would be what we would do. We didn't get far along the road before I saw a puppy hiding in the hedgerow. Of course, I said hello and she came hurtling out towards me and went crazy, attacking me with desperation and joy to see a possible rescue person. However, there was a big problem in that we were responsible for our friend's animals, one of whom was pretty poorly, and I had no idea what I would do with this puppy. I'm so ashamed to admit that I gave in to pressure and 'common sense' and that we managed to 'lose' the puppy. I spent the night worrying about where it could have gone, would it be all right and berating myself for not doing something.

Two days later we decided to walk to town again, since we had not achieved it the first time. We always went to a cafe called Elizabet's after our Spanish lesson and we always sat inside. This day our lesson was cancelled, so we went to the café a bit earlier than normal and decided this time to sit outside.

"Is that the puppy you found the other day?" I looked down and couldn't believe it - she was there. "There is no way I am leaving this dog a second time!" As we sat there I made a few phone calls and meanwhile, a young couple with a pit bull came and sat near us. The puppy went over to them, and they made a fuss of her. I asked them if they would want to take her with them and they said that they had just discussed this, but they couldn't.

"No worries. I will get her safe." I was lucky that I was able to get hold of one of the rescue ladies and explained my situation. We were about to go away on holiday as well. She put me in touch with another lady who at that time took in puppies for them. So I made the call and luckily she said I could bring her. Across the road was a Chinese emporium and I went to buy a collar and lead and with that, the puppy, a beautiful pincher, was taken into our care.

From when I had first encountered her she was calmer but understandably sadly more distressed. I felt that fate had decreed that she was to be with us – well me! I named her Molly, and we took her back to our friends' house, stopping en route (it was very hot) to let her play in a stream and get a drink. We secured her in the backyard to let her calm down and kept the other four-leggeds away from her. Later on we were able to take her to the lady in Orgiva, where we planned on leaving her until we came back from holiday. We were able to visit her once before we went away and at that time I was more than sure that we would keep her. She seemed meant to have been ours.

We collected her after our return to Spain and took her home to Restabal. I was surprised that I found it hard to bond with her, but nevertheless we gave her love and affection and training to be a well behaved girl. It was hard going and quite frustrating. One time we had taken her to the coast and as we normally did with our foster dogs, we went to a cafe where they were expected to be quiet and good and sit under the table where we were sitting. Not so Molly! In the end we had to put her back in the car.

Additionally, Pinchers need a lot of exercise – they are built to run and run. Taking all this into consideration, I finally agreed for her to be put up for adoption. For one thing in particular, I was not getting any younger and she needed a family to play and exercise with. From the moment she was reserved, which did not take long, she became the best behaved dog I had ever had! I fell in love with her big style, and she was more than loving back.

Every night she would lie on top of me and gaze lovingly at me with those adorable brown eyes. I was told she was going to live near Oslo in Norway and the evening before her journey when we had our usual loving cuddle, I told her that the next day she was going to be leaving us and going to live with a family. "You are going to have your own special family, Molly." I can't tell you how quite wonderful and well behaved she was on the journey to the airport.

We stopped off for a coffee and in the cafe she was the best behaved dog I had ever had. At the airport she seemed as though she had done this sort of thing all her life. As it turned out, the flight number I had been given was going to Bergen, NOT Oslo. I was surprised. Bergen is a lovely place, but it always rains, and Molly loved the sun. Another couple with a rescue dog and myself were informed at check-in that our dogs were not booked on the flight. Was this the moment I should have said that we would keep her with us? There had been a mix up with paperwork at the Norway end of things, but we were able to book her onboard. The decision was made. Another family had fallen in love with Molly, and they were waiting for her. I had to let her go. I took her to the pet boarding gate and settled her in the travel crate, reassuring her with a couple of treats. Then she was gone.

I know I did the right thing, but I still miss her. It has been hard to write this, and I still cry because I will never see her again. She has a great life in the country, on a farm with two other dogs and some ducks. We found out later that she has leishmaniasis, which is treatable with medication, but if we had tested her before she went, there is no way she would have been allowed to go. So it seems fate that she is loved by another family in another country and lives a good and happy life. I can never wish for more than that for her.

Poacher's Story
By Anne Blondel

HELLO EVERYONE! LET ME INTRODUCE myself – I'm Poacher, a five-month-old rescue puppy! You may think at this time I haven't much to say but believe me I've plenty to bark about. I'm quite handsome or so everyone who meets me keeps saying - whatever handsome means. I think it must be a good thing as I get loads of strokes and cuddles, which I am a tad partial to.

My fur is many colours - brown, black and white. I have floppy ears, but they are starting to stick up more and more; I have a distinctive front left white paw while the other three are brown. My tail is enormous with all the colours mentioned whipped into it. It is thick and looks as if it might go curly. I have a criss-cross pattern running down my spine in my fur which is quite thick.

I have brown eyes and my tongue is quite long. I do like to bark! Well, as I have said I have a lot to say. So now I will let you join my journey so far.

I have siblings but not sure how many; I was found at three weeks old with my sister Poppy. I was fostered out with Poppy near Granada to two lovely foster parents called Jamie and Jules; straight away I felt safe, as they were both so kind and caring. I was lucky as I had Poppy with me; we snuggled up together so we were not lonely. Jamie would pick me up and rub my tummy – I enjoyed this.

Jules spoke to me all the time and had a nice soothing voice.

Poppy found her forever-family first, but I was still not chosen; the Valle Verde Animal Rescue Group put an advert on their Facebook page to see if anyone was interested in me. I found out that there was a lady who kept looking at the photos; in fact, she could not take her eyes off me! I heard she lived in Guernsey, Channel Islands, but that could have been anywhere as locations weren't my forte. This lady got in touch to find out more about me, but at the time she realised it was going to be hard to get me to Guernsey so sadly had to decline having me.

In the meantime, I was happy enough living with foster carers, who cuddled me, played with me and gave me scrummy food. I was very content and would have stayed there happily forever, but they already had three dogs of their own. Poppy and I would play fight and tease each other; I would get a toy and Poppy would take it off me and lay on it - she was a bit cheeky really. One day our carers surprised us with a paddling pool, which was great fun! Poppy and I would try to get the plug out, but we didn't manage it.

A couple of weeks later an advert went out on Facebook saying that Poppy was going to Guernsey to live, and she would be happy if someone else from Guernsey would like me. The story goes that the lady who saw me first got in touch with the rescue Centre to enquire about me again. After checks of her home and lots of correspondence it was agreed that this lady was going to welcome me to her home and life!

The foster carer would go on Messenger and tell the lady all about me; she'd send lots of photos and stories. The lady would answer, and it was like they had become friends. They would Messenger chat and appeared to have a bond.

It was that agreed I would travel on the pet bus to the UK and meet my forever family in Poole before travelling on to Guernsey. It was hard saying the goodbyes; as I know the foster carers liked me very much, and Poppy too. When the foster carer cuddled me, her cheeks were wet, and it wasn't raining - I think it was something called tears. I didn't realise this was it and would not see them again.

Poppy and I were taken overnight to someone from Valle Verde Animal Rescue. We did not really understand where we were going but hoped it was as lovely as our home with Jules and Jamie.

We spent a few days on the pet bus with two men who fed us, exercised us and gave us a cuddle; in fact, they were very kind. It was a very long journey and at the time I didn't realise where we were heading.

It was really late or early if you'd prefer, but we stopped at 2.30am! I was taken out the crate and handed to a lady and a man who appeared happy to see me.

While the pet bus people exchanged chitchat with this lady, I just wriggled around on a lead not knowing what was about to happen. The Pet bus drove away, and I was put in a car on this lady's lap; I whined a little, as I was scared and confused.

We stopped at what looked like a huge tin can - later I learned it was called a caravan... a holiday place, whatever that meant. We went inside, and the lady took the lead off, and I ran around for a bit. The lady picked me up and gave me cuddles, so that was OK. The man disappeared (later I found out he went to bed) and the lady put me in a crate like the one I had been in previously, but there was no Poppy to snuggle with. I cried, but the lady gave me more cuddles and stayed with me all night. I eventually fell asleep, but the lady didn't go anywhere, she stayed by me.

It was 9am and the man got up and called the lady 'Anne' and she called him 'Barry' then I was given some food and water, which I liked. I was allowed to run around the tin can and I kept getting into cupboards... it was fun!

Later that morning we all went out of the tin can and across the road to a grassy place. I was on a lead but enjoyed trying to run and having a good bark at EVERYTHING. I liked to bark, but it appeared Anne and Barry were not so delighted with this and kept trying to stop me with treats. This was a bad move, giving me so many treats - I think they regretted that, ha!

We spent another night in the tin can, but I didn't mind going in the crate and fell asleep about 10pm; Anne was there at 5.30 in the morning... she had gone to bed but got up to take me out!

The car was loaded, and I was put in the back, I didn't like it and barked. We headed to the harbour... I was scared and had no way of knowing where I was going. It was a ferry! I had to stay in the car... at first, I cried but then, exhausted, I fell asleep! The next thing I knew, Anne and Barry were there, and we were driving away from the ferry.

So as we reached our final destination we had to go up some steps - I was let in to my new home! I ran around wagging my tail. I had some mishaps but wasn't told off - Anne just cleared them up and said 'never mind Poachie!'

At first, I slept in the crate, but I liked it and never cried as I knew Anne would be back. Every day she would take me outside; the garden was big, and I was allowed to run around… I loved racing around (I still do). I learned that this was my forever home on Guernsey - an island between UK and France and one of the Channel Islands - this was OK I realised quickly.

I am now six months old, and I know Anne and Barry love me, they must do, to want me to come all the way from Spain to the UK to be picked up then to Guernsey. I have met all the family, and they all love cuddles and play.

I have a lot to learn as I do not like going in the car, and it appears that I am a bit frightened by it, but Anne tries to reassure me nothing bad will ever happen to me. I'm still wary of others and bark, but I'm learning fast that I have to try not to bark (I get treats when I am calm). I've been to the beach, the park, on exciting walks, but my favourite place is home - I'm loved so much and am grateful that the Rescue Centre found me and that they ensured I would have a brilliant life.

I hope more puppies and dogs get homes just like me! Love and gigantic licks,

POACHER

Printed in Great Britain
by Amazon